DATE DUE

			PRINTED IN U.S.A.

SEASONS OF PLENTY

Amana Communal Cooking

Written by Emilie Hoppe

Illustrated by Rachel Ehrman

A project of the Amana Arts Guild, Amana, Iowa

Iowa State University Press / Ames

EMILIE HOPPE publishes *Willkommen,* a guide to the Amana Colonies, and has written numerous articles about Amana history and culture. Hoppe is an Amana native and enjoys sharing the Colony foods that are part of her family's communal Amana heritage.

THE AMANA ARTS GUILD is a nonprofit organization dedicated to preserving traditional Amana folk arts and crafts and to promoting the fine arts.

RACHEL EHRMAN is a resident of the Amana Colonies and exhibits her artwork throughout the Midwest.

Book design by Kathy J. Walker

Iowa State University Press
2121 South State Avenue
Ames, Iowa 50014

Orders: 1-800-862-6657
Office: 1-515-292-0140
Fax: 1-515-292-3348
Web site: www.isupress.edu

Authorization to photocopy items for internal or personal use, or the internal or personal use of specific clients, is granted by Iowa State University Press, provided that the base fee of $.10 per copy is paid directly to the Copyright Clearance Center, 27 Congress Street, Salem, MA 01970. For those organizations that have been granted a photocopy license by CCC, a separate system of payments has been arranged. The fee code for users of the Transactional Reporting Service is 0-8138-2659-4/98 $.10.

♾ Printed on acid-free paper in the United States of America

First edition, 1994 (two printings)
First paperback edition, 1998
ISBN: 0-8138-2659-4

THE LIBRARY OF CONGRESS HAS CATALOGED THE HARDCOVER EDITION AS FOLLOWS:
Hoppe, Emilie.
    Seasons of plenty: Amana communal cooking / written by Emilie Hoppe.—1st ed.
        p. cm.
        ISBN 0-8138-2242-4 (hardcover)
        1. Cookery—Iowa—Amana—History. 2. Amana (Iowa)—Social life and customs. I. Title.
TX715.H7864 1994
641.59777'653—dc20   94-21238

The last digit is the print number: 9 8 7 6 5 4 3 2 1

Be aware that He seeks you to comply with these words: "Whatever, therefore ye eat, or drink, or whatsoever ye do, do all to the glory of God " (I Corinthians 10:31) and that everything good and worthy which you accomplished will be pleasing to Him who gave you everything you can call your own; to Him who deserves all your gratitude, including that for your daily bread. Yes, to Him be ever thankful and follow Him faithfully.

 J. F. Rock, February 13, 1738,
Cusel, Switzerland.
Early translation.

CONTENTS

PREFACE

Amana is a community with a history so vibrant it resonates today even above the noise of modern life. Like a melody that cannot and should not be forgotten, it comes to mind again and again, especially at those moments when you see the geese arc above the Iowa River or the children playing beneath *Opa*'s apple tree or in an Amana Church when sunlight falls upon the white pine benches and the hymn begins. This book is about Amana yesterday and Amana today. It is about the foods prepared and shared here, the customs and songs and stories of a community so very different from any other in the world that there are, perhaps, only a few hundred people who know the song and can sing the melody and it will not be many more years before the tune is heard no more.

The Amana Arts Guild, a nonprofit organization, comprises people who wish to preserve that song and who are working to collect, record, and perpetuate the folk culture of the Amana Colonies. Established in 1978 by Gordon Kellenberger, the Amana Arts Guild sponsors many activities and programs including the annual Amana Communal Supper, local folk art classes, a children's summer art workshop, the Amana Folk Arts School Curriculum, summer week-long art workshops, adult education classes, the Amana Tomorrow Cultural Heritage Program, and the annual Amana Festival of the Arts. Many of these events and classes are held at the Amana Arts Guild Gallery and Folk Life Center in High Amana.

It makes sense, then, for the Amana Arts Guild to have worked toward the creation of this book. As a project of the Amana Arts Guild, partial funding for the research and the writing of *Seasons of Plenty* was obtained through an Iowa cultural grant administered by the Iowa Department of Cultural Affairs.

All royalties from the sale of this book will benefit the Amana Arts Guild and its programs.

Seasons of Plenty was the brainchild of Julie LeClere, West Amana, who visited me one day a few years ago and told me about an idea she had for a book. With Julie's help and that of artist Rachel Ehrman of South Amana, whose magical drawings bring this book to life, *Seasons of Plenty* came to be. Lanny Haldy and Barbara Hoehnle at the Museum of Amana History were invaluable sources of help and advice. Marietta Moershel, who was asked to read the manuscript, corrected my faulty German and gave great encouragement, as did my mother, Janet Zuber, my husband, Bob Hoppe, and so many good friends.

A Note about the Recipes

There are three types of recipes in this book: original communal kitchen recipes gleaned from notebooks kept by *Küchebaase* and recalled by those who were taught how to cook in the Amana kitchens; recipes that have been adapted from communal kitchen recipes; and finally, recipes that were not used in the communal kitchen but have since 1932 (the end of the communal era) become a part of the Amana culinary tradition.

All the recipes in *Seasons of Plenty* were contributed by Amana cooks who cheerfully and obligingly opened their hearts and their recipe books for this project. Those men and women, above all, deserve acknowledgment and thanks, for they are the ones who keep alive traditional Amana. In telling the stories, in tending the gardens, and in preparing good colony food, they are keeping faith with the past and teaching us the song of Amana.

ALL TO
THE GLORY

CHAPTER 1 FAITH SUSTAINS

*Your goal and way shall proceed westerly
to the land that is still open for you and for
your faith. I am with you.*

Inspired testimony, Christian Metz,
Germany, July 27, 1842

Amana began as prophecy: impassioned words spoken to a people who then dared to dream of a place where they might live in peace and worship in freedom. First the prophecy, then the dream, finally the reality of seven Amana villages in a broad green valley of eastern Iowa where the Iowa River winds and where the sun casts light across the meadows gold.

It may have been the light, the gentle amber haze of the Iowa prairie spring, that comforted the four German men as they scouted for land along the Iowa River. After the bleak hostility suffered in Germany and 10 years spent in the wild, shadowy forests of western New York State, the sunlight on windblown grass and on the silvery leaves of cottonwood trees may have been a welcome change. At any rate, the men wrote to their brethren in Ebenezer, New York, and within a few months bought thousands of acres of land along the Iowa River.

That was in 1855, and by the end of the year the first of seven villages, Amana, was under construction. In subsequent years, West Amana, South Amana, High Amana, East Amana, Homestead, and Middle Amana were established. Within 15 years, the villages were nearly complete and the farmland cultivated. In addition to the various small crafts, two woolen mills, sandstone quarries, brickyards, lumberyards, gristmills, and a calico works were operating. The orchards were planted and flourishing, the gardens, too, and the vineyards, row after row of trellised grapes on the slopes, a scenic reminder of the European homeland.

The wine regions along the Mosel River, the Black Forest *Dörfer,* the walled cities and rural villages of Alsace, of Swabia and Hesse, the Alpine retreats of Switzerland—these were the places Amana families left behind. These were the places where the religious Community of True Inspiration originated in 1714 with roots in mystic and pietist teachings and where a small group of worshippers struggled to survive despite persecution that took the form of discrimination, beatings, imprisonment, and forced relocation. After a prophecy in July 1842, leaders determined that a move west to the New World offered the best hope for a better life. Under the guidance of leader Christian Metz, four community members traveled to New York, scouted for land, and then purchased 5,000 acres near Buffalo. About 800 men, women, and children packed up their books, their tools, and their treasures and embarked on a journey to this new place, which they called Ebenezer.

In Ebenezer they found the opportunity to build the utopian community of fellowship and prayer for which they were willing to sacrifice a great deal. Members had pooled their wealth in Germany in order to provide capital with which to buy the Ebenezer land and to transport those who wished to go. It was hoped that, once in America, those who had contributed would be repaid and the land divided among the community members. It soon became obvious to Metz and to the others, that this would not occur, so in order to keep the community from disbanding they proposed that an organized communal structure be established. In Ebenezer communalism was formally adopted by constitution.

When Ebenezer's population topped 1,200, attempts were made to buy more land. Nearby, the city of Buffalo had grown, causing land prices to soar. Any available land was beyond the Inspirationists'

means, and the city, with its urban temptations, was an unwanted neighbor. In Ebenezer the community suffered a number of setbacks, including an epidemic of "miliary fever" (rampant TB accompanied by high fever), which claimed 30 lives in a few short months. So it must have seemed that Ebenezer was not the peaceful haven the Inspirationists had longed for. The Inspirationists had heard that vast tracts of land were available in Kansas and in Iowa, so scouts were dis-patched, and preparations were made to move west. When community leader Carl Winzenried and his companions found the Iowa River land, the long search for a home was over.

It took compelling motivation to establish a community despite persecution, to transport that community across the ocean, to build a new home, and then to relocate yet again. The religious beliefs shared by the community members provided that motivation.

The Community of True Inspiration, today also known as the Amana Church, is built upon the "sure foundation" of the Bible and the teachings of Jesus Christ. Using Christ's life as a guide, Inspirationists believe in God's fundamental desire to reach humankind and to communicate with humankind. Believing that God can and will bestow spiritual gifts upon those who pray and seek the Lord, those who attain the gift of inspiration or prophecy are considered divinely guided. In Germany, and later in America, the sect had a number of inspired men and women, known as *Werkzeuge* (instruments). Their teachings and writings are still being applied within the Amana Church. The Holy Spirit, at work within the community, is believed to give other gifts as well: "There are varieties of gifts, but the same Spirit; and there are varieties of service, but the same Lord; and there are varieties of working, but it is the same God who inspires them all in every one" (*Glaubensbekenntniss* 1839).

At the turn of the century the village of Amana was encircled by gardens, vineyards, and orchards. Although agriculture was important to the community, textile production was vital to its economic base. Smokestacks pictured are for the Amana calico works and the woolen mills. Reprinted with permission from the Museum of Amana History.

Faith, piety, a loving heart, and a humble spirit, these gifts are sought by the members of the Amana Church. Their worship services reflect the desire to attain humility and piety, to remove the overt trappings of organized churches and to replace them with sincerely moving expressions of faith. As form follows philosophy, the churches in Amana are plain structures without adornment: no altar, no crucifix, no grand facade, no steeple tall. The aspirations of each human, sinner though he or she be, should not take the form of mere architecture: the soul is where the holy edifice is to be constructed and the offering made.

It was this religious faith, kindled in Germany and carried within the hearts of Inspirationists to Iowa, which provided the energy to build the Amanas. That faith, like a light, could not be hidden. It shone forth and mixed with the prairie sunshine, invigorating and strengthening each man and each woman so that within a few years, brick upon brick, stone upon stone, the seven villages were built—or so it must have seemed to those who stood in the valley and saw that light cast across the land to the villages in the distance, illuminated, rose and gold upon green like an altarpiece.

The interior of an Amana *Saal* (meeting room/ church). Photo by Joan Liffring-Zug. Reprinted with permission from the photographer and the Museum of Amana History.

The Community

It is difficult to imagine a place where everyone works for the benefit of the community, a place where no one receives a wage and no one needs a wage. It is difficult to imagine that such a place ever existed in the United States, but from 1855 until 1932 the Amana Colonies were just such a community.

Amana's communal system, like everything concerning the colonies, has its roots in Germany. A very informal communal way of life took shape there as wealthier members helped the less fortunate. In Ebenezer communalism was formally adopted by constitution. That constitution was reaffirmed when the Inspirationists incorporated and adopted bylaws in Amana in 1859.

The constitution provided the legal basis for the communal system, but a system is a lifeless thing unless you believe in it and are willing to make it a way of life. The men and women of Amana were willing to do just that because they were motivated by a strong desire to work for the good of the community, to aid in its maintenance and improvement. This desire was rooted in the quiet spirit of self-sacrifice and brotherly love inherent in the teachings of the Amana Church. The religious conviction felt by the members of the Amana community made communal living a reality.

> Take my silver and my gold
> Not a mite would I withhold;
> Take my intellect and use
> Every power as Thou shalt choose.
>
> (F. Havergal, "Take My Life and
> Let It Be," *The Amana Church
> Hymnal*)

During Amana's communal era, able-bodied men and women worked at assigned jobs on farms and in factories, in craft shops and kitchens, in gardens, orchards, and vineyards. They received no pay but were given an allowance for clothing and household items. Food, housing, medical care, and education were provided by the community, the *Gemeinde*.

Each family was assigned a home, often sharing a large house with relatives. Community doctors and dentists, sent to a state university or to Europe for their education, kept offices and made house calls. Medicines, some prepared by community pharmacists, were made available.

Schoolteachers, also educated outside the community, taught all children ages 5 to 14. Upon reaching age 14, most boys were assigned work on the farms or in apprentice positions in the craft shops and stores as their talents determined. A few young men were selected to attend college to prepare for careers as teachers, doctors, or pharmacists.

Girls were assigned kitchen work and fulfilled their duties until marriage and parenthood interrupted. When youngsters were four or so, old enough to attend *Kinderschule* (daycare) or to be cared for by grandparents, a young housewife was reassigned to kitchen work or to work in one of the large vegetable gardens. Women with infirm elderly relatives or numerous children to care for did not work outside the home.

Versammlungen

Gathering for worship, *versammeln*, 11 times each week, the Amana villagers followed a weekly schedule of Sunday morning and Sunday afternoon services, daily vesper prayer meetings, and Wednesday and Saturday morning services. Work and school schedules were adjusted to allow time for everyone to attend services. Only those who were caring for young children or were too ill to attend were excused from V*ersammlungen* (prayer meetings).

Each village had several men who served as church elders. Elders conducted all worship services, leading prayers, reading from the Bible, and giving testimony. This is still the case in today's Amana Church. According to the "Register of All Elders," compiled by the Amana Church Society from 1816, when the register was begun, to 1970, when the document was printed, 328 men had served as elders in the Inspirationist Community. Since 1970, other men and women have volunteered and have been appointed.

Whether the service was an evening prayer meeting or a Holy Communion, the singing of hymns, in German and without accompaniment, was important. The *Vorsänger* (song leaders; both men and women) led the congregation in singing from the *Psalterspiel* (hymnal), which contains both traditional German hymns and songs written by community members. Christian Metz, perhaps Amana's foremost leader, was particularly gifted in writing poems and songs. Some of Amana's most beloved hymns were composed by him and by church founders Eberhard L. Gruber and his son, Johann A. Gruber.

The *Grossebruderrat* and the *Bruderrat*

Decisions, both temporal and spiritual, having an impact upon the community were considered and determined by the *Grossebruderrat* (board of trustees). According to the constitution and bylaws of the community adopted in 1859, 13 trustees were elected from among the church elders on "the first Tuesday of December" by a ballot of the adult male community members, widows, and single females over the age of 30 who "are not represented by a male member." How nominations were accepted and whether or not a single slate of nominees was offered the voters is not specified in the bylaws of the Amana Society. It does seem clear that, whether by rule or by standard practice, each village had at least one representative trustee on the *Grossebruderrat* and that leadership responsibilities rested primarily with a few men who were elected repeatedly to the board of trustees.

The *Grossebruderrat* met the first Tuesday of each month, alternating from one village to the next. It was the *Grossebruderrat* that decided where, when, and how the calico works would be constructed, the Mill Race canal dug, the Iowa River bridge erected. It was the *Grossebruderrat* with the leadership of Metz and others, that affirmed the community's intent to practice communal living and provided the framework within which that system functioned.

The *Grossebruderrat* assumed yet another responsibility: to approve marriages. A couple wishing to marry asked permission of the village trustee (or trustees if the intended bride and groom were

An Amana home.
Reprinted with permission
from the Museum of
Amana History.

from different villages) who brought the matter before the board. The *Grossebruderrat* considered the question and either gave permission to the couple or counseled that the couple not marry. Most often, the union was approved, a "waiting period" of one year assigned, and a wedding date set. There are cases reported in the community history, *Inspirations—Historie*, where permission was refused for one reason or another.

While the *Grossebruderrat* dealt with larger questions, specific day-to-day village concerns were the providence of each village's *Bruderrat* (council of elders). Each *Bruderrat* had between 7 and 19 members elected by the colonists from among the village church elders. The village trustee was also a member of the village *Bruderrat* and served as a communication link between the *Grossebruderrat* and the village. The *Bruderrat* met weekly, sometimes even daily, and discussed such topics as crop planting schedules, construction projects, and labor assignments. When appointing foremen or *Baase* to head various village enterprises and hearing regular reports from them, the *Bruderrat* tried to cultivate and use the skills and talents of their community members.

Housing also was assigned by the village *Bruderrat*, which considered both family space requirements and practical questions such as proximity to work. For instance, the head schoolteacher and his family were often housed on the second floor of the school. The keeper of the general store and his family usually had a home adjoining the store. The communal kitchen *Baase* and their families resided in the kitchen houses.

Obviously, disagreements with the *Grossebruderrat* and the *Bruderrat* occurred, and more than one community member left Amana because a work assignment did not appeal, permission to marry was denied, or some other conflict arose for which no acceptable resolution was found.

When the Bell Rang

This rather spare account of Amana communal life leaves much to the imagination, and though time past separates us from those old communal villages, we can, if we try, imagine how it must have been when the sun topped the horizon as the women walked to the kitchen house, long calico skirts brushing dew damp grass, to fetch their families' breakfasts.

Each village had its apiary. Honey was collected and distributed equally among the households. Photo by William Noé. Reprinted with permission from the Museum of Amana History.

After breakfast, an early meal because there was work to be done, the village bell was rung, and the farmers walked to the barns, which stood clustered at the edge of the village, and fed cattle and hogs or hitched teams of horses or oxen to work in the fields. Although Amana's economy was diversified and the woolen and calico mills provided significant income, agriculture was necessary to the well-being of the community. They farmed to live, and nearly everything produced was consumed by the community. Surplus crops were sold and the money returned to the community treasury.

The men of each village farmed land surrounding their particular village, anywhere from 1,200 to 1,800 acres. Historian Bertha M. H. Shambaugh reported that in 1900 the total yields (all villages combined) for major crops were 55,208 bushels corn, 42,464 bushels oats, 31,622 bushels potatoes, and 9,779 bushels onions. Wheat, barley, and rye were grown in large quantities, but Shambaugh gave no figures. At that time, the community had 2,580 swine, 930 steers, 607 dairy cows, 272 horses, and 18 teams of oxen. Shepherds counted 2,817 sheep.

Sheep were kept for the wool, and swine were kept for the pork. Pork was consumed in quantity in Amana. In tiny East Amana during the course of a winter over 150 hogs were butchered and enough ham, bacon, and sausage were cured and smoked to feed the village through the summer. In the village of Amana three times as many hogs were butchered annually.

Each village kept a large herd of dairy cattle, or "shorthorns." The shorthorns were pastured and driven, twice daily, to the milking barn. In winter they were fed hay. Generally, the village dairy herd produced about 200 gallons of milk each day, this according to former dairyman Fred Schinnerling. During the spring and summer, when pastures were lush, milk production increased, and of course, during the winter it dropped. All of the milk was divided and distributed by wagon to the various kitchen houses. During an interview conducted shortly before his death in 1986 at age 87, Schinnerling described the Middle Amana farm where 16 teams of horses were needed to cultivate cropland and where horses were ridden to herd cattle and keep track of swine in pasture. More than 20 Middle Amana men and a number of hired hands kept the Middle farm. It was much the same in each Amana village.

Having experienced drought in Germany and having seen how adverse farm conditions can debilitate regional economy, Amana's leaders were in-

It was not unusual for oxen to be used on colony farms. Reprinted with permission from the Museum of Amana History.

tent upon diversifying the economic base of the community, a fact stated in the community's 1859 Amana Constitution and Bylaws, ARTICLE III:

> Agriculture and the raising of cattle and other domestic animals in connection with some manufacturing and trades shall under the blessing of God form the means of sustenance for this Society. Out of the income of the land and the other branches of industry the common expenses of the Society shall be defrayed.

Textile production was perhaps the most successful Amana endeavor and earned for the community a reputation for fine woolens and handsome calico. This too had its origin in Germany as several Amana families had owned textile weaving or yarn factories in Germany. The brightly patterned blankets and the rich woolen cloth were shipped to wholesale markets in Chicago, St. Louis, and New York and to buyers across the settled states. So were the cotton calicos, printed in the Amana works and read-

ied for market at the warehouse in Homestead. The deep blue calicos and elegant cream-colored cottons sprigged with navy were offered in hundreds of patterns: florals, geometric designs, whimsical motifs. The plainer patterns, navy blue or black cotton with narrow white stripes or tiny white flowers, were kept for the Amana women who, of course, sewed their own clothes, practical long-sleeved dresses with long, full skirts.

For years communal Amana tailors sewed suit coats for colony men, but by the turn of the century it was believed to be more economical to stock ready-made menswear in village general stores. Black serge or wool suits were favored for church and social occasions, but for work, overalls and dungarees, chambray shirts (sewn by Amana women), and straw hats were typical.

Men worked on the village farms, in the butcher shops, bakeries, general stores, and craft shops. They milled grain and ground flour; they made wine, brewed beer, or baked bread. They kept bees, tobacco fields, and orchards. They sawed lumber, built furniture, and carpentered buildings; they cut stone or made brick; they blacksmithed or tinsmithed. They made clocks or machined locks. They sewed

Draft horses "pulled their weight" on colony farms. Reprinted with permission from the Museum of Amana History.

harnesses and cobbled shoes. They tailored coats, cut lampshades, tanned hides, mended umbrellas, wove carpets, or threw pots. They wove baskets or turned brooms. They taught school, minded the general store, and kept the books. They did all those things necessary to keep a community of 1,500 or more people well provisioned.

Women worked in the home, in the kitchen houses, and in the gardens. They sewed and did needle crafts of all types. They quilted. They hooked or braided rugs. They made mattresses and braided rope. They did laundry and cleaned house. They planted and tended berry patches, herb gardens, vegetable gardens, and started seedlings in hotbeds and cold frames. They grew flowers. They ran the kitchens, cooked, and baked. They pickled, canned, and dried foods. They kept chickens and made cheese and butter. They operated the village preschools. They nursed the sick; they raised the children and took care of the elderly. They did all those things necessary to keep a community of 1,500 souls well provisioned.

Each kitchen had its own two- to three-acre garden tended by the *Gartebaas* and several helpers. Photo by John Barry. Reprinted with permission from the Barry family and the Museum of Amana History.

After the Work Was Done

Do not for one moment imagine that life in communal Amana was all work and no play. During the course of the year there were holidays to commemorate: Christmas and Easter most notably. Weddings were celebrated with enthusiasm and almost any social occasion required good food, song, and stories.

In the spring they went fishing, had picnics beside the farm ponds, and walked through the meadows collecting wildflowers. They took long walks and hunted morel mushrooms, gathered the bluebells, and looked for jack-in-the-pulpit.

On Sunday afternoons in the summer when it was hot, they walked along the river and the Mill Race and collected the pearly freshwater oyster shells that lay on the banks and sandbars. The shells were used to border flower gardens, the shells edging beds of pansies and four-o'clocks. Or they brought chairs out on the lawn in the cool shade of the trees. Friends came to call, and *Saftwasser* (fruit juice and water) was served. Adventurous youth went swimming in the ponds or in the swift-moving Mill Race. Baseball, like card playing, dancing, and dice, was forbidden in communal Amana by elders who believed that such "worldly" play was bad for one's spiritual health. For years ball games were played in secret by young men who risked a scolding from their parents and a verbal rebuke from the elders if caught. Finally, in the mid-1920s the ban was lifted, and baseball became a respectable leisure activity for a young colony man.

In autumn Amana colonists went for long walks in the woods, gathered nuts, and looked for "button" mushrooms. They took buggy rides and had bonfires and picnics in the timber, where the leaves dropped russet and flame.

In the winter the young people went ice-skating on the ponds, the Lily Lake, or some Iowa River oxbow where the black sheet of ice was overhung by the branches of tall trees. They went on sleigh rides, a favorite pastime of courting couples. Those children and young men and women who lived in West Amana, South Amana, High Amana, or Middle Amana rode their sleds down nearby hills given names to describe their height, slope, or location. The *Katzebuckel* (Cat's Back) bluff near South Amana was a popular sledding spot. The *Huppel-di-hup* (Bumpity-bump) in High Amana was famous for jolting sled riders, and in Middle Amana the daring chose the hilly meadows along the forest or the *Apfelbaumberg* (Apple Tree Hill, west of the cemetery). North of West Amana adjacent to the *Schafbusch* (Sheep Woods) were hills of almost mythic stature where West Amana youngsters played.

No matter what the season there was needlework to do and woodcrafts to practice. There were books to read. The community printed and distributed a variety of religious works, prayer books, and journals written by German theologians and gifted community members. These were a part of every resident's collection of books. Works of fiction were hard to come by, but newspapers and journals were passed from household to household. Phonographs, and later radios, were frowned upon, but music was a part of Amana life. Men sang in choirs called *Sängerbunde,* and the talented took up guitar, zither, violin, or accordion. The songs they sang and played were the gentle folk songs of Germany, the choral works of classic composers such as Mozart, and the familiar hymns of the *Psalterspiel.* If time were not a wall but a door and you could step back and walk through an Amana village at dusk when the work was done, you might have heard their melodies and the sweet echo of their harmony.

CHAPTER 2 GIVE US THIS DAY OUR DAILY BREAD

We ate well. We had a great variety of foods; the fruits and vegetables . . . the kinds of soup we had, the kinds of vegetables and pickles, the salads, if you made a list of all the foods, it would be pages and pages . . . and it varied with the season.

Elizabeth Schoenfelder, Amana

There is a story in Amana of a young man who left the *Kolonie* to try his luck in the "outside world." The young man stayed away for nearly a year. Then one day in early spring he returned. When asked why he had come back to Amana, the prodigal said, "Because there is nothing fit to eat in the world."

While trying to pursue his dream, the young man had encountered slumgullion reality and began dreaming of home, where there was bread hot from the oven, savory dumpling soup, pickled yellow beans and "sour onions," tender beef roasts spiced to perfection, hot horseradish sauce, riced potatoes with onion, sweet rhubarb pie, feather-light apple fritters, and cream puffs bigger than a man's fist.

They ate well in communal Amana and that fact contributed to the success of one of America's most prosperous communal societies. Unlike some religious communities and communal societies where little thought was given to victuals, in Amana a great deal of time and effort was spent in growing, preparing, and serving food. The hearth-baked breads and coffee cakes, the hickory-smoked hams and sausages,

the grape wines, the beer, the honey, the cheeses, and all the rest of the foods prepared and served here were the result of a conscious decision and a collective effort.

A religious community, like an army, marches on its stomach. As the Inspirationist leaders must have understood, good food in satisfying quantity provided the nutritional fortitude to keep men and women productive. Perhaps more importantly, good food, well prepared and cheerfully served in the kitchen houses, was a comfort and a blessing enjoyed by one and all—this too the Inspirationists seemed to have understood.

The Amana Kitchen

The communal kitchen system was created to provide meals as efficiently as possible. During the height of the communal era, there were 55 communal kitchens in the seven Amana Colonies, according to maps drawn from a 1932 tally in the archive

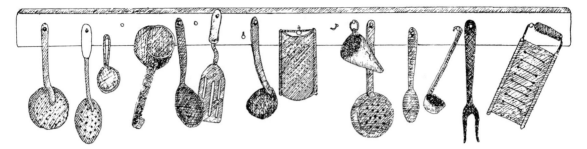

of the Museum of Amana History. The largest village, Amana, had 16 kitchens, while the smallest village, East Amana, had 4 kitchens. High Amana, nearly as small, also had just 4 kitchens; West Amana and South Amana had 6 each. There were 9 kitchens to feed the residents of Homestead, while 10 were required in Middle Amana.

Each kitchen was assigned 30 to 45 residents; usually these were families, single folk, and hired hands living nearby. The kitchens were operated by the *Küchebaas* (kitchen boss), her *Vizebaas* (assistant boss), and *Rüstschwestern* (those who prepared fresh vegetables for cooking) and two or three young cooks. These women, appointed by the *Bruderrat,* presided over the kitchen, kept chickens, made butter and cheese, baked pies and cakes, pickled and preserved foods, and served their patrons three meals a day, every day, all year. In addition, the kitchen crews prepared midmorning and midafternoon "lunches," usually coffee, wine, bread and cheese, for the farmers, gardeners, or anyone who required additional sustenance.

Like the homes, churches, and shops in Amana, each of the communal kitchen houses was built using one of several basic floor plans. Usually a kitchen was located in a large two-story brick, stone, or frame house constructed with a one-story addition adjoining the main structure. The kitchen and dining room were located on the first floor or in a walk-out lower level of this addition. The *Küchebaas* and her family, perhaps including single relatives and parents, lived in the larger residence portion of the kitchen house.

As time went on, the kitchens were slightly modified to suit the women who worked there, and eventually each kitchen came to have its own unique functionality and atmosphere. Equipped with a large brick hearth stove and a wood- or coal-fired oven, the kitchen also contained a six-foot-long sink and washstand. Originally, water had to be pumped outside at the nearest well and carried to the kitchens, but as colony waterworks progressed, the kitchen houses were the first to receive an indoor hand pump and eventually a cold water faucet. Tall shelves, "pie safes," and cupboards provided storage, and a huge icebox stood in one corner or in a hallway. Baskets and outsized basins and tubs were hung from hooks and stored beneath the sink. Curtains made from white cotton calico framed the windows where potted geraniums and violets bloomed on the sill.

Each kitchen contained all the hand tools and gadgets required, everything from apple peelers and cherry pitters to cheese molds and noodle boards. Tin pails, pudding molds, cookie cutters, sieves, ladles, spoons, and pots and pans were made and repaired at the nearest tinsmith shop. Tinsmith shops were located in East Amana, West Amana, Homestead, and the village of Amana. Simply by placing an order with the tinsmith, a *Küchebaas* could have a new pail or a boiler made. Wooden buckets, barrels, half-barrels, and casks were made by the village cooper, who also produced the huge barrels for wine making. Brooms, all shapes and sizes, were made by the village broom maker, and while a new broom could be had for the asking, good brooms

Four-pound loaves of bread bake in the stone hearth of a colony bakery. Photo by John Barry. Reprinted with permission from the Barry family and the Museum of Amana History.

were taken care of, and every young cook learned the proper way to clean, air, and store a broom, for the handiwork of craftsmen was never taken for granted and never misused.

The Common Dining Room

In Ebenezer and in the Amanas for many years, residents ate their meals in the large dining room at the kitchen house to which they were assigned. Men sat at one long table; women and their children sat at another table; hired hands or guests were seated at a third table. Meals were taken home to the ill or to mothers with infants.

The meal always began with a German prayer. After the blessing, bowls and platters of food were passed about as the *Küchebaas* and her helpers watched and refilled as necessary. Mealtime was not meant to be a social occasion. Conversation was not encouraged at the dining table and any light-hearted jocularity was thought in the worst possible taste.

Once the meal was complete, a second prayer was offered. No one lit a cigar or lingered over a cup of coffee; the residents got up, gave the *Küchebaas* their thanks, and went home to prepare for evening prayer services.

Not surprisingly, after 60 years of silent suppers Amana residents began to wonder if it might not be more enjoyable to eat at home. Sometime after the turn of the century, the common dining room tradition was abandoned. Instead, housewives, baskets in hand, went to their assigned kitchens at mealtime to pick up the meal and carry it home. Single men and women and the *Küchebaas* and her family still met at the dining room for their meals.

Each kitchen kept a flock of 300 or more chickens. Reprinted with permission from the Museum of Amana History.

Serving Guests

Although the kitchen houses existed to serve community residents, visitors were not turned away. When transportation was limited to horse-drawn buggy or train, few "outsiders" found their way to the Amana Colonies. Even so hotels, complete with kitchens and dining rooms, were built in Amana, South Amana, and Homestead to lodge salespeople and railroad travelers who stopped there. In the 1920s, when automobiles made visiting the Amana Colonies easier, outsiders occasionally stopped at one of the village kitchen houses for a meal and were served in the common dining room. There seems to have been no set rule as to whether or not strangers were charged for meals in the village kitchen houses. Accounts vary from village to village. In some villages these early tourists were charged 15¢ to 25¢ per meal, and the cash was added to the kitchen's account at the village general store. In High Amana for instance, the keeper of the High Amana General Store sometimes sent his very best out-of-town customers to one of the kitchen houses for dinner. A type of voucher system was worked out between the High Amana General Store and the kitchens, as the store repaid the kitchens for meals served to those outsiders who shopped for paint, tires, and farm supplies at the High store before dining at a High Amana kitchen.

Visiting relatives were another matter. If possible, a resident expecting guests from the "outside" informed the *Küchebaas* in advance so that arrangements could be made for additional servings of the main course and side dishes to be prepared. A *Küchebaas* might also make a special dessert, perhaps red raspberry pie or *Eispudding* (Ice Pudding). Few cousins complained of the food while spending time with colony relatives.

Lending Her Name to the House

A kitchen house was known by its *Baas*'s last name. If Louisa Frey kept the kitchen beside the butcher shop, it was known to one and all as "Frey's *Küche*." Sometimes it was confusing when a younger woman took over after a *Küchebaas* retired. It could take years before folks, especially old folks, remembered to call the kitchen by the "new *Baas*'s" name, and conversations that should have progressed with little confusion became nearly impossible to follow unless both parties had the management changes of each kitchen house clearly in mind.

Taken from a list kept by former village baker and Amana historian Henry Schiff, here are the names of all 16 Amana kitchen houses as of 1932:

The Moershel *Küche*	The Frey *Küche*
The Heinze *Küche*	The Graf *Küche*
The Leichsenring *Küche*	The (Mrs. John) Noé *Küche*
The Goerler *Küche*	The (Mrs. Charles) Noé *Küche*
The Neubauer *Küche*	The Osterle *Küche*
The Christen *Küche*	The Hertel *Küche*
The Zimmerman *Küche*	The Rettig *Küche*
The Winzenried *Küche*	The Hotel

The *Küchebaas*

As her title specifies, the *Küchebaas* was the boss in her kitchen. Sixty years after the end of Amana's communal era, the *Küchebaas* is commonly regarded by Amana folk as some archetypal kitchen goddess, part thunder and lightning, part breezy solicitude, wholly frightening and wholly good. The truth, of course, is that she was none of those things and all of those things.

The *Küchebaas* was appointed by the village *Bruderrat*. As was the usual procedure, when the elders had reached a decision as to who might manage a kitchen (or any other village enterprise), one elder paid a visit and made the request. Elizabeth Schoenfelder, Amana, explained: "That's the way it was. When they wanted my mother to be *Baas,* one of the elders came to our house and asked her if she would take the kitchen. At first my mother did not want it. It was a lot of work. My grandmother and I said we would help her. Then she thought, *Ja,* she would do it. It was her decision."

Once appointed, a *Küchebaas* stayed until illness or age forced a retirement. The new *Baas,* having already spent years working in a kitchen, knew the routines and the requirements of her post. Although it may have happened during some hour of Amana's history, no Amana resident interviewed in the course of preparing this book recalled ever hearing of a *Baas* being asked to resign because of incompetence. One colony resident quipped, "No one fired you if your dumplings were as heavy as rocks, but you sure heard about it!" No *Baas* wanted her kitchen to be known for poor meals or small portions. Every *Baas* worth her salt hoped to earn praise from her patrons and strived to turn out delicious meals.

Great-Aunt Henrietta

Having grown up in a community where relatives live up and down and across the street, and have done so for generations, I did not have one great-aunt but several. One had a pointed nose; one was almost deaf; one had a sharp tongue; one was somewhat aloof, at least towards children.

Then there was Great-Aunt Henrietta. She was short and plump; she had a round face and laughing eyes and lips curved in a smile. Her iron-gray hair was parted in the middle and combed back smoothly on either side of her head with no strand out of place. Usually she covered her hair with a net. Her dress was the conventional Amana style—long sleeves, high neck, full skirt. Only on very hot days did she wear a less close-fitting bodice and skirt and elbow-length sleeves. She wore an apron most of the time: calico in the kitchen and black cotton or silk for dress-up occasions.

What appealed to me especially, when I was a youngster, were her culinary accomplishments. Her homemade ice cream, her coffee cake, her currant and strawberry syrups for cool drinks on a summer's day, and her strawberry shortcake were rare delicacies. Since my mother's birthday was in the middle of June, when strawberries are at their most luscious ripeness, Great-Aunt Henrietta always baked a strawberry shortcake for my mother's birthday instead of an ordinary angel food or devil's food cake. I can still taste the layer of cake topped with a thicker layer of sweetened berries and then, finally, the heavy whipped cream covering and completely hiding the two layers underneath. No other shortcake has ever tasted so delicious.

Before reorganization in 1932 (the end of the communal era) it was customary for Amana girls to leave school at 14 and to begin work in one of the community kitchens. I had completed eighth grade and was attending school until my fourteenth birthday, so I "graduated" in February. A few days later Great-Aunt Henrietta (sister to my late grandmother) came for a visit—first to see my grandfather, who was a member of the *Bruderrat,* and then to see my family, principally me, to announce that next week I was to begin work in the kitchen of which she was the *Küchebaas.* I had expected this and was secretly pleased that I was assigned to her kitchen and not another. So with both anticipation and anxiety I looked forward to the following Sunday.

The principal lessons were in cooking, from simple fried potatoes for breakfast to the sweet rolls and coffee cake made of yeast dough and kneaded by hand. As did most women of her day, Great-Aunt Henrietta knew the standard recipes by heart and used a cookbook only for cakes and some newer recipes. I followed instructions for cooking soup, creaming spinach, roasting meat; and at first it was fun, as long as she

The *Rüstschwestern* (paring knife sisters), the *Küchebaas,* and her helpers prepare green beans for canning. Photo taken mid-1920s. Reprinted with permission from the Museum of Amana History.

told me what to do. But after a few weeks, when some of the dishes appeared on the menu again, she expected me to remember what ingredients to use and in what proportions. To my dismay I discovered that I had forgotten many of her earlier instructions. I dared not ask her, yet I hesitated to blunder ahead and perhaps spoil the meal for all the people served in that kitchen. Finally, I did ask her—was the farina for the soup put into a dry skillet, or was the lard melted first and the farina added? She showed no annoyance, she did not scold, but her answer I'll never forget. A few years ago, she said she had a girl working there who could not seem to remember simple recipes, and she told this girl to get a little book and write down ingredients and instructions. Apparently this solved her problem. To me this seemed a humiliating solution, and I resolved, henceforth, to pay closer attention. Needless to say, I fared much better.

Cleaning the stove, sink, and cupboards and scrubbing the floors were part of the weekly routine. Friday morning we rose early and had much of the work completed before breakfast. I wasn't fond of this type of work, especially in winter, when it was cold and we worked by the light of kerosene lamps, but my aunt's never-failing good humor and her energetic bustling self made the work pleasanter. In fact, I enjoyed surveying the finished work and learned to take pride in shiny floors and gleaming kettles.

My aunt, in the years I saw and worked with her daily, was in her early 60s and was busy in the kitchen almost all day. Besides the routine cooking and baking, there were vegetables and fruit to be canned and dried, cheese to be made, butter to be churned, chickens to be tended. She never complained, and her cheerfulness and energy helped me to become more unselfish so that I tried to save her steps by running errands for her.

In the two years I was under her wing, Great-Aunt Henrietta taught and influenced me very much. She died in 1932, shortly after the community kitchens forever closed and each family began to cook its own meals. To me, Great-Aunt Henrietta typifies the *Küchebaas* who occupied such an important place in communal Amana.

Henrietta Ruff, South Amana

Spring cleaning in an Amana kitchen house. Photo taken by Dr. C. Herrmann. Reprinted with permission from the Museum of Amana History.

Kitchen Management

The management of the kitchen, from cellar to attic, was the sole responsibility of the *Baas*. She kept track of supplies and obtained what she needed from the village butcher shop, flour mill, bakery, dairy barn, orchard, and icehouse. Deliveries from each were made on a regular schedule.

Coffee, tea, molasses, rice, cocoa, spices, raisins, vinegar, kerosene, and occasionally rennet for cheese making were obtained at the general store. In theory and in practice the kitchens were run as small businesses. At various times during the year, eggs and surplus garden produce were delivered to the village general store, and their value was credited to each kitchen's account. A detailed record of the kitchen's account was kept by the storekeeper. Individual kitchens traded goods, such as sugar and coffee beans, against the sale of the credited produce, facts that were noted in the record books. The eggs, onions, onion sets, kraut, and beans were sold in the store to "outsiders" or were shipped and sold at markets in surrounding communities to help offset the enormous cost of feeding some 1,500 hungry Amana residents.

If a kitchen's egg production was down or if the cabbage crop failed, the kitchen operated "at a loss" on the storekeeper's books until the amount was "made good" by the village treasury. A better than average harvest or extremely productive hens meant that the kitchen began its fiscal year with a surplus in the budget, and the *Küchebaas* could breathe a sigh of relief and throw an extra handful of raisins into the coffee cake dough without worrying about her bottom line.

Homestead women cut cabbage for sauerkraut. Photo taken mid-1920s. Reprinted with permission from the Museum of Amana History.

Coffee, Sugar, and Tea

In 1868 the Middle Amana storekeeper kept this account of the coffee, sugar, and tea consumption during one week in each of Middle's kitchen houses. Middle Amana was under construction at the time and had only 6 kitchen houses, so each was serving a fairly large number of residents and an additional number of hired men engaged to help with the construction of the Middle Amana Woolen Mill and the canal. Eventually 10 kitchen houses would operate in Middle.

Coffee, sugar, and tea for week ending July 16, 1868.

KITCHEN	NUMBER SERVED	COFFEE	SUGAR	TEA
Murbach	56	10 lb 8 oz	14 lb	14/16 lb
Ruedy	44	8 lb 4 oz	11 lb	11/16 lb
Herr	47	8 lb 10 oz	11 3/4lb	12/16 lb
Krienstler	56	10 lb 8 oz	14 lb	14/16 lb
Meyer	58	10 lb 14 oz	14 1/2 lb	14/16 lb
Winzenried	52	9 lb 12 oz	13 lb	13/16 lb

The Kitchen Gardens

Each kitchen house had its own large garden managed by a *Gartebaas,* a woman with an exceptionally green thumb, appointed by the *Bruderrat.* The garden, known by the name of the kitchen it served, was located alongside the kitchen or on the outskirts of the village. Each garden, roughly two to three acres in size, was tended by the *Gartebaas* and her crew of three or more women. Usually an older man, retired from farm work, was assigned to help at the garden as well. There were times when more hands were required, for instance when the garden was raked smooth after spring plowing or when the cabbage crop was harvested. Then older schoolchildren and women from the kitchens were recruited for a day or two.

The Communal Kitchen Menus

When describing the Amana communal kitchen, and considering the system of store accounts and records, the wonderful efficiency of bakery and butcher shop deliveries, the economy of the kitchen house gardens, and the management of the kitchen house itself, we should remember that we are describing not 1 but 55 kitchens in seven different villages. Each village, each kitchen, did things just a little differently from the next, but certain practices were standard in all seven colonies. These practices evolved between 1855 and 1932 as a means of feeding a community of hardworking folk and as a way to insure the equitable distribution of food. To guard against any one group of residents receiving more than its share, menus were standardized to a great extent. For instance, the typical Saturday night fare in all Amana kitchen houses was pork sausage or cracklings, boiled potatoes, cottage cheese with chives, and *Schmierkäse* (a soft caraway cheese spread on bread). In addition, on Saturdays there was always freshly made coffee cake. On Sunday at noon you could have visited any of the kitchen houses and received rice soup, creamed spinach, fried potatoes, boiling beef, *Streusel* (coffee cake), and coffee or hot tea. So it was for each day of the week.

The menus did change with the seasons. During autumn and winter, when keeping meat was not a problem, fresh meat was delivered to the kitchen houses frequently, and so boiling beef, ground beef dishes, roasts, and ribs were served. In winter milk and egg production dropped, so milk- and egg-rich desserts and main dishes were replaced on the menu by dishes requiring less of both. Dried and canned fruits and vegetables were used almost exclusively. Certain root vegetables such as salsify and horse-radish were buried in barrels of sand in the cellar and kept well enough to use all through the winter to supplement the diet of dried beans, spinach, and kale and canned and pickled vegetables.

In the spring and the summer when the dairy-man brought extra cans of fresh milk to the kitchen and the egg baskets were overflowing, cakes and custards and cheeses were served regularly, and butter was plentiful. Garden vegetable dishes, salads, and fruits were on the menu, while fresh beef and pork were replaced with ham, bacon, and sausage.

The Kitchen Week

Efficient kitchen management demanded adherence to routine. Each *Baas* established weekly routines for her kitchen and saw to it that the routines were maintained and work accomplished on schedule. The weekly routine varied little from kitchen house to kitchen house:

MONDAY was laundry day, so meals were less complicated and no dessert was prepared.

TUESDAY a special dessert was served with the noon meal.

WEDNESDAY was baking day, and coffee cakes were baked in the kitchen house, in addition to meal preparation.

THURSDAY a special dessert, perhaps pie or pudding, was served with the noon meal.

FRIDAY was cleaning day, and the entire kitchen was scrubbed from floorboard to lamp shade. As a result, meals on Friday were usually simple. In the village of Amana on Friday each kitchen sent someone to pick up supplies such as coffee, tea, and spices.

SATURDAY was baking day, and coffee cakes, or occasionally rolls, were baked in the kitchen house. In other villages on Saturday one of the women was sent to the village store to pick up supplies.

SUNDAY was the day of rest, but hot meals were prepared and served nonetheless.

The younger women who assisted the *Baas* and the *Vizebaas* (vice boss, or second in command) worked on a weekly rotation. One week a young cook would be in charge of actually preparing the meals, frying potatoes, making soup, baking pie, or doing whatever was required. When it was her "week to cook," as the kitchen workers called it, she was the first to arrive at the kitchen, sometime before 5 A.M., and began by lighting the wood-burning stove and making coffee. The following week, the young worker was "off" and need not appear in the kitchen before 6 A.M. Additionally, she was allowed a longer afternoon break. That week she accomplished chores as assigned and helped the *Baas* mix cake batters, collect eggs, or make cheese. The third week she arrived a little early to set tables and stayed a little later to wash dishes, but rarely did anyone wash dishes alone in communal Amana, where most jobs were done by a group rather than an individual. As one former Amana kitchen worker explained, "We always helped one another . . . I remember in the evening when we washed the dishes after supper we sang together, you know, all the old songs." So singing all the old songs, they carried through the week a day-by-day melody of friendship and cooperation.

SPRING

The trees leaf out, the grass is green,
The bees are humming for their queen,
All Nature seems to harken.
The tulips and the daffodils
Are nestled round the rocks and rills
In God's prolific garden.

The lark flies up into the blue
The flowers drink the morning dew
And swallows tend their fledgling.
Oh, hear the gifted nightingale
Pour forth her song o'er hill and dale
From tallest tree to hedgling.

Paul Gerhardt,
"Go Forth, My Heart and Soul, Awake,"
translated by Erna Fels,
The Amana Church Hymnal

CHAPTER 3　**SPRING**

And in the spring, one Sunday, my Dad would say,
"Today, we'll go see the lambs." And we all walked out
to see the baby lambs in the field. That was something
we looked forward to, going to see the lambs.

Lina Moessner, Middle Amana

When patches of dirty snow and ice are all that remain of winter and the meadows grow green and the trees show signs of budding, the smell of the earth coming to life brings Amana residents outdoors. So it is now and so it was then.

Springtime in communal Amana sent the *Gartebaas* to work and to worry over her cold frames and hotbeds and prompted the *Küchebaas* to initiate the spring rite of cleaning her kitchen. Every colony housewife had her own ritual of window washing, floor scrubbing, and rug beating in which every able-bodied person in the household took part. All that whisking, washing, and scrubbing was followed by the arrival of the village whitewashers who made the rounds from house to house repainting a room or two with the light blue wash used in Amana homes. Once that was done, the rag rugs were relaid, the furniture was polished and set back in place, the freshly laundered and starched curtains were hung, and the pictures were replaced. Perhaps the last thing hung back upon the wall was the cherished *Haussegen,* or house blessing, carefully embroidered upon cloth or gold-embossed paper. "Bless this home, now clean," the Amana housewife could have added.

Combating dirt on every front, Amana women dealt with the perennial problem of muddy streets and yards and muddy men who returned from early spring fieldwork, feedlots, and stalls with filthy boots and work clothes. During the years just after the Amanas were established, women lugged their laundry to a village washhouse, where rainwater was heated and laundry done in oversized tubs. Later on, each house had its own washhouse, and the common washhouse system was abandoned. In West Amana the huge copper washtubs once used for the village laundry and kept in the walk-out cellar of the village school were refitted and used to dry hops for beer making.

Laundry Day

Monday was laundry day. Gardeners were excused from work and kitchen workers adjusted their schedules and took turns doing chores so that they could do their laundry. Preparations actually began on Sunday when a fire was lit in the washhouse boiler and rainwater pumped by hand from the cistern to the boiler. By Monday dawn, the water was steamy, and wash day commenced. The tubs were filled with hot water, and the laundry was soaped and scrubbed on washboards and then wrung out and rinsed repeatedly. On a fine morning the wash was hung on the clothesline (the only truly grassy area in a colony yard, where fruit trees, grape arbors, and berry patches competed for sunshine with the flower beds and the lilacs). If it was raining, the wet laundry was

lugged in baskets into the house and up two flights of stairs to the attic, where it was hung on lines suspended beneath the rafters. Attics were kept dust-free for just such days.

Lye soap, bleach, and sunshine were the only things available to remove stains. A white shirt stained with berry juice was left in the sun for hours until the stain faded. If all such remedies failed, a shirt or apron was newly colored with dye from the Amana or Middle Woolen Mill.

Soap for laundry and housework was made at the soap works in the village of Amana. Located at the edge of the village, the soap works was run by two men who made lye, rendered lard, and made different types of soap for various purposes.

The soap works, like so many things in Amana, depended upon the thrifty habits of the residents. In each home and shop, wood ashes were swept from stoves and hearths and taken to a village collection box. When the box was full, the ashes were removed and taken to the soap works. To make lye, ashes were packed into a barrel. Water was drawn through the barrel and the result was liquid lye. Lye added to lard, rendered from the animal scraps of each village butcher shop, was cooked in an open kettle for nearly three days (according to research conducted by Jeanene D. Hoppe on file at the Museum of Amana History). Once it reached the proper consistency, it was poured into barrels or forms. A soft soap, *Schmierseif,* was made and delivered by the barrel to each kitchen house for dish washing, household cleaning, and laundry. Smaller casks of the smooth, creamy lye soap were given to each household. Yellow bath soap was made in 15-inch-long bars and distributed to all. For the delicate skinned, there was a facial soap, pure and white as snow, available in small bars only upon request.

Spring Routines

The first really sunny spring day when the breeze seemed almost balmy, the village beekeeper brought out the bee boxes. Before anyone knew that domestic bees can weather winter outdoors, bee boxes were hauled into a basement for the cold months. Snoozing in their hives, the bees were known to emerge on unusually warm winter days when the cellar temperature rose. For that reason the basement of some unoccupied building was chosen to house the hives. No one wanted to risk having a cellar buzzing with irritable bees.

Come spring the heavy boxes full of soporific bees were lugged up the cellar stairs and into the orchard. The beekeeper—one was appointed for each

Amana village—probably enlisted the help of several strong-backed, fearless young men. Once the bee boxes were set up in the village orchard near the gardens and grapevines, the beekeeper looked forward to summer when he could tend the hives, collect the honey, and divide it equally among the households.

Strong backs were also needed to mend fences and to muck stalls, to plow and to harrow, to help farrow and calve, all the heavy spring chores of farming. In the village of Amana at the Mill Race workmen brought the dredge boat out of dry dock, and preparations began for a spring and summer spent slowly cruising up the six-and-one-half-mile Mill Race canal dredging its bottom and repairing levees and gates.

Meanwhile the Iowa River, swollen with spring runoff, washed through the forested valley. Before a raised road and bridges were constructed between West and South Amana, if you needed to travel from one village to the other, you went by water, and boats were built for that purpose. A shallow-bottomed boat just big enough for two men was outfitted with a crude mast, rudder, and sail. But the wind was no sure thing, so more often than not, you rowed. It was a long pull to South Amana against the uncertain currents and backwashes of the swollen river. The trip was undertaken only if absolutely necessary, but Harry Zuber of West Amana once told of a young man who rowed across each spring Sunday to court his South Amana sweetheart. The suitor came back across the river at sundown, his oars stroking black water just as the moon was rising and the sun was falling. The young man and his love were eventually married, and all that rowing was thought worthwhile.

Weather Watch and Moon Phases

Consulting her almanac and the journal she kept through previous planting seasons, the *Gartebaas* determined her planting schedule. There were, of course, no weather forecasts available, no long-range rainfall predictions, no daily weather reports beyond what was published in the *Farmer's Almanac* and what the *Gartebaas* knew to be true of Iowa.

For a short time in the village of Amana the farm boss and the train station manager collaborated to deliver a daily weather report via telegraph. When the station master received the morning report on the telegraph, he sent word to the head farm boss, who chose an appropriate flag from the collection kept for just that purpose and ran the flag up a tall pole beside the Amana General Store. The triangular flags, decorated with various ingenious symbols, notified residents of partly cloudy or stormy or sunny days, of windy weather, frosts to come, or blizzards. The system worked for a time and then was abandoned, perhaps because Iowa weather defies simple description and the farm boss got tired of running up a different flag every time the wind changed. The flagpole came down two generations ago, but the flags, a bit tattered, still exist in the collection of the Museum of Amana History.

With or without the aid of flags and telegraph, the *Gartebaas* watched the weather and the moon. Planting by moon phase is an ancient custom in many lands and was practiced here by the *Gartebaase*. The wisdom was that everything that bears above the ground, such as peas and beans, should be planted when the moon is on the increase from new moon to full moon. Everything that bears below the ground, potatoes, carrots and the like, should be planted when the moon is waning from full to new moon. During the moon's dark phase nothing should be planted, though it may be a good time to plow or pull weeds. As one *Gartebaas* noted in her journal, "Peas you should sow when the moon is rising so that you won't get the bugs."

Amana gardeners grew as much of their seed as possible. Preferring not to spend community dollars on seed, they harvested their own and spent winter days sorting, weighing, and labeling the precious seed. Special care was taken with several rare plant varieties unavailable in American seed catalogs but cultivated by community gardeners because they were dependable producers. These plants may have come from Germany, or they may have been first developed in Amana. Historians know that seed for favorite varieties was brought from Germany to

Ebenezer when the community first settled there. In 1844 artist and avid gardener Joseph Prestele confirmed in letters that seed brought from Germany had been planted and had flourished beyond expectation. As is noted in a variety of sources, throughout the history of Amana there have been members of the community who were enthusiastic gardeners and talented nurserymen. They would have had the knowledge to develop new plant varieties or to enhance old ones.

Preserving a Priceless Treasure

In a project initiated by the Amana Preservation Foundation and now carried on by the Amana Heritage Society, Larry and Wilma Rettig of South Amana are working to perpetuate historic plant varieties via the collection and distribution of seeds.

Since 1985 the Rettigs, as volunteers, have operated the seed bank. They established the bank with a handful of precious seeds given to them by an Amana *Oma* (grandmother) who was afraid that the traditional varieties would be lost. Within a few years, by growing the plants and harvesting and sharing seed with other gardeners, the Rettigs have built a stock of these Amana varieties:

Amana Stargenbohnen (string bean)
Ebenezer Zwiebel (onion)
Eiersalat (leaf lettuce)
Vielfarbiger Rettich (many-colored radish)
Zitronenmelone (citron melon)
Knollensellerie (celeriac)
Schwarzwurzel (European black salsify)
Kapseltomatte (ground-cherry)

When talking with the Rettigs, you can understand their wholehearted commitment to the Amana Seed Bank. The beds of radish and celeriac, the yellow-leafed *Eiersalat*, and the tall pole beans are as much a part of Amana as the stone buildings and the great barns.

By Easter

In March the hotbeds were planted; each 12-foot-long glass-topped bed was sown with radishes, lettuce, and greens. Every *Baas* hoped to present her kitchen with fresh lettuce on Easter Sunday, and with luck and sunshine quite often the goal was accomplished. Boxes of seedlings were nurtured in sunny window wells and in the *Altans* (side porches). Plants that could withstand cold went in the ground as soon as possible. A special winter cabbage that had been fall transplanted from the garden to a dirt bed in the kitchen house cellar was replanted in early spring and encouraged to shoot seed. The seed was replanted, seedlings transplanted, and the cabbage harvested late summer. Gardeners hoped to have their potatoes in the ground by Easter even if it meant working in mittens and shawls.

From the *Gartebaas*'s Journal

Writing notes in a small, canvas-bound notebook, Marie Murbach, *Gartebaas* for the Ruedy Kitchen House in Middle Amana, kept account of her gardening progress. In the spring of 1900, Mrs. Murbach was 37 years old and already a veteran gardener. Mrs. Murbach continued as *Baas* for nearly 30 more years, living in Middle and working alongside two daughters, one of whom would eventually become a *Küchebaas*. The journal was translated from German by Susanna Hahn of Middle Amana, Mrs. Murbach's granddaughter.

Excerpt from the Year 1900

Today the 22nd of March we planted the hotbeds and some salad in the *Rabatt* [raised bed along a building foundation]: celeriac, Henderson [seed variety] kraut and Kitzingen savoy, red cabbage, leeks, and several kinds of tomatoes, cauliflower, and kohlrabi.

23rd of March. More salad in the *Rabatts* and one row of beets. And we planted the horseradish.

9th of April. We had some plowing done.

10th of April. We started planting onion sets through the 14th of April. All the sets were planted. Ten bushels of sets.

19th of April. We plowed again and put the onion out for seed. On the 20th we spaded the asparagus patch and put out the garlic. Planted salad and radishes, spinach, salsify and peas, beets, carrots. We planted late cabbage and onion seed. In 36 plots, each 22–24 feet long, we planted beans, cucumbers, and the last beets and carrots.

May 1 we planted more cucumbers, the last peas, and summer endive.

May 2 we planted six rows of kraut plants and all kinds of other plants, rest of cabbage and so forth.

4th of May we put in one plot of pole beans, one plot of celeriac, and other plants. Sowed the cabbage plants to plots between the onions and cauliflower, late and early Savoy, and cabbage. We planted the rest of the early cabbage .

Easter

Easter was celebrated with loving reverence. Bible passages describing the last days of Christ's life were read in sequence in special church services held each noon of Holy Week. The German Bible verses, spoken in hushed voices, nonetheless echoed across the *Saal* (church meeting room); each chapter a canto in Christ's elegy.

Hymns written especially for Holy Week were sung, including this 380-year-old German hymn:

> Lord Jesus Christ, my Life, my Light,
> My Strength by day, my Trust by night,
> On earth I'm but a passing guest
> And sorely with my sins oppressed.

> (Martin Behemb, "Herr Jesus Christ,
> Mein's Lebens Licht," [1608]
> *The Amana Church Hymnal*)

Good Friday was a day of fasting: bread and water was all that was served to most except the very young, the very old, and the ill. Work continued but was punctuated by morning, noon, and evening worship services.

On Easter the sequence of worship services culminated in a joyful commemoration Easter morning. "Ere yet the dawn hath filled the skies / Behold my Savior Christ arise," the congregation sang in German, the melody sweeping through the open windows out across the flowering gardens, out to the jonquils and bleeding heart and the budding forsythia.

After the lengthy service worshippers in all seven villages went home to the customary Easter meal: asparagus, fresh lettuce salad, tiny new red radishes, *Spätzle* soup, smoke-cured ham, mashed potatoes topped with toasted bread crumbs, and rice pudding with sweet canned apricots or plums. Gathered around a table in the "good room," the family, *Oma, Opa,* and any other relatives living in the house,

enjoyed the first, and perhaps best, meal of spring; that too was a tradition of the season.

Easter Baskets

Every child had an Easter basket made just for him or her by the village basket weaver. Empty baskets were not allowed on Easter, so each kitchen house planned Easter egg hunts for the children it served and children related to the cooks. Since a child usually had aunts, sisters, mothers, and grandmothers employed in kitchen houses or gardens throughout the village, it was typical for a child to attend two, three, or more egg hunts. Baskets in hand, the children searched for colored eggs and sugar cookies among the shiny tinware in the kitchen or, if the weather was fine, out in the garden beside the kitchen house, where eggs were nestled under the lilacs and amid the new growth of daylilies.

Filling those baskets took some effort by the kitchen workers. During or just before Holy Week, eggs were dyed in each kitchen house, the cooks coaxing chickens and hoarding eggs just for Easter. Eggs were dyed using onion skins. Cooks saved onions skins for weeks, hoping to collect enough for several dozen eggs, which attain a rich honey-colored hue in a pot of simmering onion skin broth. Sometimes cooks tied thread around the eggs or used warm, softened, beeswax to draw patterns on the eggs. Using a wax stylus, the poet wrote German rhymes upon the eggs, delighting the children with a brief verse regarding spring flowers or Easter tidings. When the eggs were placed in the onion skins, the coloring did not adhere to the beeswax and the eggs emerged decorated with delicate designs or poetry.

Eggs were also colored using vivid dye from the woolen mill's dye works mixed with glue from a woodworking shop. The dye and glue were cooked in a double boiler until bubbly, poured into cups, and then allowed to cool to a rubberlike consistency. Roll hot newly hard-boiled eggs on the jelled dye, and the result is a wonder. How anyone hit upon this method is a mystery, but the resulting eggs are so brilliantly colored that they defy description. Red, yellow, purple, green, and blue eggs, plus the rainbow-colored eggs favored by all Amana children, were made by the kitchen house women and are still made to this day by enterprising colony women who have found modern means for replicating the old-fashioned eggs. The recipe for Amana Easter Eggs is a secret, shared only among the colony women, but if you come to Amana at Easter time, ask to see a dozen Amana Easter eggs.

Onion Skin Easter Eggs

Wilma Rettig of South Amana was happy to share her technique for coloring eggs with onion skins. There is no formula for this process. Like many things, it is accomplished with a little practical know-how, a little patience, and a little luck. There is no right or wrong to dying Easter eggs; that is why it is a perfect Easter activity to share with children.

Onion Skin Easter Eggs

Skins from yellow onions, at least 1 ½ quarts, but more is better
Beeswax, a crayon or a chunk
1 or 2 dozen white eggs, raw

Collect a lot of onion skins. In fact, at Christmas it may be best to begin collecting the whisper thin brown and yellow outer skins and placing these in a coffee can with lid or some other airtight container. Do not mix skins from red and yellow onions, or the resulting eggs won't be as nice.

Soften edge or tip of beeswax a bit and then gently draw upon raw eggs. Draw whatever you like.

In a stockpot or kettle simmer onion skins in enough water so that you can immerse the eggs. Allow to simmer about 20 minutes or until you have a brown broth. Allow to cool. Then add eggs to cooled liquid (adding cold eggs to hot liquid will cause cracks) and turn up heat. Cook just as you would to hard-boil eggs. When eggs are hard-boiled, remove kettle from heat, add cold water to onion skin broth, and remove eggs. Discard broth and onion skins. Wash off eggs. Refrigerate eggs until ready to place in baskets.

To remove wax from your soup pot, swish with hot water and then scour.

Makes 1 to 2 dozen colored eggs.

Rabbit Cookies

Henry Schiff, Amana, was a baker in communal times, and as a young apprentice in the bakery he drove the horse and wagon through the village, delivering bread and coffee cake to the village's 16 kitchen houses. An amiable youth, ready with a smile and a friendly word, he was, as anyone could tell you, a favorite of the kitchen house *Baase,* who remembered him at Easter when the rabbit cookies emerged from the oven, hot and ready to be frosted. As he tells it, "At Easter time I would make my rounds, and the cooks would say, 'Would you like a cookie?' and by the end I had 16 of those big rabbit cookies. I just couldn't say no. Those rabbit cookies were just too good!"

Made with cookie cutters fashioned at the village tin shop, there were chickens and squirrels, lambs and deer, but everyone loved the 8-inch-long rabbit cookies. Shaped like a hare on the run, the long cookies with raisin eyes were frosted white and perhaps decorated with shredded coconut or colored sugar. In addition to a few smaller cookies, one rabbit cookie was given to each child, and though time has a way of enhancing all such memories, those cookies, as any colony native will tell you, were the best ever tasted.

Oster Hasen
Easter Rabbit Cookies

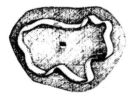

2 ½ cups granulated sugar
2 ½ cups brown sugar
1 ¼ cups vegetable shortening
1 ¼ cups butter
15 eggs
13 teaspoons baking powder
15 cups flour
2 ½ cups milk
1 to 2 cups raisins or chocolate chips
Vanilla frosting (page 211)

In a large mixing bowl cream sugars and shortening and butter. Beat in eggs, blending well after each addition.

In a second bowl mix flour and baking powder. Stir flour mixture into batter, alternating with 2 cups milk. Add final ½ cup milk only if the batter seems too dry (the size of the eggs used may make batter too moist or too dry). This forms a very soft dough.

Dough must be refrigerated at least overnight. Since this is a soft dough and can be difficult to roll and cut out, you may want to place dough in freezer 1 hour before baking. Roll out portion of dough on well-floured board. Keep the remaining dough in the freezer or refrigerator while you are rolling and cutting. Using a rabbit cookie cutter, cut into shapes and place a raisin or a chocolate chip in each for the bunny's eye.

Bake at 350° for 10 to 11 minutes. Allow cookies to cool before icing with vanilla frosting.

Yields about 10 dozen cookies, depending upon the size of the cookie cutter.

Zuber's Kitchen House, Middle Amana
Dorothy and Emilie Zuber, Middle Amana

Note: Several recipes for *Oster Hasen* are used in the Amanas, but this one from the Zuber Kitchen House in Middle Amana is considered by many cooks to be the ultimate bunny cookie recipe. It originated there in the old brick kitchen house (where only raisins, no chocolate chips, were used for bunny eyes) and has been shared among colony cooks for generations.

As you can see, it makes about 10 dozen cookies, and you may wish to cut the recipe in half for your Easter baking. The recipe has been updated to include chocolate chips and the hint about using the freezer to stiffen the dough. If you like, decorate your bunnies with shredded coconut or colored sugar sprinkles.

From the Tinsmith's Shop

Cookie cutters were handmade at the village tin shop. Fashioned from strips of *Blech* (tin), the cutters were made to last for many years.

One of the few things the tinsmith produced that called for fanciful interpretation, each cookie cutter was different. He made stars and bunnies, fluted diamonds, circles, Santas, and gingerbreadmen, but the tinsmith was not limited to these few designs and could make whatever his imagination conjured. And so Amana boys and girls grew up eating cookies shaped like chickens and deer, camels and fish, bonneted ladies and leaping ponies, swallows and swans.

Elizabeth Schoenfelder's father was the village of Amana's tinsmith, and she remembers her mother asking him to make new cookie cutters. "She told him 'I'd like something different.' And so my brother said, 'I want a big cookie!' My father made a big rabbit for him. Then I said, 'I'd like a squirrel. I don't want a rabbit.' So he made me a nice squirrel. It's sitting with its tail up—really very nice. He did a good job. . . . I still have it."

Spring Forage

The earth provides. When rejuvenating sunshine brings green to the gardens and yards, colony folk go out with paring knife in hand to cut dandelion greens. So did the communal cooks and the garden workers who looked for newly sprouted dandelions in the yards and meadows. Many Amana gardeners actually cultivated dandelions, keeping a bed near the garden and covering it with straw late in the spring to prevent the dandelions from maturing. This was in keeping with old-world ways. In Germany, particularly the southwestern regions, dandelion salad, called *Löwenzahn Salat* (lion's teeth salad), was a common dish, and dandelion greens could be purchased in the marketplace. According to gardening expert Louise Riotte in her book, *Sleeping with a Sunflower*, dandelion greens were also typical early American fare, and dandelion seed was available in American seed catalogs by 1870.

To the uninitiated, the thought of eating weeds is difficult to overcome, but Amana residents consider a *Zigorriesalat*, dandelion salad with creamy dressing, a delicacy to be relished.

Zigorriesalat
Dandelion Salad

4 cups prepared
   dandelion greens
1 tablespoon diced
   onions
2 tablespoons bacon fat
   or vegetable shorten-
   ing
2 tablespoons flour
¾ cup water
2 tablespoons vinegar
3 cups hard-boiled eggs,
   chilled and sliced
⅓ cup cream or half
   and half
Dash salt and pepper

Find a grassy area where no chemical fertilizers or pesticides have been used, ever. In March or April select young green dandelions from this yard. (By the time the dandelions bloom, the leaves are too bitter to eat.) Spread newspaper on work area and then place greens on paper separating inner, tender leaves from darker, tougher leaves. Discard outer leaves. Wash inner leaves over and over again in cold water to remove grit. Chop greens into small bits. Place in colander and rinse again. Allow to drain.

In a medium-sized skillet sauté onions in fat or shortening. Add flour and stir until smooth. Combine water and vinegar and pour both into skillet. Stir until thickened. Remove from heat. Place sliced eggs in empty salad bowl; add cooked dressing and cream or half and half. Stir and add salt and dash pepper. Allow dressing to cool; then toss in prepared greens.

Serves four to six.

Spring Nettle

As unassuming as the lowly nettle is, the weed was valued by colony residents who gathered nettle tops from barnyard, ditch, and canal levee by the bushelful in the spring. Nettle greens were considered to be a healthful dish, a blood purifier, a rejuvenator and a kind of spring tonic. Combined with dandelions or lettuce, nettle greens were eaten in salads. Nettle greens were also cooked solo or in combination with any fresh greens available and prepared very much like kale or spinach.

Gekochte Nessel
Cooked Spring Nettle

5 cups prepared nettle
    tops
4 tablespoons butter or
    margarine
3 to 4 tablespoons
    water
1 to 2 cups beef stock
    (page 44) or
    vegetable stock
    (page 46)
2 tablespoons minced
    onions or the tops of
    several green
    onions, chopped
2 tablespoons flour
Salt and pepper

In early spring find some stinging nettle plants in an unmowed area where no chemicals of any type have been used. By late spring or early summer the nettles have matured beyond their culinary prime and may contain juices harmful to humans.

Wearing gloves, grasp the nettles and remove the green tops. When you have a full large pail, remove tender green leaves from the tops and wash over and over. Chop into pieces.

Place greens in a kettle or large saucepan with melted butter or margarine and several tablespoons water. Cook over medium-low heat, stirring occasionally, until very tender. Drain.

Return greens to pot; add beef or vegetable stock and onions. Stir in flour to thicken and salt and pepper to taste. Cook slowly about 1 hour.

Serves six.

Note: You must use sound cooking judgment when preparing this recipe. Depending upon the amount of nettle greens you have, you will need to make adjustments in the amount of beef stock and flour you are using, or the result will be soupy.

Morel Mushrooms

Iowa, like a few other midwestern states, is blessed with a climate, woodlands, and soil favorable to morel mushrooms. Amana is no exception, and the forests here have their secret places where the mushrooms appear each April and May.

Taking a hint from their Iowa County neighbors, some communal Amana residents discovered that the golden morels, more rare than truffles, were one of nature's best gifts. Spring hours were spent in search of the tender, sponge-topped morel (*Morchella esculenta*) hidden among the first spring flowers and plants of the woodland. For many years in Amana morel mushroom hunting was pursued only by a few

well-informed colonists who brought home their morels and fried the mushrooms on the washhouse woodstove in an iron skillet borrowed from the kitchen house. Since the end of the communal era in 1932, morel mushroom hunting has gained popularity among those who enjoy a walk, even a long one, in the woods.

No one has been able to grow morels for commercial sale, and so you won't find them conveniently placed on your grocer's shelf. In fact there is nothing convenient about getting a few morels. All you can do, really, is find a likely looking forest, get the owner's permission to search there, wait for a spring day, and tramp about with sack in hand hoping you will get lucky. If you are a novice morel mushroom hunter, find an expert or a book about mushrooms and make sure your morels are indeed morels. There are varieties of mushrooms that appear to be morels but are, in fact, imposters, and it would not do to become ill from eating wild mushrooms.

If you should be so lucky as to find a few yellow morels standing like tiny sentries beneath an old pine tree or under the multiflora rose bushes or alongside the trunk of a dead elm tree, here is a recipe for preparing your spring treasure.

Gebratene Pilze
Fried Morels

Morel mushrooms
¼ box saltine crackers,
    crushed
2 eggs
Melted vegetable
    shortening, ¼ inch
    deep in skillet

Wash the morels very carefully, trimming off the soiled end of the stem and any dark brown or spoiled portions. The object is to save as much of the mushroom as possible. Rinse thoroughly, removing grit. Gently drip dry and blot with towel.

Cut medium- or large-sized mushrooms in half lengthwise. Crush saltine crackers until you've got a fine crumb. Pour the crumbs into a sturdy plastic bag.

Beat eggs with a little dash of water. In a heavy skillet melt shortening. Dredge mushrooms in egg and throw in crumb sack. Shake gently until mushrooms are coated. It's best to dredge and shake just a few mushrooms at a time. When all the mushrooms have been breaded, fry in hot shortening until deep golden brown. Drain on paper towels and pat dry. Serve hot.

Note: Fried morels are rich and need only be accompanied by a light meal. If you are not interested in fried foods, you may want to try morels in a 3-egg omelet. Or sauté the morels in butter and add to a rich meat gravy to top a choice cut of beef or pork.

Spring Pursuits and Pleasures

With farm work to be done, gardens to be sown, and dozens of other chores to be accomplished, there was little time in spring for Amana residents to spend on hobbies or other pastimes. When at leisure, more often than not, they went to the forest where the bluebells spread a turquoise carpet. A favorite picnic spot for Homestead and Amana residents was the wooded bluff overlooking the Indian Dam. Built of glacial boulders, the V-shaped fish trap, or weir, was believed to have been constructed by Native Americans over 200 years before the Inspirationists arrived in the valley. Now flooding and sedimentation have changed and even destroyed portions of the dam, but in communal times when the colonists saw it and walked upon it, the trap was nearly whole and quite impressive.

Another Sunday walk took residents in High Amana, Middle Amana, East Amana, and Amana to meadows near their villages where the shepherds kept the sheep and newborn lambs played in the clover. Not every village had a herd of sheep, but those that did kept them for the wool, not the mutton. Walking out to see the lambs, following the farm lane up over the hill to the green meadow where the sheep roamed, was considered the very best way to spend a spring day.

CHAPTER 4 **SOUPS**

Soup we always had with the noon meal.
Good soup.

Louise Wendler Noé

Nourishing and easy to prepare in quantity, soup can be made from ingredients commonly found in a well-stocked kitchen and from otherwise unsuitable joints of meat. Therefore, soup was perfect for Amana communal meals. Every day of the year there was soup simmering on the stove in the communal kitchen. The kettle, carefully tended by the cook, bubbled, and steam rose carrying the smell of delicious soup. Preparing and then straining the stock were important tasks, and young cooks were carefully instructed in the art of soup making. From a rich beef stock, clear chicken broth, or vegetable stock a variety of soups were made: *Fransozensuppe* (French vegetable), *Klösselsuppe* (dumpling), *Riebelsuppe* (egg white), *Linsensuppe* (lentil), and *Kartoffelsuppe* (potato) just to name a few. On Sundays it was usually chicken rice or chicken with *Spätzle* (part noodle, part dumpling), and on very special occasions there was chicken rice with tender bread dumplings. Soup, hot and savory, was an essential element in communal Amana cooking.

Rindknochenbrühe
Beef Stock from Beef Bones

3 ½ to 4 pounds beef
  bones, raw
4 quarts cold water
1 small leek, coarsely
  chopped
3 carrots, coarsely
  chopped
Several stalks celery,
  including tender
  yellow inner stalks,
  chopped
3 sprigs fresh parsley or
  2 teaspoons dried
  parsley

Choose beef soup bones with some meat clinging to them. In a preheated 400° oven, roast beef bones in a roasting pan about 20 minutes until browned.

Using a large stockpot or kettle, add roasted beef bones to water. There should be enough water to cover bones. Add vegetables and parsley. Bring to a boil and then turn down the heat. Simmer uncovered or partially covered 2 ½ to 3 hours. Strain stock, discarding bones and vegetables. Refrigerate overnight and then remove fat. The resulting beef stock is excellent for a variety of soups and may be frozen for future use.

Yields 3 quarts stock.

Note: The colony cook used leeks from the kitchen garden for beef stock, and indeed, leeks add delicious flavor to beef stock. If you are unable to find leeks, onions may be substituted to good effect. This recipe calls for celery, which is common in today's gardens and grocery stores, but in communal Amana the cook would have used celeriac, sometimes called "root celery." Nowadays, celeriac is difficult to come by unless you grow it yourself.

Rindfleischbrühe
Beef Stock from Soup Meat

1 to 2 pounds boiling
  beef or other
  inexpensive cut of
  beef with bone
3 to 4 quarts cold water
1 small leek, coarsely
  chopped or 1 large
  onion, chopped
2 carrots, coarsely
  chopped
Several stalks celery,
  chopped
2 sprigs fresh parsley or
  1 ½ teaspoons dried
  parsley

In a large stockpot or kettle add meat to water. Add vegetables and parsley to the kettle. Bring to a boil. Turn down heat and allow to simmer uncovered or partially covered about 3 hours or until meat is tender. Drain, discarding vegetables. Allow meat to cool enough to handle. Trim meat from bone in bite-sized pieces. Discard bone. Reserve meat and refrigerate. Refrigerate stock overnight. Remove the fat and re-heat stock, adding meat for beef barley, beef vegetable, or beef lentil soup.

Yields about 3 quarts stock.

Hühnerfleischbrühe
Chicken Broth

3 pounds chicken
    wings, backs, or
    necks, raw
4 quarts water
1 onion, chopped
3 carrots, chopped
Several stalks celery,
    chopped
$\frac{1}{2}$ teaspoon thyme
3 sprigs fresh parsley
    or 2 teaspoons dried

Wash chicken and then add to stockpot or kettle containing 4 quarts water. Add vegetables to kettle. Add thyme and parsley. Turn up heat and bring slowly to a boil. Reduce heat and simmer 1 to 2 hours. Remove chicken from bones and refrigerate for future use. Strain broth. Refrigerate or freeze broth until ready to use.

Yields about 3 quarts stock.

Hühnerknochenbrühe
Chicken Broth

1 cooked chicken (or
    turkey) carcass
2 to 3 quarts water (or
    enough to cover)
1 onion or leek,
    chopped
1 carrot, chopped
1 to 2 sprigs fresh
    parsley or 1
    teaspoon dried
$\frac{1}{4}$ teaspoon thyme

Remove any large pieces of meat from carcass and reserve for soup. Cut leftover carcass into several manageable pieces and place in kettle containing about 2 quarts water or enough to cover. Add vegetables to kettle. Stir in parsley and thyme. Bring broth to a boil; then turn down heat and simmer $1 \frac{1}{2}$ hours. Strain. Discard vegetables and bones and reserve meat and broth. Refrigerate or freeze until ready to use. Remove fat before reheating. Chicken broth is an essential ingredient in the Amana stalwart *Hühnersosse,* creamed chicken.

Yields 1–2 quarts broth.

Salting the Soup

When making broth or stock, the goal is to produce a flavorful base from which soup can be made. You will notice that none of the recipes for broth or stock call for the addition of salt or pepper. Because cooking stock in an open kettle can reduce the liquid by nearly half, it therefore intensifies the salty flavor. It is best to wait and to add salt and pepper during the last stage of soup making after all other ingredients have been allowed to simmer at length. At that time the soup has attained nearly full flavor, and it is much easier to judge how much salt and pepper is required. Be cautious with the salt and pepper, please. Too much of either can ruin your soup, and as one Amana cook conceded, "*Ja,* there is nothing worse than salty soup."

Gemüsenbrühe
Vegetable Stock

2 tablespoons butter or margarine
1 cup chopped yellow onion
3 to 4 carrots, chopped
Several stalks celery, including yellow inner stalks, chopped
½ cup diced turnips or kohlrabi (optional)
2 quarts water
1 to 2 sprigs fresh parsley or 1 teaspoon dried
½ teaspoon thyme

In a small kettle, melt butter and sauté chopped yellow onion until just tender. Add other vegetables and just enough water to cover. Add parsley and thyme. Simmer slowly until vegetables are tender, about 1 hour. Remove from heat. Strain and discard vegetables. Refrigerate or freeze vegetable stock until ready to use.

Yields about 1 ½ quarts stock.

Note: Vegetable stock, light and wholesome, is a suitable base for tomato soup, vegetable soup, or potato soup. It can be substituted for beef stock if necessary, although the resulting soup will not be as flavorful. Vegetable stock can be used to prepare the traditional Amana dishes: creamed spinach, creamed kale, *Krautgemüse,* and *Kartoffelgemüse.*

Fransozensuppe
French Vegetable Soup

2 quarts beef stock
   (page 44)
1 quart home-canned
   tomatoes or
   1 46-ounce can
   tomato juice
1 to 2 cups cubed
   cooked beef
   (optional)
2 quarts shredded or
   finely chopped
   cabbage (1 large
   head)
3 medium onions,
   chopped
3 medium carrots,
   chopped
Salt and pepper to taste

Combine stock and canned tomatoes or tomato juice. Add cubed beef (if desired) and vegetables. Simmer on medium-low heat until vegetables are tender. Add salt and pepper.

Yields 12 servings.

Linda Selzer, Homestead

Note: As a young cook in the Graesser Kitchen House in West Amana, where her mother was *Baas,* Mrs. Selzer was taught to prepare *Fransozensuppe.* When Mrs. Selzer prepares it, she shares with neighbors and friends, "It makes so much I end up giving it away, but it does keep well in the refrigerator or freezer."

Fransozensuppe ohne Fleisch
Light French Vegetable Soup

2 quarts vegetable stock
   (page 46), chicken
   broth (page 45), or
   instant chicken
   bouillon
2 quarts shredded or
   finely chopped
   cabbage (1 large
   head)

3 medium onions,
   chopped fine
3 medium carrots,
   chopped fine
1 large can tomato juice
   (46 ounce)
Dash salt and pepper

Prepare stock or broth and, if necessary, add water to increase to 2 quarts. Bring slowly to a boil; add vegetables and tomato juice. Simmer until vegetables are tender. If you are using instant bouillon, do not add salt. If you are using homemade stock, you may want to add a dash of salt and pepper. Taste your soup before adding the salt.

Yields 12 servings.

Linda Selzer, Homestead

Note: Mrs. Selzer adapted the original *Fransozensuppe* recipe to conform to her family's low-fat diet.

Gerstesuppe
Beef Barley Soup

2 quarts beef stock
   (page 44)
Reserved meat, cut into
   small cubes
½ cup barley,
   uncooked
Salt and pepper to taste

Prepare beef stock, reserving meat. Strain and remove fat. In stockpot or kettle bring stock to a boil; then turn down heat and add barley. Simmer until barley is tender. Salt and pepper to taste.

Yields about 10 servings.

Linsensuppe
Lentil Soup

½ pound green lentils
1 pound bratwurst
1 gallon beef stock
   (page 44)
1 cup chopped celery
1 cup carrot, chopped
1 chopped onion

Wash lentils and soak for an hour. Drain and rinse well.

Remove skin from bratwurst and form sausage into small balls. Brown in skillet, drain, and pat dry.

Meanwhile bring beef stock to a boil and then add vegetables. Let boil up once and then add lentils. Simmer until lentils and vegetables are tender. Ten minutes before serving, add sausage balls and bring to a boil. Turn down heat and allow to simmer. Serve steaming hot.

Yields about 12 servings.

Helen Kippenhan, Homestead

Note: Mrs. Kippenhan knows her soup. Taught the art of cooking in a Middle Amana kitchen by Lina Hahn, after all communal kitchens closed in 1932, Mrs. Kippenhan became a cook at the Homestead Sandwich Shop and later at Bill Zuber's Restaurant in Homestead. For 27 years, Mrs. Kippenhan minded the soup kettle at Zuber's and there perfected the recipes she was taught as a girl.

"Burnt Barley Soup?"

Only rarely did an Amana cook try something new in her kitchen, but once in a great while if a recipe sounded as if it could be managed for 30-plus diners and if it appeared worth the risk, the *Küchebaas* gave it a try.

So it was when Elizabeth Schoenfelder's mother, an Amana *Baas,* heard about lentil soup. As Mrs. Schoenfelder tells the story,

> Lentils were unknown in the Amanas. My mother had gotten the recipe and the lentils from friends in Cedar Rapids. So my mother said, "We're going to try something new. We're making *Linsensuppe.*" And when the people came, they had their containers. It was Wednesday, see; lentil soup came close to vegetable soup that we usually had on Wednesdays, and the ladies looked at the soup, and hardly anyone took soup. My mother said, "That's strange!" Well, we found out later that they had thought it was barley soup and that we had burnt the barley cooking it, and so they hardly took any. But the little they took, they asked the next day if there was any left. They liked it. It was good. After that it was served frequently. But at that time in Amana no one knew about lentils.

Klössel
Dumplings for Soup

3 eggs, separated
¼ cup butter, softened
1 ½ cups water
1 ½ cups flour
¼ t salt

Beat egg whites until very frothy. Set aside. Beat yolks lightly; then add butter, water, and flour alternately. Fold in egg whites. Drop by teaspoon into simmering beef stock or chicken broth.

Makes enough dumplings for one large kettle of soup.

Schaefer Kitchen House, East Amana

Note: This dumpling recipe was handwritten by Lena (Magdalena) Schaefer in her kitchen journal alongside recipes for dill pickles and oatmeal cookies. There were, and are, many different dumpling recipes used in Amana kitchens. A few are listed here, and others exist in the memories of good colony cooks. In a community where dumplings were, and still are, considered "good for what ails you," there is no one basic recipe.

Mrs. Kippenhan's Dumpling Soup

¼ cup butter or
    margarine, softened
2 to 3 eggs
¼ teaspoon seasoning
    salt
Pepper
Dash freshly grated
    nutmeg
3 cups fresh bread
    crumbs
1 gallon chicken broth
    (see recipe, page 45)
    or beef stock (page
    44)
½ cup dry Cream of
    Wheat

Into softened butter, add 2 eggs, salt, dash pepper, and nutmeg. Whip. Gradually stir in bread crumbs. If the mixture seems dry, add the third egg. Knead by hand until dough achieves a firm consistency. Form about 1 teaspoon of dough into ball. Place on plate or cookie sheet, cover, and refrigerate.

Heat broth or stock to a boil and add Cream of Wheat while stirring. Let simmer. About 10 minutes before serving, add dumplings and simmer hard until dumplings float to the top of the kettle, about 5 to 10 minutes.

Yields about 30 dumplings.

Helen Kippenhan, Homestead

Erbsensuppe mit Klössel
Split Pea Soup with Dumplings

Use preceding recipe and omit Cream of Wheat. You may substitute vegetable stock (page 46) for chicken broth (page 45) or beef stock (page 44).

Wash ½ to ¾ bag of dried split green peas. Cook slowly in 1 gallon stock until peas are tender. When peas are soft, mash in pot with potato masher or turn through food mill or blender.

Prepare dumplings as stated in preceding recipe. Add dumplings to pea soup and simmer near boiling point until dumplings float to top and are cooked through. Serve hot topped with croutons or bits of buttered toast.

Yields about 12 servings.

Helen Kippenhan, Homestead

Suppe mit Spätzle
Chicken Soup with *Spätzle*

For chicken soup

1 chicken, cut into
    pieces

Water

Bay leaf

1 ½ cups finely diced
    celery

Salt to taste

2 14 ½ ounce cans
    chicken stock

For Spätzle dough

2 ½ cups flour

1 teaspoon salt

Pinch baking powder

1 cup milk

2 eggs, beaten lightly

Wash chicken and place in kettle with enough water to cover; add bay leaf. Simmer until tender, about 1 ½ hours. Remove chicken and refrigerate until cold. Strain stock and refrigerate. Remove chicken from bone and cut meat into bite-sized pieces. Refrigerate chicken and celery.

Remove desired amount of fat from chilled stock. Reheat stock in soup kettle, adding salt to taste and chicken stock.

For *Spätzle* measure flour and sift with dry ingredients. Pour into a mixing bowl and form a well. Add milk and stir with wooden spoon. Add eggs, slightly beaten, and stir until soft dough is smooth.

When broth is at a low boil, add *Spätzle* using either a handheld *Spätzle*-slicing machine (available in gourmet shops) or the old-fashioned method as follows: Hold bowl in one hand and sharp knife in the other. While slowly tipping bowl and pouring batter, cut with knife, dropping noodle-sized *Spätzle* into bubbling soup. *Spätzle* should be smaller than your little finger. It's best to dip the knife in hot soup after each slice.

Stir in celery and chicken. Cook about 5 to 8 minutes more (or until *Spätzle* bob to the surface of the kettle) and serve. Do not overcook or the *Spätzle* will toughen.

Yields about 12 servings.

Mary Wendler, High Amana

Note: When Mrs. Wendler contributed this recipe, she wrote, "The Amana people have always been known for the sharing of food. Perhaps it could be traced to the communal kitchen philosophy. It is a tradition and a Christian gesture that should be preserved. This recipe will make enough for your family with extra to bring a friend. It comprises the old Amana *Spätzle* recipe with modern techniques."

Mrs. Wendler also noted that the *Spätzle*-slicing machines now available make this soup much easier and more enjoyable to prepare.

A Taste of Swabia

There is no accounting for *Spätzle*. Part noodle, part dumpling, the German contribution to world cuisine defies description. Even its origin is obscure. Attributed to Swabia, a region of southwestern Germany, *Spätzle* may have been the invention of an unknown *Hausfrau* laboring over a steaming kettle in some medieval Swabian inn, or it may have been brought to the area by a Roman soldier of ancient times. Whatever the case, *Spätzle* caught on in Swabia and eventually gained popularity throughout Germany and Austria.

Hundreds of years later when the Inspirationists, some Swabian-born, packed up their belongings, they did not neglect to bring their recipe books or their taste for excellent *Schwabishe* cookery. *Spätzle* in soup, in pot pie, or as a side dish to *Sauerbraten* or roast pork was served in Ebenezer and in Amana. Today it is still being prepared and served in Amana homes and in local restaurants.

Spätzlesuppe
Beef *Spätzle* Soup

2 quarts beef stock
(page 44)
Spätzel (see preceding
recipe)
Several sprigs fresh
parsley

In a large kettle bring beef stock to near boiling. Prepare *Spätzle* batter and slice into stock. Simmer well until noodles bob to the surface, about 5 minutes. Garnish with parsley sprigs.

Yields about 10–12 servings.

Spargelsuppe
Asparagus Soup

2 tablespoons butter
3 tablespoons flour
2 leaves of leek,
　　chopped fine, or
　　½ onion, minced
2 quarts beef stock
　　(page 44) or
　　chicken broth (page
　　45)
2 pounds fresh aspara-
　　gus, cut into
　　1 ½-inch pieces
¼ teaspoon thyme
1 cup cream
Salt and pepper to taste

Melt butter in kettle and sauté chopped leek (or minced onion). Stir in flour. Turn down heat; add stock or broth, stirring well. Add asparagus and thyme. Allow to reach a boil. Reduce heat and simmer about 30–45 minutes. Tender asparagus stalks require less cooking time.

Cream asparagus mixture with food grinder or use electric blender or food processor. Stir in cream. Add salt and pepper to taste. Heat and serve.

Yields about 12 servings.

Note: Every *Gartebaas,* and some kitchen bosses, kept an asparagus patch, working it with extravagant care. More than likely the patch was planted by a mother or grandmother, for a well-tended asparagus bed may last years and years. It was the custom then to sprinkle salt on the bed each spring, a practice now thought to be unnecessary to the well-being of asparagus.

Tomatensuppe
Tomato Soup

3 ½ quarts tomato juice
6 stalks celery
7 sprigs fresh parsley
3 bay leaves
10 cloves
3 large onions, chopped
⅜ cup flour
3 tablespoons sugar
3 teaspoons salt
½ teaspoon pepper

In a very large kettle bring tomato juice, celery, parsley, bay leaves, cloves, and onions to a boil. Allow to simmer until celery stalks are tender and then some. Strain.

To strained soup sift in flour and add sugar. Stir in salt and pepper. Simmer slowly about 1 hour.

Yields about 16 servings.

Kippenhan Kitchen Journal, South Amana
Annie Kephart, South Amana

Of Home-canned Soup and Kitchen House Journals

Annie Kephart, South Amana, grew up in what was once the Kippenhan Kitchen House. Born in 1942 just 10 years after the end of the communal era, Mrs. Kephart grew up in transitional Amana, where older residents were coping with a new way of life and younger Amana folk were embracing that way of life, eager to disassociate themselves from time-worn communal ways. Amana residents then were learning to speak and write English; they were starting businesses, taking on new jobs, remodeling their homes, buying cars and radios, sending their children to high school and even college. Communal Amana was gone, but not forgotten, and although each passing year brought change to the villages, the residents clung to their church and their songs and stories. They tended their gardens and they cooked their colony food.

In those days then, former *Küchebaas,* Lina Kippenhan, like many other colony housewives, made all the good old colony recipes held dear in memory and in the flour-smudged, yellow-paged recipe journals. This recipe for tomato soup is hers, written in her communal kitchen journal. When she prepared it, however, she started with 7 quarts of homemade tomato juice, and she made it to be canned in sterilized quart jars, a hedge against future icy winter winds.

Today Mrs. Kephart keeps the Kippenhan Kitchen House journal, and while she counts it among her most-treasured things, she was happy to share this and other recipes. After all, she said, good things are worth remembering and sharing.

Kartoffelsuppe
Potato Soup

2 quarts beef stock (page 44) or vegetable stock (page 46)
2 pounds potatoes, raw, peeled, and diced
1 tablespoon chopped fresh parsley
1 large onion, peeled and chopped fine
Salt and pepper to taste
2 tablespoons butter or margarine
1 cup bread cubes

In a large kettle add stock and simmer potatoes, parsley, and onion until potatoes are tender, about 20–30 minutes. Mash potatoes with potato masher until nearly smooth. Add salt and pepper and simmer.

Just before serving, in a heavy skillet melt butter or margarine and brown bread cubes until toasted. Serve soup very hot topped with bread cubes.

Yields about 12 servings.

Die Geschichte vom Suppen-Kaspar
The Story of Soup Kaspar

Colony children who would not eat their soup were reminded, with a joke and a smile, of a storybook character well known in communal Amana, *Suppen-Kaspar,* who came to a very bad end and was buried beneath a soup tureen because he refused to eat his soup, crying, "O' take the nasty soup away. I won't have soup today!"

Soup Kaspar's story can be found in a German children's book popular in Amana, and in all German-speaking communities, titled *Struwwelpeter* (Slovenly Peter). Written and illustrated in 1844 by Dr. E. Heinrich Hoffman, *Struwwelpeter* is a collection of cautionary tales for children. Often silly, sometimes surreal, and occasionally downright macabre, the fate of children who play with matches, are rude to their elders, or tease their schoolmates is set forth in vivid detail with oddly engaging illustrations. Hoffman originally wrote *Struwwelpeter* for his son but was persuaded by friends to have it published and was astonished when it became a top seller in Germany. Later Hoffman wrote other children's books including *The Nutcracker,* which was the basis for Tchaikovsky's magical ballet of the same name.

Rahmsuppe
Cream Soup or Dead Man's Stew

2 tablespoons butter or
   margarine
1 slice of bread, cut into
   cubes
2 cups whole milk or 1
   cup cream cut with
   ½ cup water
¼ teaspoon salt

This makes one serving of soup. Melt butter or margarine in heavy saucepan or skillet, add bread cubes, and brown lightly over low heat. While stirring, add milk and salt. On low heat, simmer about 10 minutes. Do not allow the milk to boil or scald. Serve hot.

Serves one.

Note: In communal Amana, *Rahmsuppe* was served to ill folk and new mothers. It occupies a special place in Amana folklore exciting strong opinion: either you love it or you hate it. Some colony residents are sure that it was the dish *Suppen-Kaspar* died refusing.

CHAPTER 5 # SALADS

*When you needed a whole pail of radishes to make a salad,
you planted a lot of radishes!*

Elizabeth Schoenfelder, Amana

They served what they had when they had it in Amana's communal kitchens. In spring, nettle and dandelion greens combined with hotbed leaf lettuce more than sufficed until the gardens brought forth head lettuce, endive, spinach, kale, tomatoes, cucumbers, and onions, all the makings of summer salads. In late summer, cabbage and other hot weather crops peaked, and the variety of salads offered in the kitchen houses expanded. In autumn, the very last of the fresh vegetable salads appeared, served alongside pickles and relishes. By winter, pickled vegetables and relishes and the occasional hot celeriac *Salat* were all the salad there was, and folks thought longingly of spring when the *Gartebaases* would ready the hotbeds and fresh greens would appear again to everyone's delight.

Colony Dressing

2 ½ tablespoons
vinegar
4 tablespoons mayon-
naise or sour cream
½ cup half and half
3 green onions, chopped
fine
Salt and pepper to taste
1 hard-boiled egg, sliced

Combine vinegar, mayonnaise or sour cream, and half and half. Stir until smooth. Add onions; salt and pepper to taste. The dressing's consistency should be thin and creamy smooth. To make a traditional colony salad, prepare this dressing and pour over a tossed salad made of leaf lettuce and several sliced radishes, and one sliced hard-boiled egg.

Yields about ¾ cup dressing.

Janet Zuber, High Amana

Note: Mrs. Zuber makes this dressing several times a week and always on Sunday when the Zuber family dinner is served and children and grandchildren are invited. Although this recipe can be made with sour cream, Mrs. Zuber prefers mayonnaise. Communal Amana cooks made their own mayonnaise from egg yolks, olive oil, dried mustard, and sour cream, but modern-day cooks may find store-bought mayonnaise more convenient.

French Dressing

4 tablespoons vinegar
8 tablespoons olive oil
Juice of 1 lemon
1 tablespoon sugar
1 heaping teaspoon
paprika
Dash celery seed
Salt and pepper to taste

Stir together ingredients and chill. Serve over lettuce or chopped tomatoes.

Yields about ⅔ cup dressing.

Kippenhan Kitchen, South Amana
Annie Kephart, South Amana

Sour Cream Dressing

½ cup sour cream
¼ cup whole milk or
half and half
1 tablespoon minced
chives
Salt and pepper to taste

Whip sour cream and milk or half and half until creamy. Stir in chives and salt and pepper. Chill until ready to serve.

Yields about ¾ cup dressing.

Rettichsalat
Radish Salad

2 dozen or so radishes,
 thinly sliced
½ teaspoon salt
½ cup sour cream
1 tablespoon vinegar
1 heaping tablespoon
 chopped green
 onions
Pepper to taste

Sprinkle radishes with salt and set aside. After ½ to 1 hour drain liquid from radishes. Place radishes in glass serving dish. Stir together sour cream and vinegar. Pour over radishes; add green onions and pepper to taste. Toss and chill. Serve cold.

Serves four.

Just Passing Through

In the spring they arrived like the hummingbirds; that is, they simply appeared one warm day. These were the "hobos," the homeless who passed through the Amana villages on the road to someplace else and received meals from the kindhearted cooks who would not turn them away hungry. In the colonies just after the turn of the century each village had a "constable," who issued free meal tickets to the hobos and made sure they did not disrupt village life. Some itinerants stopped in a village for a day or two and were never seen again. Some were regular visitors, staying for weeks at a time and taking up residence in one of the "hobo hotels," rough little houses built on the outskirts of the village to shelter these homeless men. Those who were able worked for their meals, chopping wood and performing other odd jobs. A few stayed all summer, helping with the gardens and the field work, earning wages in addition to room and board. Come autumn they jumped a train and headed south, preferring southern winters to the Iowa variety.

Amana lore is filled with stories of Peg-leg and Hair-breath Harry, Texas Ben, and Indian Joe, colorful characters who charmed Amana folk with their stories of life on the road. There was One-eyed Robert, a former circus acrobat who delighted the children with his tumbling routines, Zither Franz, who carried a zither in a burlap sack and played tunes for the kitchen house women while they did their work, and Fire-down Williams, who was said to be a titled Welsh or Scottish aristocrat on the lam.

Romantic stories aside, the wanderers who passed through Amana in the early 1900s were without community, luckless refugees who, for one reason or another, could not or would not make a home. In the days before national Social Security and federal and state welfare programs, those people without income or family were truly without support, and many were forced to wander. Others, perhaps, simply chose the hobo life. In Amana they received food, shelter, and compassionate treatment, and although they could have stayed, few ever did. Instead, they moved on, and whatever became of them is another story, or rather 1,000 other stories.

Rettich und Selleriesalat
Radish and Celery Salad

1 dozen red radishes,
    thinly sliced
6 white radishes
2 cups chopped celery
1 cup mayonnaise
Salt and pepper
Several large leaves of
    lettuce or endive

Combine radishes and celery with mayonnaise and dash salt and pepper. Chill. Serve a spoonful of dressed radishes and celery on a leaf of lettuce or endive.
    Serves four.

Carrie Shoup, South Amana

Note: Mrs. Shoup copied this recipe into her recipe journal. Alongside it was a recipe for homemade mayonnaise, a much livelier stuff than the store-bought variety. If you are using store-bought mayonnaise, you may wish to enhance the flavor of this recipe with a dash of paprika or seasoned salt.

Tomatensalat
Tomato Salad

6 tomatoes, chopped or
    quartered
1 large onion, cut into
    rings
1 green or red pepper,
    coarsely chopped
3 tablespoons sugar
3 tablespoons vinegar
½ teaspoon salt
Pepper to taste

Combine vegetables. Stir together sugar, vinegar, salt, and pepper and pour over vegetables. Toss vegetables. Chill well before serving.
    Serves six.

Erna Pitz, High Amana

Gurkensalat
Cucumber Salad

9 cups peeled, thinly
    sliced cucumbers
2 tablespoons salt
1 cup sugar
1 cup vinegar
1 cup sliced onions
1 cup chopped green
    pepper
1 tablespoon celery seed

Place sliced cucumbers in colander, sprinkle with salt, and allow to drain in sink about ½ hour. Squeeze cucumbers to remove liquid. Combine sugar and vinegar. Place cucumbers, onions, and peppers in large serving bowl; top with celery seed and sugar and vinegar. Cover and refrigerate overnight. Serve cold.
    Serves six.

Helen Wolf, West Amana

Gurken mit Sosse
Cucumbers in Sour Cream

2 large cucumbers,
    peeled, grated, or
    sliced very thin
1 teaspoon salt
1 medium onion,
    chopped
¼ cup sour cream
¼ cup mayonnaise
2 tablespoons vinegar
Pepper to taste

Place cucumbers in colander and sprinkle with salt. Allow to stand in sink about 10 minutes until liquid can be squeezed from sliced cucumbers. Place cucumbers and chopped onion in a glass serving dish. In a small mixing bowl combine sour cream, mayonnaise, vinegar, and a dash of pepper, stirring until smooth. Pour dressing over cucumbers and onions. Cover and refrigerate at least 2 hours before serving so that it attains its full, zesty flavor.
    Serves four.

Helen S. Krauss and Ginger Myers, Amana

Tomaten und Gurkensalat
Tomato and Cucumber Salad

2 large tomatoes, cut
    into chunks
1 medium cucumber,
    peeled and cut into
    chunks
2 green peppers, cut
    into chunks
1 small or medium
    onion, coarsely
    chopped
Salt and pepper to taste
French dressing (page
    58) or sour cream
    dressing (page 58)

Prepare vegetables and combine with dash salt and pepper. Serve cold with French dressing or sour cream dressing.

Serves four.

Janet Zuber, High Amana

mothers salad— she
served it on a bed of
Lettuce with miracle whip
dressing. she always
used the sweet, red onion

Krautsalat
Coleslaw

1 2- to 3-pound head
    white or red cabbage
1 teaspoon salt
¾ cup vinegar
¾ cup sugar
⅓ cup vegetable oil
1 onion, chopped
1 ½ teaspoons caraway
    seeds

Remove the cabbage's outer leaves. Cut head into quarters, remove core, and shred. Place in large mixing bowl and add salt. Pound cabbage with a potato masher or mallet until it seems less stiff. Pour off any liquid.

In a saucepan mix vinegar, sugar, and oil until sugar is dissolved and bring to boil. Remove from heat and allow to cool. When cool, pour over cabbage and leave standing about 15 minutes. Then add onion and caraway seed and mix thoroughly. Cover and refrigerate until serving time.

Serves six.

Creamy Coleslaw Dressing

1 cup mayonnaise
2 tablespoons sugar
2 tablespoons vinegar
1 teaspoon prepared
    mustard
1 teaspoon celery seed
1 teaspoon caraway
    seed

Combine ingredients and blend until nearly smooth. Pour over shredded cabbage and toss. Cover and refrigerate until serving time.

Yields about 1 ½ cups dressing.

Endiviesalat
Endive Salad

1 tablespoon minced
    onion
½ tablespoon vegetable
    shortening (or bacon
    fat)
¾ cup water
2 tablespoons vinegar
2 tablespoons flour
¼ cup half and half
3 hard-boiled eggs,
    chilled, peeled, and
    chopped
1 pound endive,
    chopped and chilled

Sauté onions in vegetable shortening or bacon fat until tender. Combine water and vinegar; add to onions and stir. Sprinkle flour into mixture and stir until smooth. Heat until thickened into a creamy sauce. Slowly add half and half and stir.

Combine chopped eggs and endive in a salad bowl, top with warm dressing, and toss. Serve immediately or chill until ready to serve.

Serves four to six.

Janet Zuber, High Amana

Note: Endive salad was the communal kitchen accompaniment to fried side pork and boiled new potatoes.

Knollenselleriesalat
Celeriac Salad

2 medium celeriac,
  peeled and sliced or
  grated
2 cups beef stock (page
  44) or
  vegetable stock
  (page 46)
1 teaspoon salt
1 onion, chopped
3 tablespoons vegetable
  oil
2 tablespoons vinegar
1 teaspoon sugar
1 tablespoon flour

Place celeriac in boiling beef stock or vegetable stock to which a ½ teaspoon salt has been added. When tender, after 15 to 20 minutes, drain celeriac and place in a serving dish.

In a skillet sauté onion in vegetable oil; then add vinegar, sugar, remaining salt, and flour. Stir and cook over medium-low heat until bubbly. Pour over celeriac and serve hot.

Serves four to six.

Louise W. Noé, High Amana

Note: Buried in sand in the kitchen house cellar, celeriac kept well through much of the winter. Hence this hot dish made from the wintering celeriac was prepared and served in place of fresh greens unavailable during the cold months. Like so many foods served in communal Amana, *Knollenselleriesalat* is a traditional German dish, and various recipes for it can be found in German ethnic cookbooks.

SUMMER

Ye forest leaves so green and tender,
That dance for joy in summer air;
Ye meadow grasses, bright and slender;
Ye flowers, so wondrous sweet and fair;
Ye live to show His praise alone,
With me now make His glory known.

Johann Menzer,
"Oh, That I Had a Thousand Voices" [1704],
The Amana Church Hymnal

CHAPTER 6 # SUMMER

When you till the ground, pray to the heavenly gardener
that He may prepare your spiritual garden for the right harvest,
that He may turn your mind heavenward and away from all
earthly thoughts.

From the *Kinder-Stimme*, a book of
religious instruction for youngsters written in 1717 by
J. A. Gruber and other members of the community.
Translation by Bertha M. H. Shambaugh.

The same south wind that carries spring warmth and blows rain hard against the windowpanes brings summer, and as quickly as the last of *die drei kalte Männer* (three cold men) passes (May 12, 13, and 14) and the threat of frost is over, summer takes hold.

When a summer breeze blew just right, residents of communal High Amana could hear West Amana's bell gently tolling. Likewise, when the wind blew just right, residents of West Amana could hear High Amana's bell gently tolling. Rolling across the green meadows and through the trees on the banks of the *Ochsengrabe* (a stream that flows between the villages), the carillon intoned the long-held beliefs of a community, the bittersweet, baritone song of tradition.

Each village had its bell and its bell tower. The village of Amana had two bell towers: one located near each end of the village. The bells were rung four times daily, Monday through Saturday, and three times on Sunday. On summer workdays the bells were rung at 6:00 A.M., 11:30 A.M., and 12:30 P.M. and again at 6:30 P.M. On the Sabbath the bells were rung at 8:00 A.M., at 11:30 A.M., and at 6:00 P.M. The man living nearest the bell tower was asked to take charge of its ringing and as a result kept track of the correct time for the entire village. Synchronizing the wall clock in his home and his pocket watch with the accurate regulator clock in the railroad station or in the general store, the bell ringer tried to be as precise as possible in his ringing. On Sunday morning he went to some trouble to make sure that the first peel of the bell rang exactly at the stroke of 8:00 A.M., for throughout the village folks were checking and changing their watches and their wall clocks.

It may appear odd to us now that a place beyond the rule of time clocks and wage keepers would care at all about the measure of time. In fact, time as measured in seconds, minutes, hours, days, weeks, months, seasons, and years was of great importance to the Inspirationists. In Amana villages there were watchmakers and clockmakers who labored to insure that time would be measured accurately, and there were the bells sounding daybreak, noon, end of noon, and day's end each day, every day, round the year, year after year until the summer of 1932, when the communal era ended and the bells stopped ringing. Why should they have cared about time at all, living as they did in a valley purposefully chosen because it was beyond the world's clamor? The clue may be contained in this hymn written by Christian Metz:

This song is for the fleeting days;
Swift arrows through the air.
Be hasty, Soul, recall the ways
Which thou must still prepare.

The years of life pass swiftly by.
These numbered days will end.
Oh heart, recall how time does fly.
Remember now thy Friend.

What lives this day will live no more.
Life changes as the sun.
No sooner is the seedtime o'er
Then the reaper's work is done.

("This Song is for the Fleeting
Days," translated by
Glenn Wendler,
The Amana Church Hymnal)

If the goal is to seek and find Christ and the best means to attaining that goal is a life of prayerful fellowship with like-minded individuals, then establishing a community of such individuals is the means to that end. The establishment of communities in Germany, in New York, and finally in Iowa was a well-organized effort by the Inspirationists to attain the finite goal of true Christian life on earth. Life does not last forever, so the ultimate, infinite goal for Christians is salvation and eternal heavenly communion. "Be hasty, Soul," use your time on earth to seek that "Friend" which is Christ, so teach the Inspirationists. Time is a gift, the Inspirationists say, and wise folk do not squander their gifts. They do not waste the most precious gift of all.

This may be the reason why from the start Inspirationists, unlike the Amish, embraced laborsaving devices. If a thing could save time, increase productivity, was no detriment to quality, and provided no distraction from religious life, they were willing to give it a try. As Bertha M. H. Shambaugh wrote of Amana just after the turn of the century in *Amana: The Community of True Inspiration*, "The latest inventions, the newest improvements in machinery, in truth anything that is designed in any way to facilitate work are promptly tested."

The telephone is one example. In 1876 Alexander Graham Bell discovered the principles of sound transmission via wire. One year later the Bell Telephone Company was founded. In 1878, Iowa's first telephone exchange was installed in Keokuk. As Museum of Amana History research indicates, two years later clockmaker Friedrich Hahn of Middle Amana built several telephones and switches using plans he found in a copy of *Scientific American*. With the help of Adolph Heinemann, also of Middle Amana, who copied and sometimes improved upon the electrical circuitry and coils found in commercial telephones, Hahn built telephones and installed the works in handmade walnut cases. The pair even built their own transmitters and switchboard. Within four years of Bell's discovery, telephones were in use in the Amanas.

The system worked so well that within a few years nearly 50 telephones were located throughout the seven villages in depots, stores, factories, shops, and doctors' offices. Telephones were not installed in private homes with the exception of the doctor and the head village elder; telephone use was restricted to business concerns and emergencies. Greatly improving communication between the villages, the telephones were considered cost-effective and very practical.

If an innovation saved time, improved productivity, and helped to insure the continued security of the community, it was incorporated into village life. In many cases limits were imposed by the *Grossebruderrat*. For instance, when automobiles became common throughout America, the Inspirationists considered them practical for deliveries and business transportation. However, individual ownership of cars was strongly discouraged by the elders, who may have feared the trouble that might arise from private ownership of such a potentially liberating machine. Hence, most Amana residents did not purchase cars until after the end of the communal era in 1932. When gasoline tractors came into being, Amana farmers gave them a try but, due to the expense of modernization, were slow to give up their horse-drawn implements. Horses were used on Amana farms until after World War II when they were replaced by the most modern farm machinery available.

Summer Sounds

In communal Amana during the summer you would have heard the pounding of hammers, the shouts of carpentry crews, and the sound of horse-drawn wagons bringing brick, lumber, and other materials to building sites. From 1855 until about 1910 barns, shops, and homes were being constructed in the Amanas with peak construction occurring between the years 1855 and 1870.

It took four years to build the Mill Race, a six-and-one-half-mile-long canal that redirects a portion of the Iowa River downstream to provide power for Amana mills and shops. Work began in 1865 when Christian Metz, Friedrich Heinemann, and Carl Winzenried examined the Iowa River west of West Amana and discussed how best to harness the natural power before them. After Metz determined just where the first control structure should be built and the canal begun, a team of workers from each village camped on the site and worked dawn to dusk, digging the canal bed and building levees. In 1867 the half-dug canal was flooded, and a dredge barge was launched. Moving up the ditch, crews worked alongside the dredge as it dug out the canal bed. Finally in 1869 the canal was completed, and the waterwheels began turning in the woolen mills, the calico-printing mill, the machine shops, and the gristmill. The Mill Race was constructed to flood a slough between Amana and Middle Amana, perhaps as a convenient source for block ice. Each summer the pond produced a surface bouquet of yellow lilies and eventually became known as the Lily Lake. Members of the Sac and Fox tribe living on the reserva-

tion near Tama, Iowa, visited the lake each summer to harvest the bulbous lily tubers, which they said were a delicacy when properly roasted.

After the Mill Race was completed, a steam-powered dredge boat was used to keep it free of silt. Whenever news reached those villages located nearest the canal that the dredge was coming into view, every child in town found an excuse to be on the levee to watch as the dredge puffed upstream, its whistle blowing, its captain and crew shouting hello. Watching the dredge work, seeing it shovel up great mountains of muck, was the best summertime entertainment for youngsters who spent after-school hours on the levee, where elderberries grew thick amid wild grapes and green willows.

Summer School

Although playing on the levee or in the green fields was a temptation, there were no "lazy days of summer" for Amana children. Children between the ages of 5 and 14 attended public school year-round, six days a week. Each village had its own schoolhouse and its own teachers, usually men. The schools were public, not parochial, and thus were governed by the laws concerning public education in the State of Iowa. Lessons were conducted in German until the World War I prohibition against the use of German in public places abruptly ended that practice. Thereafter, teaching was conducted in English Monday through Friday. After World War I German language classes were held on Saturday. Monday through Friday the school curriculum was heavily based upon the standardized Iowa public school curriculum. On Saturday, religion, music, and German grammar were taught in the morning. Saturday afternoon the teachers usually took the children out to the apple orchards or to the *Schulwald* (pine forest), and they spent the warmest part of the day in the shaded calm of fragrant trees.

Windfalls

Our teachers also were in charge of quite a large orchard and during the summer—we had school all year round—would take us all to the orchard to pick up windfalls, which the older boys would deliver to the kitchens where they were used for pie and apple sauce. We used to find a special nice apple and on our way home we took it to the bakery and asked to have it made into an apple loaf. The following day, when school let out for the noon hour, we would stop at the bakery and pick up our apple loaf. Oh, how good that tasted, fresh, still warm bread with the apple center. If we happened to think of it, we would have one made on a Friday evening as a sweet dough was prepared then for the Sunday bread, it was similar to coffee cake.

Emma S. Setzer, South Amana,
from an essay written by Mrs. Setzer in 1961,
Museum of Amana History

The *Schulwald*

There is something magical about the *Schulwald*. Imagine a place where pine trees grow in straight lines as orderly as an honor guard, so tall that the birds in the branches above seem quite far away and the tops of the trees seem to poke holes in the clouds. Imagine a place where the wind sings and the flatland fragrance of prairie grass is overpowered by the snow mountain scent of spruce. That is the *Schulwald*.

According to research by the staff at the Museum of Amana History, in the 1850s pine seedlings were brought from the Canadian forests of Ebenezer because Iowa had no native pines. Groves were planted near South Amana, East Amana, and the village of Amana. Planted and maintained by schoolchildren, the *Schulwälder* were special places where little boys built imaginary castles, families retreated for picnics, and lovers took long walks.

The last pine trees in the Amana *Schulwald* were felled during World War II, but the groves near South Amana and East Amana still stand. Homestead now has its own pine grove just east of the village. Thousands of pines were planted on a rise of sandy ground in the 1950s, and today they shelter the deer and provide a pleasant destination for afternoon walks. In the 1970s Amana teacher Phyllis Burgher and her sixth-graders planted and watered pines near the site of the old Amana *Schulwald*. This small grove has taken hold and flourishes on the banks of Price Creek. Some day soon it may be the perfect place for youngsters to defend imaginary castles, for families to picnic, and for friends to walk under a green canopy of pine boughs.

The Threshers' Parade

In communal Amana, men working in the brickyards, the sawmills, the quarries, and the building crews labored long hours. Still they put down their tools to help plant fields and harvest grain. Bread being more important than bricks, building ceased when extra hands were needed in the fields.

Farmwork reached a fever pitch in the summer when hay making and threshing were accomplished with help from the older schoolboys and hired hands. Because there was often more work than workers, hired hands were employed in the Amana Colonies throughout communal days. Group labor was necessary to achieve quick results. The team effort was coordinated by the *Ökonomiebaas* (agriculture manager) and various other village *Baase* who released men from regular chores in order to help with special tasks. Threshing grain, for instance, required more than 20 men and as many draft horses.

Carl Schuerer, born in 1906, recalls helping with the threshing in East Amana, the smallest Amana village, where he has spent nearly all his life.

> We had six teams of horses and six teamsters in the field, and then maybe four or five men pitching bundles [of grain]. One hauling grain up, four to stack the straw. One at the elevator to push the straw onto the wagon before you hauled it away. Two to haul the straw and one to haul the chaff. Two to unload the grain sacks in the granary. . . . Threshing was quite an operation. Everyone had their job and they had to know how to do it well. There was a lot more to it than you might think!

The day threshing was finished in Middle Amana, the farmers decorated the wagons with shocks of grain and the teamsters bound pale yellow lilies from the lake to the horses' harnesses. All who had helped thresh climbed aboard the wagons, and as the "Threshers' Parade" wound its way through the village, the older *Kölonisten* (colonists) smiled and indulged the young people who were happy simply because the threshing was done.

A Summer Song

Whenever groups of men or women worked together, there was sure to be some grumbling, some complaining, some laughter, and some song. They sang whatever came to mind and whatever seemed to suit the occasion. More than a few songs were written in Amana by talented men and women who enjoyed setting to rhyme the puns and parodies of colony life, poking fun, sometimes none too gently, at their friends and at themselves. These songs were sung, or *deklamiert* (declaimed or recited), at work and at social gatherings. Generally, the songs were in German, but a few were written in English and parodied the accents and mispronunciations of a German people whose English was laced with German.

THE THRESHER SONG

When Emil blows the whistle
And Rind says let er go
And Kiesling says where's Oehlers
    Ernest
I am sure I do not know.

Chorus
O we ain't gone to tresh no mo, no mo.
We ain't a gone to tresh no mo.
So how in the hell can Ludwig tell!
That we ain't a-gone to tresh no more.

(Contributed by Lillian H. Krauss [originally from the late Philip Dickel, Middle Amana] to the Museum of Amana History)

The songs and jokes kept spirits up when the sun grew hot, when no breeze would lift the sultry air and the rows of bundled grain stretched on, as if for miles. It's hard to complain when you are laughing. It's hard to be discouraged when you are laughing. So they told the jokes and they made fun of one another as if they were one family where the rivalries and tensions were dissolved in good-natured teasing like dust in a rain barrel.

CHAPTER 7 POTATO AND OTHER VEGETABLE DISHES

The elder came and asked me if I would work in the garden. I said I would but that I didn't know anything about gardening. He said they would teach me, and the Gartebaas, *she did. We had fun together there. We all got along.*

Helen Seifert Krauss, Amana

From the gardens, hotbeds, and orchards came all the good things to eat. Each kitchen house had its own garden located somewhere on the edge of the village. These gardens were large, averaging about 2 acres. In 1908 Iowa historian Bertha M. H. Shambaugh wrote that well over 100 acres of Amana land was used for vegetable gardening. She did not include the enormous potato fields or the onion fields in her estimate.

Women were assigned to kitchen or garden work by the village council of elders. Because garden work was seasonal and considered lighter duty than kitchen work, housewives with family responsibilities were often chosen for the gardens. Enjoying the quiet routines of the garden, some women preferred it to kitchen work, and they asked to be assigned to a garden.

Gardeners worked from 7:30 A.M. until 4:00 P.M. with an hour-long noon break and a short midmorning and midafternoon "lunch" break. They worked at the discretion of the *Gartebaas,* who might excuse them on Monday, laundry day, or send them home early when the afternoon heat made work unbearable. The *Gartebaas* might also ask them to stay late or come Saturday morning during the busiest times.

Garden Tools

Many of the gardens had a one-room garden house where an orderly array of tools and implements, baskets and buckets, was stored. There were hand tools for every garden task. For hoeing the herb beds and the *Mistbeete* (hotbeds) there were small, narrow hoes with shorter handles. For weeding row crops there were much wider, heavier hoes with longer handles. Highly valued by the gardeners, the hoes, rakes, and shovels were kept clean and well oiled. Tools were brushed clean each evening and hung in the shed. Some of these tools were made by the village blacksmith; others were store-bought. Special hand cultivators that could be walked through a garden smoothly and easily were made by the village blacksmith. Tin buckets used for gathering produce were made by the local tinsmith. A *Gartebaas* need only ask the tinsmith to have a new pail or watering can made. The cooper supplied wooden buckets for carrying water or half-barrels for catching rainwater. From the village carpenter, the *Gartebaas* got her wheelbarrow called a *Schubkarren*. No garden work could be accomplished without a *Schubkarren* to carry baskets of seedlings, weeds, or harvested vegetables. Trays for drying seeds, sturdy wooden rakes, and pitchforks were also made in the village woodworking shop and stored in the garden house.

The Garden House

Amid the tools and baskets, the *Gartehaus* (garden house) had a table and chairs where the women could rest while they ate their midmorning and midafternoon lunch. Cheese spread on thick slices of freshly baked bread or a slice of sugared coffee cake served with hot coffee was the usual lunch break fare. Lunch was brought to the garden by one of the kitchen house girls, and everyone looked forward to that pleasant respite in the cool *Gartehaus*. The ladies had noon dinner at the communal kitchen dining room or at home with their families.

Sometimes mothers brought their preschool-age children to the garden to play near the *Gartehaus* while they worked. Generally, children ages three to five spent their day with grandparents or at the village *Kinderschule* (preschool or day-care center), but more than one indulgent mother saw nothing wrong with a morning spent playing along the garden paths or digging in the mounded earth beside the *Gartehaus*.

To Manage the Garden

Like the cooks, the garden ladies worked together as a team and made the day more enjoyable by chatting and joking as they did their chores. The *Gartebaas* may have been more earnest in her labor, however. Garden management, which included growing some of the seed used in the garden, was a heavy burden. Having gained her knowledge from years of experience and from various gardening books and seed catalogs, the *Gartebaas* was responsible for growing all the produce the kitchen would need to feed its 40 villagers. The *Gartebaas,* like her kitchen compatriot the *Küchebaas,* was a woman to respect and obey. Her word as to how the garden should be managed was law.

There was a friendly rivalry between the *Gartebaase* as to who grew the most, the best, the biggest. In communal Amana, competitiveness was not encouraged by the church elders, who taught humility and selflessness, but pride, like a morning glory, is a hard thing to keep down, and hardworking *Gartebaase* naturally took great pride in their straight furrows and weedless plots. It can be said that a little gentle boasting did as much as fertilizer to ensure the harvest outcome.

Common Sense, Garden Sense

Because a bucket of shelled peas or a bushel of beans was needed for just one meal, the *Gartebaas* planted in quantity. Row upon row of peas, string beans, lima beans, yellow beans, navy beans, beets, and kohlrabi were planted. There were 20-foot-long beds of asparagus, spinach, celery, celeriac, radishes, cucumbers, tomatoes, carrots, red and green peppers, kale, cauliflower, leeks, endive, garlic, and citron melon. There were huge beds of onions and even larger gardens of cabbage.

The wise *Gartebaas* tried to extend the growing season by allowing some crops to reseed themselves and by replanting others so that a second harvest could be obtained. Squash, pumpkins, horseradish, salsify, and other cool weather crops were planted

later in the summer and carefully tended for autumn harvest.

Gardens were watered only when necessary. For many years water was hauled by tank wagon to the gardens, but at the turn of the century a more-sophisticated waterworks was installed, and water was piped to each garden. Even so, water was conserved. Straw was spread between the rows to keep down weeds and to hold moisture. New plantlets were sprinkled, and the delicate celery plants were covered with wet sheets to prevent sun damage.

Pesticides were unheard of in those days, but gardeners used common sense and whatever was handy to protect crops. Ashes and dust were sprinkled on cucumber plants to keep away insects, and salt water was used to kill cabbageworms. Grubs and other pests were plucked from plants before too much damage could be inflicted. Marigolds were planted between beds to discourage insects. Rags or even old sheets were tied on sticks to scare off birds. A good scolding took care of youngsters who scavenged for strawberries and new peas, but occasionally the boldest and quickest could pluck a handful and be gone.

One Main Amana gentleman, who smiled when he recalled this story, told of a moonless summer night when he and two other young boys stole the largest, ripest melon from a likely looking patch and ran to a nearby woodshed. Excited and afraid, the boys cut the melon and ate eagerly, only to discover that they had stolen a tasteless citron melon, acceptable for pickling but hardly forbidden fruit and not worth risking one's good name.

The Onion Harvest

Onions and onion seed were grown as a cash crop in communal times. This was a labor-intensive endeavor that required cooperation between the *Gartebaase,* the kitchen workers, the farm *Baas,* and his farmhands.

When the farmers planted the village onion fields, they expected help when necessary from the gardeners and anyone else in the village willing to rake, plant, and hoe. Come mid-July when onions were ready for harvesting, nearly everyone in the village turned out to help, beginning the work before dawn to avoid the heat. Older children were released from school and may have been the only ones to regard the onion harvest as a holiday, although the *Baase* tried to make the day as pleasant as possible and sometimes brought ice-chilled bottles of soda, an extravagant treat, to the helpers.

Onions were cleaned and sorted according to size. The best onions were divided equally among the kitchen houses. The rest of the large onions were stored in a barn or put into burlap sacks and taken to the nearest train station where they were transported to city markets. The average quantity of onions produced annually in communal Amana is not known, but several Middle Amana gardeners, who still recall helping with the harvest there, noted that fields in Middle often produced well over 2,000 pounds of onions.

The *Gartebaase* and their helpers planted and maintained beds of onion sets and plots for onion seed. In her journal Middle Amana *Gartebaas* Marie Murbach recorded onion seed harvests topping 40 pounds. If each of the 10 kitchen gardens in Middle Amana did as well, the village produced over 400 pounds of onion seed a season. Some of this seed was set aside for next year, but a large portion was taken to the general store for sale to out-of-state seed companies.

In early August, onion sets were dug, placed on drying racks, and sorted. Involving the *Gartebaas,* her workers, anyone who could be spared from the kitchens, and the older school-age girls, this task usually took more than a week to complete. Once cleaned of dirt and sorted by size, the onion sets were divided, some taken to the depot for shipment to seed companies and the rest carted to the kitchen house cellars for storage.

A Letter from Mr. Heinemann
regarding the Onion Seed

Marketing the onion seed, onions, kraut, and pickled ("sour") beans produced by the kitchens was generally the responsibility of the village business manager or storekeeper. In Middle Amana about the turn of the century John Heinemann ran the Middle Amana General Store and saw to it that the village received a fair price for its produce and regularly dealt with seed salesmen and grocers in Iowa and throughout the country. Here is a copy of a letter he sent in 1906 (Museum of Amana History, Archive Collection). It is one of several written to out-of-state dealers regarding onion seed:

Mes. Schilder Brothers
Chillicothe, Ohio

Dear Sirs:

Our onion seed is originally from Germany and we always try to keep it as pure as possible. The hardiness or keeping quality is what we aim to improve, and our onions have of late years had a reputation and were a good success in the markets as we try to get them out early, we will try to send you a small sample of them that you may see how they are. We have been selling our onion seed to dealers at $1.15 and $1.00 [per pound] net. We have about 30 pounds of 1905 and about 150 pounds of 1906 seed [left].

Awaiting your favor we remain
yours truly,

Amana Society
Middle Amana
John Heinemann

The Potato Harvest

The village farmers planted and tended the potato fields, but when it came time to harvest the potatoes, everybody set aside their regular work and went to the fields to help pick up and sort. The dirty, tiresome job was made much easier by the use of a specially designed horse-drawn harvester that unearthed the potatoes and tossed them backward to be collected. The cheerful fellowship of a day spent working together helped to pass the time as jokes were shared and songs were sung. Those who helped with the potato harvest or the onion harvest anticipated the afternoon breaks when sweet lemonade or a vat of homemade ice cream or a laundry basket of fresh-baked cookies was brought to serve the workers.

Potatoes were sorted according to size and quality with a number of bushels set aside for seed. Each community kitchen received a quantity of potatoes; the number of bushels per kitchen was determined by the size of the harvest and the number of folks to be fed by each kitchen. Small potatoes were used right away, while the larger potatoes were stored in the cellar for winter use.

This is a simple explanation of the potato production in communal Amana and should, by no means, leave the reader with the impression that potato production was a simple matter. In fact, many a farm *Baas* and many a *Küchebaas* sweated the outcome of the potato harvest. It took hard work and planning to ensure a successful harvest. And how did they measure success? As recorded by the Amana Society secretary, at the turn of the century the average annual potato yield was 31,622 bushels. A good potato harvest could yield well over 40,000 bushels. Anything under 20,000 bushels would have been thought a disaster.

Potato Dishes

With potatoes in such abundance, the communal cooks used and invented many recipes for potatoes: creamed potatoes, pan-fried potatoes, raw-fried potatoes, potato pancakes, potato salad, crumbed potatoes. Potatoes, in one form or another, were served with nearly every meal, including breakfast.

Rohgeröste Kartoffel
Raw-fried Potatoes

5 large potatoes, peeled,
    thinly sliced ($\frac{1}{4}$
    inch to $\frac{1}{8}$ inch
    thick)
4 tablespoons vegetable
    shortening
Salt

Soak potatoes in cold water to crisp. Drain well and pat dry with towel. In a large heavy skillet melt shortening over medium-high heat. Shortening should be hot when potatoes are added. Be careful: shortening may splatter! Lower heat a bit and fry until potatoes are crusty and golden brown. Turn once or twice. Remove and place on a dish or colander lined with toweling. Salt and serve very hot.

Serves four.

Note: Communal cooks used lard and achieved a perfectly browned, crispy fried potato. You get nearly the same results using shortening, but traditionalists insist that lard produces the tastiest fried potatoes.

Schnellerkartoffel
Quick Fries

6 to 8 small round
   potatoes
4 tablespoons vegetable
   shortening
Salt

Boil potatoes in their jackets and cool enough to peel while hot. It's best to chill the peeled potatoes, even overnight, so that they are firm enough to cut and fry. Cut chilled potatoes into slices (about $\frac{1}{4}$ inch thick or less) or thicker chunks. In a heavy skillet melt vegetable shortening (or if you prefer, lard) and, when shortening is quite hot, carefully add potatoes. Fry until nicely browned. Salt and serve.

Serves four.

Note: Prepared in the communal kitchens for breakfast or dinner, the fried potato has a place all its own in Amana culinary tradition. A favorite still, *Schnellerkartoffel* are frequently served today in Amana Colony restaurants.

Queller

When I stand at the kitchen sink peeling *Queller,* I think of experiences I remember from my younger years. When my Amana *Opa* (grandfather) died, my *Oma* (grandmother) moved to Homestead, where my family lived, to an upstairs apartment in Bergers' house. She became *Rüstschwester* in Beck's kitchen next door—one of the women who prepared vegetables for cooking. Sometimes, when I was eight or nine, I spent the night with her. In the late afternoon she and two or three other women often sat near a window in the dining room peeling *Queller,* small potatoes culled from the larger ones stored in the kitchen cellar. These potatoes had just been cooked and were still hot.

It was cozy sitting with the women, listening to grown-up talk, not always understanding it, smelling the warm, steamy, delectable potato smell. Sometimes when *Oma* had peeled a potato that seemed to her especially tasty, she gave it to me to eat. Speared on her knife, from which I took it, the potato was almost too hot to hold. How good it was—pure potato flavor, without butter or salt.

When I was myself a kitchen girl peeling *Queller* for frying, I found them even hotter to handle. I was almost grown-up (at 14) and did not dare complain because I knew that *Queller* are easier to peel when hot. Peeling them was a regular kitchen chore because fried potatoes were a breakfast staple in all kitchens.

Now I peel only a few for myself, to fry whole or sliced. I sample one. Somehow it doesn't taste nearly as good as when I was 8.

Henrietta Ruff, South Amana

Majoram Kartoffeln
Marjoram Potatoes

Fry potatoes as stated in the preceding recipes and add ⅛ teaspoon sweet marjoram.
Serves four.

Note: Marjoram, a perennial herb of the mint family, was grown by some colony cooks. Wilhelmine Zimmerman Baumgartner of South Amana grew it in quantity and sold it via advertisement. She used marjoram in a variety of vegetable dishes, including potato dumplings.

Fried Potatoes with Onion

When frying the potatoes, as stated in the preceding recipes, add ¼ cup finely minced onion.
Yields four servings.

Note: There is a story in Amana of an elderly lady who professed to detest onions and demanded that her food contain no onions. In her communal kitchen, it was customary to add a handful of minced onions to a pan of frying potatoes. So the *Küchebaas,* trying to please the old lady, always took the time to fry her a portion of potatoes without onion. One day, the cook forgot and served the elderly woman onion potatoes. That evening when the old woman came for her supper, she grasped the cook's hand and exclaimed, "Oh, such a dinner we had today! Those were the best potatoes I've ever tasted!" After that, the cooks served the old woman onion potatoes, and everyone was pleased.

Browned Bread Crumbs

The efficacy of browned bread crumbs is not to be questioned or so the Amana communal cooks believed.

Communal cooks browned bread crumbs or coffee cake crumbs in butter and used them on potato dumplings, boiled potatoes, mashed potatoes, noodles, vegetable dishes, and even yeast dumplings and liver dumplings. To place a dish of *Spätzle* on the table without a generous sprinkle of toasted bread crumbs was unthinkable. Serving Amana's beloved *Gefülltenudeln* (beef noodle pockets) without their crown of golden bread crumbs was heresy.

Just about any pale, bland food can be made more delicious and eye appealing with a sprinkle of browned bread crumbs. Anyone who has tasted ordinary boiled potatoes topped with browned bread crumbs knows the power of this magic stuff. The flavor contrast between the crunchy buttered crumbs and the potato makes this very plain dish delicious. Add a portion of boiled beef or a link of sausage and a fresh salad with sour cream dressing and you have a fine meal in the Amana kitchen house tradition.

Browned Bread Crumbs: The Basic Recipe

2 tablespoons butter or margarine
½ cup dry bread crumbs
A little salt, if you like

In a medium or small skillet, melt butter over medium heat. Add bread crumbs and stir or turn with a fork or spatula. Allow crumbs to brown evenly, turning or stirring frequently. Add a dash of salt. The bread crumbs tend to burn, so monitor heat and do not allow the skillet to become overheated. Once mahogany brown, remove from heat or leave on very low heat until ready to use.

Note: You can use store-bought bread crumbs, but why buy, when homemade bread crumbs are so easy to make? Preheat oven to 250°. Break day-old bread or nonfrosted coffee cake into pieces and place on a baking sheet. Bake at 250° until bread is toasted dry and easy to crumble. Remove and allow to cool. Place bread cubes in a cloth sack (or use two plastic sacks, one inside the other) and crush with a rolling pin. Dry bread crumbs can be stored in your pantry in an airtight container.

Schmelzkartoffeln
Crumbed Potatoes

6 or 8 potatoes (red or
    white), cut in half
    lengthwise
2 tablespoons butter
½ cup dry bread
    crumbs

If potatoes are very large, cut into quarters. Boil until tender. Meanwhile melt butter in a small- or medium-sized skillet on medium heat. Toast bread crumbs until golden. Drain potatoes and place in serving dish. Top with bread crumbs; stir once so that potatoes are covered with crumbs and serve immediately.

Serves six.

Kartoffel Gunden
Mashed Potatoes with Crumbs

Mash potatoes as usual and just before serving top with ½ cup browned bread crumbs (page 81). When served with toasted bread crumbs, mashed potatoes don't require gravy. Hence, this dish is excellent with ham, sausage, or other meats that produce no drippings for gravy.

Potato Fingers or
Potato Cigars

3 cups mashed potatoes
2 eggs, beaten
¼ teaspoon salt
⅓ cup flour
1 teaspoon baking
    powder
Melted vegetable
    shortening, ¼ inch
    deep in skillet
Salt to taste

Using leftover mashed potatoes, combine eggs, salt, flour, and baking powder. Heat shortening in a large heavy skillet. Work potatoes with hands. Form into finger-length fritters and place in hot fat, frying until golden on all sides. Salt and serve hot.

Serves four.

Apple Potatoes

6 large or 10 medium
  potatoes, peeled
1 teaspoon salt
6 large or 10 medium
  apples, peeled and
  chopped
¼ cup sugar
1 cup bread crumbs
¼ cup butter or
  margarine

Cover peeled potatoes with water to which the salt has been added and cook until well done. Drain and mash thoroughly. Cook the apples in as little water as possible. When tender, mash them and add sugar. Combine mashed potatoes and apples, mixing well.

Toast bread crumbs in butter (or margarine). Top apple potatoes with browned crumbs and serve immediately.

Serves six.

Elizabeth Schoenfelder, Amana

Note: A favorite accompaniment to roast chicken, apple potatoes also complement turkey or wild game.

Frätzele
Funny Faces or Raw Potato Patties

5 raw potatoes, peeled
  and grated
2 teaspoons salt
Melted vegetable
  shortening, ¼ inch
  deep in skillet
Applesauce (optional)

Peel and grate potatoes into a large bowl. Add salt and mix well. Heat shortening in heavy skillet. Drop by tablespoons into hot shortening in frying pan and flatten with spatula (to about ½ inch thickness). Fry over medium heat until golden brown on one side and then turn and fry. Serve hot with applesauce.

Serves four.

Note: Wilma Rettig of South Amana recalls that her mother, Carrie Shoup, made *Durchgedrehtekartoffeln* (turned through or grated potatoes) and called them *Frätzele,* meaning funny faces. In the Amanas, *Frätzel* was (and still is) a favorite pet name for children.

Schupf Nudel for Thirty-six

1 kettle of small potatoes, boiled in jackets
2 handfuls salt
12 eggs
1 heaping sieve of flour

Mix well.

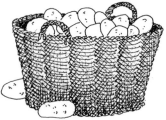

Schupf Nudel for Six

1 ½ quarts of small potatoes, boiled in jackets
1 teaspoon salt
2 eggs
½ cup flour
½ teaspoon baking powder
Vegetable shortening or lard, enough for deep fat frying
Applesauce

Boil potatoes until tender. Allow to cool and peel. Turn through a meat grinder or ricer.

Combine potatoes with salt, eggs, flour, and baking powder. Mix well. On a slightly floured board, with floured hands, roll out potatoes to form fritters about 1 inch in diameter and 3 inches long.

Fry in deep, hot vegetable shortening or lard (about the same temperature as for doughnuts) until golden brown and well done inside.

Serve hot with applesauce.

Serves six.

Elizabeth Schoenfelder, Amana

Kartoffelpfannkuchen
Potato Pancakes

6 medium potatoes,
    peeled and grated
2 eggs
4 tablespoons flour
1 teaspoon salt
½ teaspoon baking
    powder
¼ teaspoon pepper
Melted shortening or
    lard, ½ inch deep in
    skillet
Applesauce

Drain potatoes through sieve and squeeze to re-move liquid. Place in bowl. Beat eggs and add to pota-toes with flour, salt, baking powder, and pepper.

Heat lard or shortening in a large heavy skillet. Place large spoonfuls of potatoes in hot fat and flatten. Pancakes should not touch one another as they fry. Fry until golden on both sides. Remove and place on tow-eling to blot. Salt and serve hot with applesauce.

Serves four.

Janet Zuber, High Amana

Note: If you wish, add 1 small onion, minced, to grated potatoes before frying.

Some Amana residents prefer their potato pancakes thin, crispy, and fried through, while others like a thicker pancake with a creamy center; either way potato pancakes are delicious. Rich and filling, potato pancakes with applesauce, a fresh salad, and perhaps a vegetable make a splendid supper.

Kartoffelsalat
German Hot Potato Salad

2 pounds potatoes,
    boiled in jackets
3 slices bacon
3 tablespoons bacon
    drippings or lard
1 medium-sized onion,
    diced
3 tablespoons flour
2 tablespoons brown
    sugar
½ cup vinegar
½ teaspoon salt
Dash pepper
2 cups water

When potatoes are cooked, peel and slice. Fry ba-con and crumble; set aside. In drippings or lard, sauté onion; blend in flour. Add sugar, vinegar, salt, pepper, and bacon bits. Slowly stir in water and cook until slightly thickened. Pour over sliced potatoes and serve hot. This dish tastes best if it is made ahead and re-heated.

Serves four.

Henriette Roemig, Homestead

Creamed Potatoes

1 tablespoon butter
1 tablespoon flour
½ teaspoon salt
1 cup cream or whole
    milk
1 heaping tablespoon
    minced celery
2 cups thinly sliced
    potatoes

In a large saucepan with a heavy bottom, melt butter. Stir in flour and salt to form a paste. Slowly add cream or whole milk to make a white sauce—bring slowly to near boiling. Add celery and potatoes; simmer until potatoes are tender.

Serves four.

Louise Kellenberger, South Amana

Kartoffelklösse
Potato Dumplings

For dumplings
4 cups peeled, boiled,
    and riced potatoes
1 ½ cups bread crumbs,
    browned in butter or
    margarine
1 egg, beaten
1 large onion, minced
4 tablespoons flour
1 teaspoon salt
½ teaspoon marjoram
    (optional)
½ stalk celery, minced

For topping
½ cup bread crumbs
2 tablespoons butter or
    margarine

Peel and boil potatoes. Chill well as cold potatoes are much easier to rice. Rice potatoes or finely grate in food processor. Combine all dumpling ingredients. With a bit of flour on your hands, mix ingredients and shape into plum-sized dumplings. Roll dumplings in flour. Place in a large kettle with just enough salted water to cover the bottom of the pan. Bring water to a boil and then turn down heat to low and steam dumplings 10–15 minutes. Cover kettle while steaming dumplings.

Meanwhile, brown ½ cup bread crumbs in butter or margarine. When dumplings have been removed from the pan, sprinkle with bread crumbs. If you need to, you may place dumplings in warm oven until serving time.

Makes about 1 dozen dumplings.

Carrie Shoup and Wilma Rettig,
South Amana

Note: Potato dumplings are the traditional companion to creamed chicken or sauerbraten.

Nutmeg or Marjoram: A Question of Taste and Tradition

Some questions are not resolved, even with the passage of time. When it comes to cooking in Amana, nothing excites conversation like the nutmeg versus marjoram question in the preparation of the classic potato dumpling.

Many communal kitchen houses prepared their dumplings using ½ teaspoon freshly grated nutmeg to season. Other kitchen houses used marjoram. To this day in Amana you will find cooks who maintain that *Kartoffelklösse* are not *Kartoffelklösse* without nutmeg and would no more think to season them with marjoram then to serve them without bread crumbs. Colony cooks with ties to Middle Amana are squarely in favor of nutmeg.

It seems that seasoning with marjoram was the custom in some South Amana and West Amana kitchen houses. Recipe books from kitchens in both those villages contain dumpling recipes (and other dishes) seasoned with flavorful marjoram. Families with ties to those villages still make their dumplings with marjoram.

A few cooks prepare dumplings without seasoning, perhaps because they are indecisive on the question or because they have members of both camps living in their household and wish to offend no one.

Three Toes

3 medium potatoes,
    sliced
1 ½ tablespoons
    vegetable shortening
½ medium red pepper
    (pimento), diced
1 small onion, diced
1 medium tomato,
    peeled and sliced
Dash salt and pepper

Fry potatoes in vegetable shortening until about half done. Add pepper, onion, and tomato and continue frying till potatoes are golden brown. Add dash salt and pepper.

Serves four.

Betty Christen, Amana

Note: Dubbed "Three Toes" because the dish contained potatoes, tomatoes, and pimentos, it was a favorite in East Amana according to Betty Christen, who used to serve it in the East Amana kitchen house where she first learned to cook.

Kartoffelgemüse
Creamed Potatoes

2 large baking potatoes,
    peeled and cut
    lengthwise into 8
    wedges
Meat stock to cover
    (about 2 cups
    chicken broth [page
    45], vegetable
    stock [page 46], or
    beef stock [page 44])
2 tablespoons margarine
2 tablespoons coarsely
    chopped onion
2 tablespoons flour

Simmer potatoes in stock until tender. Drain, reserving 1 cup broth.

In a large pan, melt margarine. Sauté onions until tender. Sprinkle flour over onions and stir until smooth. Slowly add 1 cup reserved broth and stir until smooth. Add drained potatoes. Simmer until heated through.

Serves four.

Carrie Shoup and Wilma Rettig,
South Amana

Gemüse
Vegetables

Vegetables dishes served in the communal kitchens varied in complexity. Often just a bowl of steamed green beans and a dish of sliced fresh tomatoes were served, especially on sultry days when the cooks were busy canning and the steam from kettles of corn relish and chili sauce would have made grown men weep. Other recipes, such as creamed spinach or hot horseradish sauce, required more preparation time and more thought.

Spargel
Asparagus with Cream Sauce

2 pounds asparagus,
    fresh
2 quarts water
4 tablespoons butter or
    margarine
4 tablespoons flour
1 cup milk
Salt
Pepper

If the ends of the asparagus are woody, cut them off. If necessary, cut asparagus into 3- or 4-inch lengths. Boil or steam in salted water until just tender. The cooking time will vary, but it should take about 10 minutes. Drain, reserving ½ cup liquid.

In a saucepan melt butter. Stir flour in a small quantity of water until a paste is formed. Blend flour paste into melted butter. Add milk and simmer until a light sauce is formed. If sauce seems too thick, add portion of reserved liquid. Add asparagus and simmer until hot and ready to serve. Salt and pepper to taste.

Serves six.

Bean Casserole

1 pound baby lima
    beans
½ pound raw bacon,
    cut into 1-inch
    pieces
1 small green pepper,
    chopped
1 medium onion, diced
2 cups home-canned
    tomatoes or 1 can
    tomato soup
2 teaspoons dry
    mustard
1 cup brown sugar

Preheat oven to 350°.

Soak lima beans overnight. Drain, add fresh water to cover, and cook until tender. In a 2-quart casserole dish combine beans, bacon, chopped pepper, diced onion, tomatoes, dry mustard, and brown sugar. Bake at 350° for 1 hour and 15 minutes.

Serves six.

Erma Kellenberger, West Amana

Note: Erma Kellenberger's garden beside her West Amana home is a sight to behold come summer. Rows of tomato plants, green beans, peas, radishes, and lettuce are lovingly tended by this expert gardener who has, as a result, quite a collection of recipes for fresh vegetables.

Bohnen mit Sosse
Green Beans with Herb Sauce

1 pound fresh green
    beans, cut, or
    1 9-ounce box of
    frozen green beans
1 tablespoon finely
    chopped green
    pepper
1 tablespoon finely
    chopped celery
2 tablespoons minced
    onion
2 tablespoons salad oil
1 large tomato, chopped
1 tablespoon vinegar
$\frac{1}{2}$ teaspoon garlic salt
$\frac{1}{8}$ teaspoon black
    pepper
$\frac{1}{4}$ teaspoon marjoram

Steam or cook beans until tender; drain. Meanwhile, simmer pepper, celery, and minced onion in oil for about 5 minutes. Add tomato, vinegar, garlic salt, black pepper, and marjoram—simmer on medium heat about 5 minutes longer. Pour over beans and heat through.

Serves six.

Erma Kellenberger, West Amana

Deviled Green Beans

1 pound green beans
2 tablespoons butter or
    margarine
2 tablespoons prepared
    mustard
2 tablespoons sugar
2 tablespoons lemon
    juice
2 tablespoons vinegar

Steam or parboil green beans. Set aside. Melt butter or margarine in heavy saucepan on medium heat. Add mustard and sugar stirring until smooth. Stir in lemon juice and vinegar. Add beans and combine. Heat through.

Serves six.

Erma Kellenberger, West Amana

The Paring Knife Sisters—*Die Rüstschwestern*

No communal kitchen could have functioned without two or three older women who came into the kitchen whenever they were needed to help prepare vegetables.

Known as the *Rüstschwestern,* these women, many of whom were retired from daily cooking chores, helped an hour or more a day in their neighborhood kitchens. Their tasks varied from day to day, but since potatoes were served with every meal, potato peeling was a constant. Because their work required a paring knife, called a *Rüstmesser* (preparation knife), the women were known collectively as the *Rüstschwestern* (prep sisters), or the "paring knife sisters." Individually, of course, they were referred to by name, "*Schwester* Miller (Sister Miller) . . . *Tante* Anna (Aunt Anna) . . . *Oma* Seifert (Grandmother Seifert)."

When it was hot, they worked on the porch or under a shady tree near the kitchen house. Perched on dining room chairs or kitchen stools, with a rectangular work tray called a *Rüstbrett* in their laps, the women shelled peas, snapped beans, peeled potatoes, and talked. Sometimes the *Baas* and her helpers joined the *Rüstschwestern,* and the time passed as the work was accomplished with the aid of amiable conversation and a little gossip.

Krautgemüse
Amana Cabbage

1 small head cabbage
3 tablespoons lard or
    vegetable shortening
1 medium-sized onion,
    diced
1 teaspoon salt
Dash pepper
3 tablespoons flour

Separate cabbage leaves. Wash leaves and dry. Remove ribs and cut leaves into pieces. Cook cabbage in boiling water to which a dash of salt has been added until nearly tender. Drain, reserving 2 cups liquid.

In a large saucepan, melt lard or shortening, add onions, and sauté lightly (do not brown onions). Add salt, dash pepper, and flour. Slowly add liquid and keep stirring. Bring to a boil and add cooked cabbage. Cook for a few minutes longer. This dish may be frozen and reheated.

Serves four.

Henriette Roemig, Homestead

Rotkraut
Red Cabbage

2 tablespoons lard or
    shortening
4 cups shredded red
    cabbage
1 cup water
6 tablespoons sugar
4 tablespoons vinegar

In a large saucepan, melt lard or shortening. Add shredded cabbage, water, and sugar. Cook until tender. Now the cabbage will lose its brilliant color as you cook, but do not fear: when the vinegar is added, the color will return. (Thank heaven for even small miracles.) Cook a little longer. Serve immediately or freeze for future use.

Serves four.

Katy Gunzenhauser, Amana

Note: Katy and her sister, Lina, grew up in High Amana and first learned to cook in High's communal kitchens. Years later, Lina and her husband, Bill Leichsenring, established their restaurant, the Ox Yoke Inn, in what had been the Hertel Kitchen House in Amana. Katy eventually joined the cooking staff of the Ox Yoke Inn, and there she and Lina shared the colony-style dishes of their communal kitchen training. As Katy said, "I always cook the old-fashioned way. That's what people really enjoy!"

Creamed Onions

2 cups small onions,
 peeled
Dash salt
3 tablespoons butter
2 tablespoons flour
1 tablespoon vinegar
Cream or half and half

Find some small onions about 1 inch or less in diameter. Peel and place in a large saucepan. Cover with water. Add a dash salt and boil until tender. Drain water and return onions to pan.

In a skillet, melt butter and stir in flour to brown. Stir in vinegar and just enough cream or half and half to form a thin sauce. Pour over onions and allow to slowly simmer until serving time.

Serves four.

Betty Christen, Amana

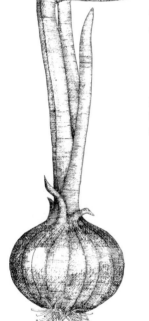

Throwing an Onion the Size of a Baseball

How a young Middle Amana ballplayer, Bill Zuber, went from his grandfather's cooper shop to Yankee Stadium is a story worth telling. Appropriately, the discovery of this homegrown baseball legend involves an onion. As author Cliff Trumpold writes in *Now Pitching: Bill Zuber from Amana:*

When Slapnicka (Cy Slapnicka, Cleveland Indian scout) came to Middle Amana to call on Zuber later that fall, he found him sitting on the north porch of his home. Nearby, his Aunt Marie rocked in an old chair while cleaning freshly harvested onions from one of the community gardens. The old worn-out story goes that Cy selected an onion approximately the size and weight of a baseball and handed it to Zuber, who of course threw it over the barn, some 250 feet away. The target, however, as designated by Slapnicka, had been the barn door, some sixty feet below the flight of the ball.

Impressed by the tall youngster, Slapnicka arranged a tryout and the rest, as they say, is history.

Gelbrüben
Creamed Carrots

4 cups sliced carrots

Salt and pepper

1 cup milk

3 tablespoons butter

3 tablespoons flour

1 tablespoon minced
   onion (optional)

Simmer carrots until tender. Drain, reserving ½ cup liquid. Return liquid to saucepan. Season with salt and pepper. Over low heat, stir in milk, butter, and flour, blending until a light sauce is formed. Add cooked carrots and minced onion and simmer over low to medium heat about 10 minutes.

Serves four.

Note: If you like, you may add 1 cup fresh or 1 small can peas to the above. Also, this recipe works well with frozen vegetables. Just follow package instructions to prepare tender (not overcooked) carrots and continue with the creamed carrots recipe.

Tomatengemüse
Stewed Tomatoes

2 tablespoons marga-
   rine

1 tablespoons chopped
   onion

1 tablespoon chopped
   celery

1 tablespoon chopped
   fresh parsley

¼ cup bread cubes

2 cups home-canned or
   commercially
   canned tomatoes

1 teaspoon sugar

Salt and pepper

Melt margarine. Sauté onions, celery, and parsley until tender. Add bread cubes and fry until golden, turning frequently. Add additional margarine if you think it is necessary. Stir in tomatoes, sugar, dash salt and pepper. Simmer until tomatoes have cooked through.

Serves four.

Carrie Shoup and Wilma Rettig,
South Amana

Spinat
Creamed Spinach

2 pounds raw spinach
    (or 3 10-ounce
    packages frozen leaf
    spinach)
2 cups boiling water
¾ cup bread crumbs
3 to 4 tablespoons
    butter or margarine
1 small onion, minced
1 tablespoon flour
2 cups beef stock (page
    44)
½ teaspoon salt
Dash pepper

Cook spinach in boiling water for 5 to 10 minutes. If using frozen spinach, cook according to package instructions. Drain, reserving ½ cup liquid. Place spinach in colander. Run cold water through spinach to cool. Squeeze out excess water. Place spinach in food processor or grinder. Chop fine.

In a large saucepan on high heat, brown bread crumbs in butter or margarine and stir in minced onion. Sauté lightly. Lower heat and add flour. Add a few tablespoons beef stock and stir until flour is smooth. Stir in spinach and remaining beef broth. Bring to a boil. Add salt and pepper. Cook on moderate heat for about 15 minutes, stirring occasionally. *Spinat* should be creamy and smooth, thickened to a porridgelike consistency. If it seems too thick, add ½ cup reserved liquid. If too thin, add bread crumbs.

Serves six to eight.

Note: Boiling beef, *Spinat,* and *Meerrettich,* an honored triumvirate in colony cooking, always accompany one another. To offer boiled beef without creamed spinach or horseradish sauce would be beyond comprehension. A few Amana families prefer beef tongue to boiling beef and serve it alongside creamed spinach and horseradish sauce. Fried potatoes and lettuce salad with sour cream dressing complete the supper. Dessert is optional, but as *Oma* would tell you, *"ein gute Obst Kuchen"* (a good yeast dough fruit cake) is recommended.

Gekochtemeerrettich
Cooked Horseradish

1 cup raw grated
　horseradish
8 tablespoons butter or
　margarine
1 cup bread crumbs
6 tablespoons flour
4 to 5 cups beef stock
　(page 44)

To grate horseradish: Wash horseradish. Grate and chop horseradish root into fine pieces. Place about $\frac{1}{4}$ cup in blender with 2 to 4 tablespoons water. Blend until finely chopped; then drain. Place in a container with a tight-fitting lid. Repeat process. May be refrigerated until ready to use, but horseradish should be used the same day it is chopped.

Melt butter or margarine in a large saucepan. Add crumbs and sauté lightly. Stir in flour and sauté a minute or so. Add processed horseradish and stir. Slowly add beef stock. Stir well and allow to boil 5 minutes. Cook on medium to low heat until ready to serve. Can be frozen and reheated.

Serves eight.

Linda Selzer, Homestead

Note: The sharp-tasting *Gekochtemeerrettich* is the traditional German side dish to boiled beef tongue, roast beef, or boiling beef. In some parts of Germany, *Meerrettich* is served as a sauce and poured directly on to the beef. Not for the fainthearted, you must actively acquire or inherit a taste for *Meerrettich*.

Schwarzwurzeln
Black Salsify or Oyster Plant

10 to 12 salsify roots
Meat broth to cover
　(see recipes, page
　44)
2 tablespoons chopped
　onion
2 tablespoons margarine
2 tablespoons flour
Salt and pepper

Scrape black off salsify roots. Cut roots into chunks, 1 to 2 inches in length. Simmer in meat broth until tender. Drain, reserving broth.

In a large frying pan sauté onion in margarine until tender. Add flour and stir until smooth. Slowly add 1 cup of reserved broth and simmer until thickened. Season with salt and pepper. Add cooked salsify and simmer until heated through.

Serves four to six.

Wilma Rettig, South Amana

CHAPTER 8 CANNING, PICKLING, AND FRUIT JUICES

We always had some kind of pickles on the table, maybe sweet or dill. And we would have the good yellow beans, dill beans. They were always my favorite!

Annie Kephart, South Amana

Great care was taken by the cooks when preparing pickled or canned vegetables. Only sterilized jars and good caps and seals were employed. Filled jars were totally immersed in a boiling water bath (212°F) to sterilize and to seal. The so-called open kettle method of canning was common in communal kitchens but sometimes resulted in poor seals, spoiled food, and waste. That particular method of canning is now considered by food specialists to be unsafe for all foods except jams and jellies.

Communal cooks kept a wary eye on the canned foods they served. Jars fetched from the cellar were checked for cracks, broken seals, seepage, and mold. If any of the above was discovered, the contents were discarded and the jar sterilized. You should check your canned goods for similar clues to spoilage, looking for tiny bubbles in the contents, mushy or cloudy foods, or off-smelling foods. These should be discarded.

If you are an inexperienced home canner, please consult your state extension service for pamphlets on safe canning procedures. Failure to use proper methods, unclean jars, imperfect lids and seals, or warm storage may lead to the growth of various lethal molds and bacteria. Food poisoning from improperly canned foods can be deadly. A recent handbook prepared by the Center for Disease Control listed home-canned tomato relish, chili sauce, pickles, and beans as prevalent carriers of botulism poisoning. So find information on safe home canning and follow it to the letter.

Pickling, Sweet and Sour

The colony cook used a high-grade white distilled or cider vinegar and pure pickling salt, either coarsely or finely ground for pickling cucumbers, beans, and other vegetables. When a recipe called for spices, the freshest available were used. Putting up a batch of pickles or dill beans, the *Küchebaas* dispatched a young girl to the garden to pick a small basket of pungent dill and to pluck a few grape or cherry leaves. The leaves added little flavor but were a natural "crisper," insuring firm pickled vegetables.

Various methods of pickling were common, including "long brine" pickling, which requires that vegetables, such as cucumbers, be packed in a crock filled with a heavy salt solution. The adage was that the brine be able to "float an egg" (about $1\frac{1}{2}$ cups salt dissolved in each 1 gallon of liquid). The crock was covered with a clean white cloth, topped with a board, and left in the cool, dim cellar for a week or more. Each day the scum, which rises to the top as a normal part of the brining process, was removed and a fresh, clean cloth placed on the crock. Cleaning off the scum was a messy, irksome job, but it was extremely important to the success of the project, and so the kitchen worker grumbled, but never balked, when it was her turn to see to the crocks. The scum contains various mold spores and bacteria. Leaving it on the brine, even for an extra day, will weaken the brine and may lead to spoilage. Once the brining was complete, usually in a couple of weeks, kitchen workers canned the pickled vegetables for winter enjoyment.

Colony Kraut

When the *Gartebaas* informed the *Küchebaas* that the cabbage was ready, all kitchen work was set aside and plans were made to harvest and cut the kraut. The next day when the morning bell rang, a crew of women recruited to help with the kraut joined the kitchen and garden workers at the cabbage patch. Baskets and baskets of cabbage were cut, cored, and washed, a task that required a full day's work by many hands.

Prior to the early 1900s the cabbage was shredded by hand, a knuckle-busting operation accomplished on giant-sized wood frame kraut cutters. Then about 1910, a pair of Amana gentlemen, perhaps after listening to the complaints of their wives and daughters, invented a kraut cutter powered by a gasoline engine that tore through a basket of cabbage faster than 10 women could work. The invention was copied in each village by a handy machinist who mounted the machine on a wagon and hauled it from kitchen to kitchen during the kraut-cutting season, making the lives of colony women much pleasanter.

Most of the shredded cabbage was packed into barrels for shipment to Chicago markets. Amana sauerkraut was a featured item on the menus of several Chicago restaurants, including, for many years, the Berghoff Restaurant.

There was no written recipe for the cabbage. As Verona Schinnerling of Middle Amana explained, "We used big crocks. We threw in a *Schüssel* [pan] of cabbage and a good handful of salt; then we stomped it down [with a wooden tamper] and threw in another *Schüssel* and more salt. So you do it until it's full. Then you cover it with a clean white cloth and a weight, a stone or a brick. Every day you have to clean off the scum on top. Then you let it ferment, maybe eight weeks or so."

According to a journal kept by Mrs. Schinnerling's grandmother Marie Murbach at the Ruedy Kitchen House in Middle Amana, they made over 200 gallons of kraut each year. In 1900, they made 165 gallons of sauerkraut for market and another 100 gallons for use in the kitchen.

Large crocks of sauerkraut were kept sealed in the cellar, and whenever the menu called for kraut, a kettleful was brought up and cooked on the stove. Kept on the heat, the kraut was boiled to kill any bacteria that it surely contained, and a small handful of *Kümmel* (caraway) was added to enhance its flavor and to aid in digestion. Colony sauerkraut was considered the perfect accompaniment to pork roast or sausage and its reputation as a colony delicacy survives to this day.

How to Make Sauerkraut

When Kenneth and Isabella Schaefer of East Amana harvested a bumper crop of cabbage from their garden, they called their friend Mary Hull of Cedar Rapids for her homemade sauerkraut recipe. This recipe is an updated version of the classic central European method and is very similar to the method used in pre-1932 Amana by communal cooks.

Sauerkraut

Prepare in the following proportions:

For 5 pounds shredded cabbage, you need 3 ½ teaspoons plain salt. (Do not use iodized or pickling salt.)

Choose a stone crock large enough to accommodate your cabbage. A 2-gallon crock holds about 15 pounds of kraut. The Schaefers used about 20 large heads to fill their 20-gallon crock ¾ full.

Remove outer cabbage leaves (do not discard); cut cabbage into halves or quarters and core. Shred cabbage and weigh. In a large bowl, mix 5 pounds shredded cabbage with plain salt. Place in stone crock. Tamp well with heavy wooden tamper until water is released from cabbage—this may take a few minutes. Repeat as necessary.

Crock should be at least ¾ full. Place clean, dry cabbage leaves on top of the salted kraut. Cover with a large plate. Then lay a clean white cloth on the plate and, finally, top with some kind of weight (a large clean stone or brick will do). The weight should be heavy enough to force the brine to come to the top of the kraut and wet the cloth. Cover the entire top of the crock with a thick layer of newspaper and tie tightly with a cord or twine. Place the sealed crock somewhere secure and warm (perhaps the garage or porch). Wait patiently four weeks for fermentation. Do not open.

After four weeks, open the crock. Skim off the thin layer of mold that has formed on the top of the kraut. Now your aromatic kraut is ready to be canned in a boiling water bath or frozen in tightly sealed containers or double-sacked freezer bags.

One 20-gallon crock makes about 15 to 20 quarts sauerkraut.

Mary Hull, Cedar Rapids

Note: Like many things, making sauerkraut requires a little patience, a little luck, and lot of common sense. Should your fermented kraut seem too moldy, mushy, or off-colored, discard it and better luck next time.

Frenched Green Beans

1 gallon water
½ cup pickling salt
½ cup vinegar
5 quarts beans, washed
    and shredded
6 or 7 quart jars,
    sterilized, with lids
    and seals

Bring water, salt, and vinegar to a boil. Add beans and boil 10 minutes. Ladle hot mixture into jars, adding plenty of liquid. Leave ½ inch of headroom at top of jar. Process for 10 minutes in a boiling water bath (212° F.) Finish seals.

Elizabeth Schoenfelder, Amana

Süszsauereroterüben
Sweet-Sour Pickled Red Beets

2 quarts beets
2 cups water
2 cups sugar
2 cups vinegar
1 tablespoon salt
2 or 3 quart jars,
    sterilized, with seals
    and lids

Boil beets until tender, dip into cold water, slip off peel. If beets are small, leave whole. If larger, cut into quarters. You should have about 2 quarts of beets. Combine water, sugar, vinegar, and salt and bring to a boil. Add beets and bring to a boil again. Pour hot beets and liquid in sterilized jars. Process in a boiling water bath about 30 minutes. Finish seals.

Connie Zuber, Homestead

Note: Connie Zuber and her husband, Bill, established Bill Zuber's Restaurant in Homestead. The restaurant is known for serving colony foods, as well as German and midwestern dishes.

Corn Relish

12 ears of corn
1 quart cucumbers,
    peeled and chopped
2 quarts tomatoes,
    peeled
1 quart peeled and
    chopped onions
1 or 2 green peppers,
    coarsely chopped
4 cups sugar
1 tablespoon ground
    mustard
$\frac{1}{2}$ quart vinegar
1 tablespoon celery
    seed
$\frac{1}{2}$ cup salt
$\frac{1}{2}$ tablespoon turmeric
10 to 15 pint jars,
    sterilized, with lids
    and seals

Cook corn and remove kernels from cobs. In a very large kettle, boil all ingredients 45 minutes. Pour into hot sterilized pint jars, leaving $\frac{1}{2}$ inch at the top of the jar. Process in a boiling water bath for 15 minutes.

Connie Zuber, Homestead

Amana vor der Höh Gurken
High Amana Pickles

Cucumbers
Fresh dill, several large
    heads
Handful cherry leaves
Fresh grape leaves,
    3 or 4

For brine
3 quarts water
1 cup salt

For syrup
1 cup vinegar
2 cups sugar
1 teaspoon pickling
    spices

Wash cucumbers. Pick several heads of fresh dill, a small handful of leaves from a cherry tree, and a few grape leaves. Wash and place these in a clean crock with the cucumbers. Mix brine ingredients and make enough to cover cucumbers.

Set crock in a cool place; cover with a clean cloth and stone. Let stand for eight days. On the ninth day, remove cucumbers and wash in clear water. Cut into slices, lengthwise, and pack into sterilized quart jars.

Bring syrup ingredients to a boil. Increase proportions as needed to prepare more syrup. Pour hot over pickles, seal jars, and process in a boiling water bath for 10 minutes. Finish seals.

Louise Wendler Noé, High Amana

Ost Küchehaus Gurken
East Amana Kitchen House Pickles

Cucumbers

For brine
3 quarts water
1 cup salt

For syrup
¾ cup water
1 cup vinegar
1 cup sugar

Mix enough brine to cover cucumbers. Wash cucumbers, place in crock or crockery bowl, and soak in brine overnight.

Remove and rinse cucumbers in clear water. Pack in sterilized jars.

Combine syrup ingredients in stated proportions and bring to a boil. Pour over cucumbers. Seal and process in boiling water bath for 10 minutes. Finish seals.

Schaefer Kitchen House journal, East Amana

Note: In a journal kept by Lena (Magdalena) Schaefer, *Küchebaas* of the Schaefer Kitchen House in East Amana, this recipe was highlighted as a no-fail pickling winner. However, the following recipe from "*Tante* Frieda" was noted as a good alternative pickling recipe.

Tante Frieda's Pickles
Aunt Frieda's Pickles

Cucumbers

For brine
1 ½ cups salt
1 gallon water

For syrup
¾ cup water
¾ cup vinegar
½ cup sugar

Wash cucumbers, place in crock or crockery bowl, and soak in brine overnight. Rinse in clear water. Pack in sterilized jars.

Combine syrup ingredients in stated proportions and bring to a boil. Pour over cucumbers. Seal and process in boiling water bath for 10 minutes. Finish seals.

Katerbohnen
Dill Beans

Yellow string beans,
    washed and trimmed
3 pints (6 cups) water
1 pint (2 cups) vinegar
⅓ cup salt
Fresh dill, several heads

Yellow beans and only yellow beans make suitable *Katerbohnen*. Using green string beans is unthinkable. Wash yellow string beans and cook in salted water until tender. Drain.

Combine, water, vinegar, and salt in stated proportions and bring to a boil. Increase amount of a syrup as needed. Pack beans in sterilized jars with one large head of dill in each jar. Pour hot syrup over beans. Seal jars and process in boiling water bath for 10 minutes. Finish seals if necessary.

Note: Some colony cooks skip the boiling water bath process and simply store their beans in the refrigerator and serve cold. This works well if you don't have more than a quart or two and like dill beans.

Gummerfischle
Cucumber Fishes

2 quarts large cucumbers, peeled and
    sliced lengthwise in
    quarters or sixths
1 large head dill per jar
½ cup salt
1 ½ cups vinegar
1 ½ cups sugar
1 ½ cups water

Wash cucumbers, peel, and cut into quarters or sixths lengthwise. (As an Amana *Oma* would tell you, cut them about as thick as a man's finger.) Place *Fischle* in a bowl and sprinkle with salt. Let stand overnight; then drain.

Put cucumbers into sterilized jars with 1 large head of dill per jar. Bring vinegar, sugar, and water to a boil and pour over *Fischle*. Seal jars and process in a boiling water bath. Finish seals if necessary.

If you are just putting up a jar or two, skip the boiling water bath and store in the refrigerator. The *Fischle* require a few days to attain full flavor.

Yields 2 quarts.

Elise Zuber, West Amana

Chow Chow

2 cauliflower heads,
  chopped
1 pound white onions,
  chopped
1 pound small cucum-
  bers, chopped
1 pound green toma-
  toes, chopped
2 green peppers,
  chopped
1 pint chopped green
  beans
1 pint chopped large
  cucumbers
1 cup salt
2 cups sugar
½ cup flour
1 quart vinegar
1 tablespoon (scant)
  turmeric
½ cup ground mustard
  (or to taste)

Wash and process vegetables, chopping as desired. Combine vegetables with salt and let stand overnight in a cool place (refrigerator). Steam vegetables until tender. Drain.

Combine sugar, flour, vinegar, turmeric, and ground mustard. Bring to a boil. Pour over steamed vegetables. Chill in stoneware or glass bowl or glass quart jars at least overnight. Serve cold.

Yields about 6 quarts or about 24 servings.

*Noé Kitchen House, Amana,
translated by Louise Miller DuVal*

A Recipe from the Kippenhan Kitchen: Mrs. Berger's Gherkins

In a recipe journal kept by Lina Kippenhan, *Baas* of the Kippenhan Kitchen House in South Amana, was this recipe for gherkins given to Lina by her neighbor and fellow South Amana cook Mrs. Berger.

Get 300 little pickles and scrub them clean. Wipe dry and place in a large basin. Take ⅔ of a cup of salt and sprinkle well through the pickles, then turn a kettle of boiling water over them. The water must be boiling hot and cucumbers well covered. Allow them to stand overnight. In the morning remove the brine, wipe each pickle dry and lay in a crock. Then take half a gallon of cold vinegar and mix it with 4 tablespoons of dry mustard, heaping same of salt, the same of granulated sugar and cover pickles with half a cup of mixed spices. Lay in a root of ginger. Pour the mixture over the pickles and stir so that each little pickle is covered. Set away in a cool place. Weigh out three pounds of sugar and each morning add a handful of sugar to the crock of pickles, stirring them well, till the whole three pounds of sugar has been used. If you follow this recipe strictly, especially regarding the adding of sugar each morning, you can not help having fine pickles. From Mrs. Berger.

Vegetable Sandwich Spread

1 gallon green tomatoes
6 green peppers
6 red peppers
3 stalks celery
1 cup salt

For syrup
1 ¼ quarts (5 cups)
   white vinegar
3 cups sugar
2 scant cups flour
1 ounce dry mustard

Wash vegetables. Grind through meat grinder or in food processor to the consistency of relish. (While grinding, catch liquid.) If using food processor, do not drain. Pour chopped vegetables (and any liquid) into large (nonmetal) bowl or crock and stir in salt. Cover and refrigerate overnight. Then drain, reserving 3 cups liquid.

In a very large kettle, combine vinegar and sugar, stirring until sugar is nearly dissolved. Bring to a boil. Meanwhile, make a paste using flour, mustard, and ½ to 1 cup reserved vegetable liquid. While stirring, add paste slowly to boiling syrup. Then slowly add ground vegetables to kettle. While stirring, return to a boil and cook several minutes more. If mixture seems too thick, add remaining vegetable liquid by ¼ cups.

If you plan to can this vegetable spread, have 10–12 sterilized pint-sized jars with seals and lids ready nearby. Fill jars with boiling hot spread, leaving headroom, adjust seals, and process in boiling water bath 10–15 minutes.

Vegetable spread can be made in smaller batches and refrigerated.

Yields about 10–12 pints.

Betty Christen, Amana

Note: Betty Christen made vegetable sandwich spread at Pauline Bahndorf's Kitchen House in East Amana, where it was so popular the kitchen workers served it the same day they made it to hungry patrons who spread the vegetable relish on slices of buttered bread. After the communal kitchens closed in 1932, Betty made vegetable sandwich spread and other communal kitchen fare for her family.

Pickled Ham

1 cup vinegar
1 cup water
1 medium onion, sliced
1 ½ pounds cooked
   ham, cut into bite-
   sized cubes

In a bowl mix vinegar and water. Set aside. Then combine sliced onion and cubed ham; fill glass quart jar. Pour water-vinegar mixture over ham and onion. Close lid tightly and refrigerate at least three days before serving. Serve cold. Store pickled ham in refrigerator.

Yields about 1 quart.

Katy Gunzenhauser, Amana

Note: Pickled ham, an original communal kitchen dish, is still an Amana favorite and is served as a side dish in colony restaurants. Communal cooks processed and sealed their canned pickled ham in a boiling water bath for pantry storage. Cooks today find it much easier and safer to simply make pickled ham in smaller quantities and store it in the refrigerator.

Saft

Then on a Sunday afternoon, Mama or Papa
hat gesagt [would say]
"Well, let's go for a walk." Dann sind mir im Busch gelauft.
[Then we went for a walk in the forest]. . . .
Then when we came home,
dann hat's Saftwasser gegeben. *[then we had fruit juice].*
The people made their own juice—raspberry,
 strawberry, and cherry.

Anna Hegewald, Middle Amana,
from a 1982 oral history interview,
Museum of Amana History, Oral History Collection.

With fruit in abundance, colony cooks made fruit juice, *Saft* or *Saftwasser*, for their families and for their kitchen patrons. Wholesome and refreshing, *Saftwasser* was the communal Amana version of the bottled fruit juices and soft drinks popular today.

Wilma Rettig of South Amana and her husband, Larry, tend a variety of fruit trees in their large yard, and each summer Wilma makes *Saft* for her family. Her advice is to wear an apron or an old shirt when making fruit juice because it can be a messy job, but the resulting juice is so purely delicious that it is certainly worth the trouble.

Kirschensaft
Cherry Juice

Wash and stem cherries. Place in large bowl or basin and mash. Let stand 36 hours.

Using a jelly bag, strain mashed cherries into a bowl. Measure juice. To each pint of juice, add 1 ½ cups sugar. Place sugar and juice in a large saucepan or kettle and simmer 15 minutes, stirring occasionally. Monitor heat carefully so pot does not boil over.

Leave headroom. Seal in sterilized pint jars. Freeze.

To serve: dilute ¼ cup juice with 1 cup of water.

Hinbeeren or Erdbeerensaft
Raspberry or Strawberry Juice

Mash fruit. Using a jelly bag, strain mashed fruit. For each pint juice add 1 cup sugar and simmer in a large kettle or saucepan 15 minutes. Monitor heat and stir occasionally. Leave headroom. Seal in sterilized pint jars. Freeze.

To serve: dilute ¼ cup juice with 1 cup water.

Traubensaft
Grape Juice

Process as you would raspberries or strawberries; however, use only ½ cup sugar per pint juice.

Wilma Rettig, South Amana

How to Make *Apfelsaft* (Apple Juice)

Perhaps intended as a reminder for herself or perhaps meant as instructions for young cooks, in her recipe box, Louise Noé, *Küchebaas* at the Noé Kitchen House in Amana, kept this brief description of her method for making *Apfelsaft*. Translation by Louise Miller DuVal.

Take 12 apples, grind them in the meat grinder, place in a pot, and cover with 5 quarts water. Set behind the stove for 24 hours, pour through a cloth, add 3 cups sugar, and fill into bottles.

CHAPTER 9 FROM THE DAIRY BARN

I can still see the Handkäse *in the crock. We used to wrap a cabbage leaf around each cheese and then put it in the crock. The green cabbage leaf wrapped around the yellow cheese. And sometimes, the cheese would have the impression of the leaf when you unwrapped it.*

Louise Wendler Noé, High Amana

Each village kept a herd of dairy cattle, and these were brought in twice daily for milking. Quite often the cattle were herded through town, so it was important to keep the three- and four-board fences mended, or gardens and flower beds were trampled under hoof. Tending the cattle and milking were burdensome responsibilities requiring long hours and complete commitment. Dairymen often rose hours before dawn and many times did not finish the afternoon milking until suppertime. As one former dairyman reported, "We used to do all the milking by hand. We had no fancy milking machines. We did it all by hand, and it was work!"

Fresh milk was strained at the dairy barn, poured into large galvanized milk cans, and delivered to the kitchen houses. The deliveries were made daily by horse and wagon. Milk delivery was considered a desirable job for a young colony man as it afforded him an opportunity to visit with each kitchen's staff and perhaps see his sweetheart. More than one romance chastely progressed while the milk cans were being set upon the milkstand or carried into the cellar.

In Cool Spring Water

Refrigeration was a problem in communal kitchens. Iceboxes fulfilled a need but were too small to contain milk cans. Therefore, each kitchen house cellar had a specially designed stone or wooden trough through which spring water was siphoned. The milk cans were placed in the water trough, perhaps covered with old rugs, and kept as cool as possible. Even so, spoiled milk was a problem that required constant attention.

Making Cheese

The most practical method of handling the summertime milk glut was to make cheese. Three types of cheese were made in communal kitchens: *Süsskäse* (sweet cheese), *Handkäse* (hand cheese), and *Schmierkäse* (cheese spread), sometimes called *Kochkäse* (cooked cheese). Each required a different process of cheese making, and as a result each had its own distinct taste and texture. Compared to

109

cheese making as practiced in Europe or Wisconsin, the process in Amana communal kitchens was very primitive, and the resulting cheese was sometimes less than perfect, but the cooks did the best they could with limited equipment, and their patrons seemed to appreciate the cheeses they produced.

Süsskäse

As its name implies, *Süsskäse* is made from sweet, fresh milk and is a soft brick cheese with a color and texture similar to baby Swiss or farmer cheese.

In the communal Amana kitchen, 5 gallons of skimmed fresh milk was heated atop the cookstove to the appropriate temperature; then a rennet tablet was added. Rennet, made from the lining of a calf's stomach, causes the milk to curdle. The congealing milk was stirred until curds formed. Then the curds and whey were poured into a cheesecloth-lined wooden press or chessit. As pressure was applied to the top of the chessit, the whey drained from the curds. About 24 hours later, the pressed cheese block or round was removed. The cook gently rubbed a handful of salt on the entire surface of the block or round. Then the cheese was wrapped in a clean cloth and placed in a special cellar pantry with a screened wooden door. There in the cool, dim cellar the cheese ripened five or six weeks.

Handkäse

Handkäse is the kind of food you either love or hate, at least that is what many colony residents will tell you. With a thick yellowish *Foulen* (rind), its semisoft center is buttery textured with a full, strong flavor and aroma.

Handkäse is made from milk that has been allowed to sour but not spoil. Usually the communal Amana cooks used 8 to 10 gallons of sour milk for one batch of *Handkäse*. This they allowed to curdle, and the resulting curds were pressed and then placed in a dishpan. Three or four handfuls of salt were added. Kneading the curds by hand, the cooks judged whether enough salt or too much salt had been added. Too much or too little salt could ruin a batch of *Handkäse,* and while nearly every communal cook occasionally had trouble making cheese (for conditions were often not ideal, and cheese can be finicky), none wanted the reputation of spoiling every batch. Once the kneading was completed, the curds were formed into balls about the size of a large peach. Then the balls were pressed using a board or a butter paddle until each resembled a round of Gouda cheese. The cheese rounds were placed on a wooden board and set to dry for about a week. Each day the rounds were turned over and their relative dryness remarked upon by the cooks who understood that humid weather slowed this process. Once dry, they were gently nested in a crock, covered, and placed in the cellar. Mold formed on each round of *Handkäse.* This was scraped off by the cooks, and the cheese was returned to the cellar. When mold appeared a second time, the rounds were placed in a washtub of water and scrubbed with small bristle brushes. This smelly, unpopular chore was repeated once or twice a week for a number of weeks until the cheese rind was a rich golden color and the smell and taste were judged suitably strong.

In Middle Amana the cooks wrapped each round of cheese in a large leaf of cabbage, to prevent the rounds from sticking together, and then carefully arranged the cheese rounds in a 5- or 10-gallon crock. Louise Wendler Noé, a former Middle Amana kitchen girl, described her delight upon removing the cheeses to discover the delicate leaf imprint upon each tender honey-colored round of cheese.

Handkäse was a favorite among colony men who enjoyed thick aromatic slices with their Saturday evening supper of boiled potatoes in jackets and bread. Occasionally, hand cheese made an appearance at the midafternoon breaks colony men welcomed while on the job. Some former communal cooks maintain that most Amana women were much less fond of *Handkäse* than their menfolk, because the women had the job of making the cheese.

How I Make Hand Cheese

I use 10 pounds dry cottage cheese, the kind you get from the dairy. I put that in a strainer for about an hour; then I put it in a large bowl and add 5 heaping tablespoons salt. Knead till nice and smooth, then form into about 15 or 16 balls, then put them on a wooden board, and turn them every day until they are very dry. It takes about one, to one and one-half weeks, depending upon how warm a place they are in. If they get moldy, I scrub them with a vegetable brush and put them back on the board. When they are hard, I put them in a crock. Cover each layer with cheesecloth soaked in vinegar. The first few weeks, I scrub them twice a week, later only once a week. It takes about three or four months before they are done. They shrink up a lot. I make *Handkäse* in the winter when the air is dry. In the kitchens we would make it when we had the milk.

The method of making *Handkäse* described by Betty Christen of Amana is a brief synopsis of a process she has perfected to near art. Before undertaking any cheese-making experiments of your own, check with your area home extension office or the public library for books on home cheese production.

Schmierkäse or *Kochkäse*

Some Amana folks call it *Schmierkäse* (smear cheese or cheese spread), and some call it *Kochkäse* (cooked cheese), but the cheese in question, flavored with caraway seeds, is a long-standing tradition in Amana and in Germany. Chef Horst Scharfenberg, a recognized authority on German regional cooking, notes in his book *The Cuisines of Germany* that *Kochkäse* is attributed to the Hesse region of Germany. In the early 1800s, the Inspirationist community found shelter from religious persecution in Hesse, and many Amana families originated in this province of central Germany; thus Hessian cooking, including *Kochkäse,* became part of Amana culture.

To make *Kochkäse,* the communal cooks rubbed pressed curd between the palms of their hands to break apart the curd. The *riebled* (rubbed) curd was placed in a stoneware bowl and left to ripen. Each day the curd became more fluid and more aromatic, and each day the patient cook stirred the ripening curd. After several days, the yellow curd was slowly cooked in a buttered iron kettle. Salt, water, and a handful of caraway seeds were added. Once cooked, the cheese was poured into a crockery bowl and allowed to cool. The finished product was a spreadable cheese delicious on bread.

Butter and Cottage Cheese

Of course, they made their own butter in the communal kitchens, and this responsibility often fell to the second in command, or *Vizebaas* (vice boss), who churned weekly or biweekly as her schedule and the dairy supply allowed. Churns were mostly store-bought and large sized; square or wooden churns with hand-cranked paddles were favored, although a few kitchens kept glass churns for the occasional small batch of butter.

Cottage cheese, sometimes called *Matte* or *Quark,* was made and served frequently. In the spring and summer, cooks added a little cream and a handful of freshly chopped chives or the minced tops of green onions to the cottage cheese, creating a traditional German dish that still finds its way to colony dinner tables and is served in Amana's family-style restaurants.

Matte mit Schnittlauch
Cottage Cheese with Chives

1 large container
 (24 ounces) small-
 curd cottage cheese
2 tablespoons sour
 cream
2 tablespoons chopped
 chives or 1 table-
 spoon minced green
 onion

Gently blend together cottage cheese and sour cream. Stir in chives or minced green onion. Refrigerate at least $\frac{1}{2}$ hour before serving. Serve cold in a glass dish nice enough for table use.

Yields about six servings.

Note: This is a refreshing addition to any meal, particularly one with a heavier or spicy meat or main dish. Amana folks often serve applesauce alongside their cottage cheese.

The Perils of Courting

There is a story of a young High Amana man who willingly, happily, walked four miles one way to visit his Amana fiancee. One evening, determined to see his fiancee even if it meant missing evening prayer services and a little sleep, the young man walked to Amana and stole through the dark village just as the kerosene street lamps were being turned down.

Believing that her intended had missed their date and giving in to her *Küchebaas* mother who insisted she wait no more, the young woman went to bed. Meanwhile, her lover crept through her mother's hollyhocks and four-o'clocks, intent upon letting himself into her home without rousing the family. Certain that his girl was waiting for him, the young man found an open window and deftly pulled himself up and over, only to land shoulder first upon a board of ripening hand cheese resting on the sill and balanced upon a chair. The board, the cheese, the chair, and the young man fell headlong with a crash upon the wooden floor of the kitchen. As lover's luck would have it, first upon the scene was the *Küchebaas,* whose fright quickly soured to anger at the sight of her soon-to-be son-in-law lying in a pile of moldy cheese. Just what happened next has been forgotten, or at least is never admitted, by colony storytellers who usually conclude by stating that the path of true love is often rocky and occasionally pungent.

AUTUMN

All the plenty summer pours;
Autumn's rich, o'erflowing stores;
Flocks that whiten all the plain;
Yellow sheaves of ripened grain—
Lord, for these our souls shall raise
Grateful vows and solemn praise.

Anna L. Barbauld,
"Praise to God, Immortal Praise" [1772],
The Amana Church Hymnal

CHAPTER 10 # AUTUMN

See how He hath everywhere
Made the earth so rich and fair,
Forests dark, the fruitful land
Living things all show His hand.

Joachim Neander,
"Heaven, Earth and Sea and Air,"
The Amana Church Hymnal

Hurrying to harvest the yield of 100 summer days, colonists worked through autumn, bringing in the corn, the barley, and the other crops, while the forests colored, the bittersweet burst burnt orange, and the wild geese took wing.

The crops were stored in granaries and barns, and carefully tabulated accounts of bushels were tallied up and compared to previous years. It did not matter what grain was selling for in some far-off marketplace. It did not matter how much farmers elsewhere were getting per bushel or per head. It only mattered that there be enough to feed the livestock and the people, and to that end they labored.

At the Kitchen House

With apples and pears wrapped in squares of newspaper, barrels of dill beans and sauerkraut, crocks of cheese or calcified eggs, bins of potatoes and onions, row upon row of jarred fruits and vegetables, braided strings of garlic or onion, linen sacks

filled with dried beans or apples, and bushels of root vegetables buried in cool sand, the kitchen house was armed against the coming cold.

Autumn was the gardeners last opportunity to make the most of the sun, and pumpkins, squash, and salsify were allowed to linger in the near-empty plot. Meanwhile, preparations were made for the following spring. A few cabbage plants were dug up and replanted in the dirt floor of the kitchen house cellar. Come spring the wintering cabbage would be planted in the garden once again and the cycle continued. After the small harvest of pumpkins, squash, and salsify was complete, the shepherd brought in a few of his flock, and the sheep grazed on spent vines and withered plants. Finally, horse manure was spread upon the garden, and it was plowed.

The Dry House

Drying fruits and vegetables, primarily apples and beans, was a practical means of preserving large quantities of food. Five of the seven Amana villages had specially constructed brick drying houses. Each of these small structures, really no bigger than a child's playhouse, was outfitted with wooden racks, a firebox or stove, and a chimney. In Middle Amana and in the village of Amana, cooks used the kilns in the woolen mills for drying foods.

Each kitchen house was given access to the drying house or to a woolen mill kiln and prepared green beans, lima beans, and navy beans for drying. Kale and spinach were blanched before being taken to the kiln. Apples and pears were peeled and sliced. These were carefully arranged on the wooden racks and a fire built in the firebox or stove. At the woolen mill, the kiln was tended by a mill worker who had long since learned how to operate the kiln for food preservation. At the mill, drying sometimes took less than a day. At the small brick drying houses, drying could take up to three days depending upon the weather, the heat produced by the fire, and the water content of the foods being dried. Once dry, the food was placed in clean linen sacks and stored in the kitchen attic or in a dry, dust-free pantry. In all, a kitchen staff might spend two weeks preparing and drying foods for winter use.

When the Grapes Were Ripe

In September or early October when the breeze carried the sweet scent of grapes from the trellised hills and the wasps buzzed lazily among the heavy clusters of arbored grapes, it was time to pick grapes and to make wine. During the course of the summer, the village vineyard had been tended by the men of the community and the trailing vines carefully tied to the trellises with willow withes. Each man who received a share of the village wine was expected to trim and care for 20 to 30 vines depending upon the size of the vineyard. Grapevines also grew on wooden trellises attached to the sides of buildings, providing both shade and fruit. Some of these grapes were taken to the press house as well, but most wound up at the kitchens and were used for pie, jam, and juice.

When it came to harvesting the ripe grapes in the vineyard, the entire village turned out to help. Schools were closed, craft shops were closed, and all regular work was postponed for the day. The cooks prepared a picnic lunch of sausage, sliced bread, cheese, hard-boiled eggs, coffee cake, or fruit, and this were taken to the vineyard in willow baskets and served to the workers who assembled there.

The grape picking, and all things associated with wine making, was organized by the village vintner. Under his direction, the bunches of grapes were placed in large willow baskets and the baskets hauled by wagon to the press house. At the press house, men unloaded and emptied the baskets and worked the heavy wooden press. Juice from the first pressing of grapes was immediately siphoned through an underground pipe to the wine cellar. Wine was made and stored in the cellar of the village general store or the *Saal* (meetinghouse), whichever had the deepest, coolest cellar. In most villages the press house was conveniently located just next door to the wine cellar.

Grape pulp from the first pressing was poured into huge vats (made by the local cooper) and allowed to ferment for several days before a second and even a third pressing was accomplished. Wine made from the juice of first, second, and third pressings varies in color, taste, and alcohol content with wine made from the third pressing the driest, darkest, and highest in alcohol content. *Tresterwein* (from the third pressing) was considered the very best the communal cellar had to offer. Most of the village wine was made from first and second press-juice. Quite often water and sugar were added to the juice in a formula known only to the wine maker and probably never recorded. The newly made wine was pumped into barrels; some of the barrels were 10 feet across and made to hold 1,000 gallons of wine.

Meanwhile, the vintner astutely judged the sweetness of the juice and its promise of greatness. The vintner, like the *Küchebaas,* the farm *Baas,* and all other managers in communal Amana, was a volunteer. He received no salary and expected no reward for his work other than the respect of his neighbors. His true reward may have been the satisfaction of producing the best wines possible. It has been estimated that each communal Amana village produced between 4,000 and 8,000 gallons of grape wine annually.

During the year while the new wine fermented, wine from previous years was shared. Each adult male and each adult female received a wine allotment or ration card issued by the village vintner who drew off the wine into bottles and jugs at a given time when those who wished to receive wine for home consumption assembled at the wine cellar. Depending upon how much wine was available, each adult male was allotted between 15 and 20 gallons per year. Each female received half that amount. Generally, families pooled their allotment cards, and those who did not drink gave their cards to those who did. Good wine gratefully shared was considered one of the gifts of community life.

More than once in Iowa's history, state law has prohibited the production of spirits, and more than once the law has been repealed, but whenever fickle legislative whim demanded, Amana wine makers sadly emptied the wine barrels and abided by the law. Henry Schiff, who for many years served as historian at the Museum of Amana History, likes to tell of the year 1917 when 19,000 gallons of wine were dumped into the Iowa River, which finds the Mississippi. As he tells it, "The next morning every catfish from Amana to New Orleans was asking for aspirin."

Amana today has a number of family-owned and -operated wineries that are direct descendants of the old communal wineries. These modern establishments produce on-site a variety of fruit and blossom wines, including grape and rhubarb wines very much like those produced by the communal vintner.

Autumn Work

In autumn they husked corn and hoped to have the corn in cribs by the end of November. Harvesting was done by hand. Each man wore a leather husking glove with an iron or steel hook sewn into the palm of the glove. Walking along a row of corn, he grasped a ear of corn with one hand and ripped it off with the hook on the other hand. The ears were tossed into the back of a wagon pulled slowly between the rows by a patient horse. East Amana resident Carl Schuerer described the long days harvesting corn with his friends, "In the morning when the frost was on the corn, your mittens got wet, and your hands got ice cold. It was hard on your hands, I can tell you that."

Harvesting corn was only one of many seasonal chores. In autumn the late potatoes were dug, fall plowing was completed, the broom corn was cut, chimneys were swept, and woodstoves were checked and repaired. A crew of men put the Mill Race dredge in dry dock. Farmers culled the sheep and brought the cattle in from the farthest pastures. They cut trees in the timber and hauled the logs in with teams of draft horses or oxen. They cut wood and delivered it to the homes, a task that continued through winter and did not end until spring mud made roads impassable.

Fall Cleaning and New Carpets

Fall housecleaning, which was almost as rigorous as the spring ritual, involved the entire household, although no one probably dreaded it more than the person to whom fell the chore of taking off the window screens and replacing these with heavy storm windows. These had to be washed before they were hauled up the ladder, an awkward job requiring great balance, and hung onto the windows.

After fall cleaning, a colony housewife gave a thought to household refurbishment and considered ordering new carpet. In communal Amana, all homes had handwoven wool or cotton carpet made from scraps of fabric collected from the household rag bag and the mending basket. Scraps and mill ends from the woolen mills or calico works were collected as well and dyed to suit. Handwoven carpet is still very popular in the Amana Colonies, and a number of weavers are kept busy filling orders for colonists who wish to replace their worn carpet.

During Amana's communal era, each village had one or more carpet weavers, usually older men, retired from other jobs. They took orders for carpeting and filled these as time allowed, usually working in the autumn and winter when cold weather made outdoor pursuits impossible. Amana carpeting was woven in 36-inch wide strips (stair runners were usually 22 inches wide), and several strips were sewn together to carpet a room. The weavers designed carpet patterns having colored stripes of varying widths repeated exactly in sequence. Black and shades of gray and blue were the colors most often used with narrow bands of brown, green, and even red as accent colors. Using worn-out clothing and scraps of fabric saved from their sewing, Amana women made their own braided, prodded, and hooked rag throw rugs. They designed their own patterns or used patterns found in magazines like *Hausfrau*. The handmade rug, both durable and decorative, added to the comfort of the Amana home.

Something Special

 Occasionally, quiet evenings at home included a snack. Without a kitchen or pantry at home, snack choices were very limited, and no Amana housewife kept candy or cookies around except at Christmastime. So Amana folks made do with what they had and improvised. A slice of bread or coffee cake skewered on a long fork and toasted over the banked fire in the woodstove was a favorite, especially when the toast was sprinkled with sugar and cinnamon. Popcorn was as popular in the Amanas then as it is today, although many colonists flavored their popcorn with sugar, rather than salt. In Homestead, it seems, chocolate popcorn was made on very special occasions when something wonderful was needed to cap an evening at home.

Chocolate Popcorn

4 quarts unsalted,
   unbuttered, freshly
   popped popcorn
4 teaspoons cocoa
2 cups sugar
1 cup hot water
1 tablespoon butter
⅛ teaspoon salt

Pop popcorn and set aside. Dissolve cocoa in hot water. In a heavy-bottomed saucepan, stir together sugar, water, and butter. Bring to a boil, slowly adding dissolved cocoa and salt. While stirring, cook mixture until the soft ball stage has been reached (234° to 240° on a candy thermometer). To test, drop a small amount of cooked mixture into cold water. The droplet should not dissolve or disintegrate but form a soft ball that can be flattened between your fingers. Upon reaching soft ball stage, remove chocolate from heat and pour over popcorn. Toss until well coated. Allow to cool before serving.

Yields about four servings.

A. Marie Hofer, Homestead

Sugared Popcorn

3 quarts unsalted,
   unbuttered, freshly
   popped popcorn
1 cup sugar
3 tablespoons water
3 tablespoons butter
3 to 4 drops food
   coloring (optional)

Pop popcorn and place in a large bowl. In a medium saucepan combine sugar, water, and butter. Bring ingredients slowly to a boil, stirring constantly. On medium heat boil for 3 minutes. Remove from heat and quickly stir in several drops of food coloring, if desired. Pour sugar mixture over popcorn and turn with a wooden spoon until popcorn is coated. Allow to cool before serving. Can be made ahead and stored in airtight container.

Yields about three to four servings.

Note: In recent years colony cooks have colored their sugared popcorn for a festive treat.

Evenings at Home

Cool weather and early sunsets brought an end to agreeable evenings spent in the flower garden or on the lawn swing. Come autumn, after the evening prayer service, folks walked home and spent their time doing things they liked to do. There were no radios and few phonographs, so the talented made their own music, teaching themselves to play mail-order zithers, accordions, or guitars. By the light of the kerosene lamp, women did needlework, skillfully creating lace circlets for the windows, embroidered pillowcases and linens, needlepoint chair covers and wall hangings, delicate knitted lace doilies, and tatted curtain ties. They knitted, a skill thought so important it was taught to children in school, and colorful, patterned mittens and hats, long thick scarves, and warm vests were made as the weather turned.

Borrowed reading material, loaned from one household to the next, was coveted as men and women looked forward to studying journals, books, and newspapers. Some men used their evenings to learn more about a particular vocation. One Amana grandmother recalled her father spending hours studying electrical engineering from manuals and textbooks the *Bruderrat* had ordered for him from a state university. Another remembered seeing her father read books on mathematics, and one Amana man taught himself drafting using books loaned to him by a friend. These self-taught men and others like them were the men responsible for designing and operating the mills, building and rebuilding mill machinery, installing village waterworks, designing furniture, and constructing bridges, shops, and barns. Formal education stopped for most men and all women at age 14, but education continued for all who wished to learn.

Renewing the Covenant

Each Thanksgiving Day for the past 130 years, one of the most important events of the Amana Church year takes place—the annual Covenant Service or *Bundesschliessung* (Renewing of the Covenant). At this most solemn worship service church members pledge, or renew the pledge, to live for the Lord. Each member acknowledges this covenant by a handshake rather than an oath. Prior to 1863, the Covenant Service was held only when "God directed." In 1863 it was determined that the Covenant Service should take place on the "annual common Thanksgiving day of the land." Ever after, the Amana Church has held its Covenant Service on Thanksgiving. So in the morning in the large sunlit *Saal* they meet and sing:

> The needy will receive God's help and
>   blessing;
> He satisfies the hungry soul.
> He strengthens those whose flame of
>   faith is lagging;
> To honor Him should be our goal.

> Christian Metz, "We Praise the
> Lord," translation by Wilhelmine
> Baumgartner and Helene Rind,
> *The Amana Church Hymnal*

CHAPTER 11

MEATS AND MAIN DISHES

Once in a while my father would get us Bratwurst *from the butcher shop in East. We lived in Amana, and they made real good* Bratwurst *here, but that sausage from East Amana was extra-good. It was something special!*

Lina Unglenk, Amana

Fresh and smoked meats were a vital part of the communal Amana diet, and while meat portions were never large, each resident received a share of what the village butcher allotted to each kitchen house. Portions were determined by the *Küchebaas*. One Amana resident who remembers going to a kitchen to get her family's meal explained, "Of the bread, soup, and vegetables you could take as much as you wanted, but the meat the *Küchebaas* cut for you, and she gave you just exactly what she thought you needed according to how many were in your house. There wasn't any extra."

Smoking, salt curing, and pickling were three methods of meat preservation practiced in communal Amana. Smoking and salt curing were by far the most convenient and reliable methods of preserving meats, and therefore, each Amana village had its meat shop and its smokehouse. When the days and nights were cold enough to allow fresh meat to be processed safely, it was time to see to the meat shop and the smokehouse.

Carl Schuerer of East Amana was born in 1906 and remembers well the days when steers were slaughtered in the East Amana meat shop and the fire in the smokehouse was kept burning November through March. There is an art to smoking meats. Carl's father, Oswald, was the East Amana butcher, and he practiced and perfected that age-old art. He taught his sons, Carl and Walter, and they, in turn, taught their nephews and sons who, in later years, managed the Amana Society Meat Shop and Smokehouse in Amana. Today the Amana Meat Shop and Smokehouses in Amana and in Homestead use recipes adapted from those used in the communal meat shops.

In East Amana prior to 1932, Carl explained, two steers were slaughtered each cold weather month. Thirty-five to 40 hogs were slaughtered five or six times during the season. Larger villages, such as Middle Amana or Amana, processed three or four times as much meat.

At just the right time, the smoked meats were removed from the smokehouse, and hung in the meat shop attic. Later in the spring, when the season's smoking was finished, those meats needed for the summer were stored in the smokehouse, and the smokehouse was filled to the rafters with racks of preserved sausage, ham, and bacon. Every so often, the butcher lit a very small sulpher fire in the smokehouse pit. The sulpher smoke kept flies away from the preserved meats.

Making Sausage

From scraps of beef and pork a variety of fresh and smoked sausages was made in the village meat shops: *Leberwurst* (liver sausage), *Bratwurst* (pork sausage), *Swartenmagen* (headcheese), *Blutwurst* (blood sausage), and *Knackwurst* (highly spiced pork sausage), to name just a few. *Bockwurst,* a pork sausage flavored with chives, was made and shared in the early spring when the chives burst green in the *Kuchebaas*'s herb bed.

Each village meat shop had its own time-tested recipes for spicing sausage, and the recipes were taught to each new generation of butchers. As Carl Schuerer reported,

We would do it by weight—so much for 100 pounds of meat. In East Amana for pork sausage we would take 28 ounces salt to 100 pounds of meat, 5 ounces ground pepper, 2 ½ ounces of allspice, and 1 ounce nutmeg. All the kitchens grew their own garlic. We used to take, oh, ½ cup and peel it and chop it ourselves. We ground the pepper ourselves. You used to have to run it through the grinder twice so it would be fine enough. And you would grind all the spices and grate the nutmeg too. The nutmeg and spices we got from the store. Usually, we would make 500 pounds of pork sausage at a time.

Curing and Smoking

Ham, bacon, and pork shoulders were packed in large wooden vats of salt brine for curing. The heavy brine was made with salt and saltpeter. Bacon took about two weeks to cure. Hams, 100 at a time, were slow-cured for four weeks. Each week the brine was removed, the meat was repacked and the brine replaced. After salt curing, the meat was hung in the smokehouse.

"You had to have a good, slow, smoky fire. Not too hot. We didn't have a temperature gauge. You just kinda knew. . . . How long it took? Well, that was a thing you didn't know. It depended upon the weather. If it was good, clear, cold weather, it was done smoking in a week. If we had weather like we sometimes have around here, grey and foggy, it would take longer," Schuerer explained. With a practiced eye, the butcher judged the sky and the smoke and carefully tended his hickory wood fire.

From the notes of one Homestead butcher scratched in an old pocket-sized notebook from the "Acme Steel and Wire Co. of Peoria," it is clear that the Homestead pork sausage recipe did not use nearly as much garlic or nutmeg as the East Amana sausage recipe. If ever historians discover the recipes for the meat shops in High, West, South, or Middle Amana, they will, undoubtedly, find other village variances in sausage making.

Fresh Meats

Fresh beef roasts, ground beef, beef liver, and beef tongue were processed in each meat shop, in addition to pork roasts, ribs, and chops. Beef steaks and other single-serving type beef cuts were thought to be impractical for communal cooking, so beef from the rib, loin, sirloin, flank, and round were cut as roasts or ground.

Preparing Meats in the Kitchen House

Because the communal cooks had to prepare a large quantity of meat as efficiently as possible, boiling and roasting were the methods most often employed. Boiled sausage, boiled beef roast and beef tongue, boiled pork ribs and chops, and boiled ham were typical communal kitchen fare. Even bacon was parboiled before it was fried to remove excess fat and reduce cooking time. Roasted meats were common, but panfrying was reserved for the occasional beef cake, and broiling, of course, was unheard of in communal Amana. Although the method for preparing meats was usually very simple, the results were savory and satisfying in the German culinary tradition of meats and main dishes.

Gekochtes Rindfleisch
Boiling Beef

3 to 4 pounds boneless
    beef brisket or arm
    roast
1 onion, quartered
1 teaspoon salt

In large kettle, boil beef brisket, enough water to cover, quartered onion, and salt. As water begins to boil, skim off foam. Cook on high to medium-high heat, covered, until fork-tender, about 2 hours.

Place meat on cutting board and cut into $\frac{1}{4}$-inch-thick slices. Return sliced meat to kettle with just enough broth to cover and warm until serving time.

Serves six to eight.

Note: Hot horseradish sauce, creamed spinach, and fried potatoes usually accompany a dinner of boiling beef in Amana homes.

Sauerbraten
Sour Beef Roast

4 to 6 pounds beef roast
    or flank steak
2 cups vinegar
2 cups water
1 bay leaf
$\frac{1}{4}$ teaspoon crushed
    cloves or 3 whole
    cloves
5 peppercorns
6 tablespoons flour
1 teaspoon salt
Dash pepper
1 tablespoon vegetable
    shortening
2 onions, sliced

Trim meat and place in a large (nonmetal) bowl or crock. Combine vinegar, water, bay leaf, peppercorns, and cloves and pour over meat. Cover and refrigerate two days. Every so often, turn meat and baste.

Drain meat, reserving liquid. Sprinkle 2 table-spoons flour, teaspoon salt, and dash pepper on meat, all sides. In a roasting pan or large skillet with lid, melt shortening and sauté sliced onion. Add meat and brown. Add marinade and cover. Stew on top of stove, covered (low heat), or roast, covered, at 325° about 1 $\frac{1}{2}$ hours.

Before serving, remove meat and slice. Pour off all but 2 or 3 cups marinade. Heat the marinade and blend in 2 to 4 tablespoons flour to thicken. While stirring, heat gravy until bubbling hot. Add sliced meat and serve very hot with potato dumplings, *Spätzle,* or noodles.

Serves six to eight.

Fleisch Küchlein
Beef Cakes in Gravy

1 pound ground beef
1 small onion, minced
1 egg
1 cup fresh bread
    crumbs
Salt and pepper to taste
1 tablespoon butter or
    margarine
1 tablespoon flour
¾ to 1 cup water

Combine ground beef, minced onion, egg, bread crumbs, and dash salt and pepper. Form into patties.

Heat butter or margarine in a skillet and brown patties until well done. Remove patties from skillet. Drain grease and deglaze skillet. On low heat, add flour and water to beef drippings in skillet and stir to form a gravy. Heat until bubbly. Return patties to skillet and simmer 5–10 minutes, turning once.

Makes 4 to 6 patties.

Lina Unglenk, Amana

Note: This Amana favorite is meant to be served with noodles or *Spätzle*.

Gefülltenudeln
Filled Noodles

3 eggs
6 tablespoons water
1 ½ cups flour
1 teaspoon salt
2 egg whites
Noodle filling or roast
    beef noodle filling
    (see following
    recipes)
Browned bread crumbs
    (page 81)

Beat eggs and water. Sift together flour and salt. Add to beaten eggs and blend to form a dough.

Roll a portion of the dough on a well-floured surface to approximately ⅛ inch thickness. Dough should be thin enough to insure tenderness and thick enough to work with. (This takes practice and patience but is worth the effort.) Cut dough into 4-inch squares. Brush surface of square with egg whites and place 1 tablespoon filling (see following recipes) on square. Top with a second square and seal edges to form a noodle pocket (raviolilike). Repeat as necessary.

Boil in a large kettle of salted water about 8 to 10 minutes. Gently remove from kettle, allow to drain a moment, place in serving dish, and top with browned bread crumbs.

Serves four or five.

Note: *Gefülltenudeln* are not served with any type of gravy or sauce. Crowned with toasted crumbs and served alongside sweet applesauce, a fresh green vegetable dish, and salad, filled noodles simply do not need a sauce. A very popular communal Amana dish, *Gefülltenudeln* sometimes made a special appearance on those days when elders from other villages were visiting.

Noodle Filling

1 pound lean ground
  beef
1 or 2 slices bread, cut
  into small cubes
1 small onion, minced

⅛ teaspoon nutmeg
1 heaping teaspoon
  minced parsley
Salt and pepper

Brown lean ground beef. Drain and pat dry. Soak bread cubes in a bit of water and then squeeze to remove excess water. Combine bread cubes, minced onion, nutmeg, parsley, salt and pepper. Spoon mixture in noodles.

Roast Beef Noodle Filling

1 smaller pot or blade
  roast (or leftovers
  from a large roast)
½ cup of gravy
1 to 2 teaspoons minced
  parsley
1 to 2 slices bread, cut
  into small cubes
Salt and pepper

Roast beef the day before (or use leftovers from your roast beef dinner). Grind beef with gravy to form a pasty consistency. Cube bread and soak in water—squeeze to remove excess water. Add parsley, bread cubes, and salt and pepper to ground roast. Fill noodles.

Susanna Hahn, Middle Amana

Leberklössel
Liver Dumplings

1 tablespoon butter
1 cup cubed day-old
  coffee cake or cubed
  bread
1 ½ pounds beef liver
1 onion, minced
¾ cup flour
2 eggs
Salt and pepper

Melt butter or margarine in a skillet and brown very small coffee cake cubes (or substitute bread). Set aside.

Grind liver. Add minced onion, flour, eggs, and browned coffee cake cubes. Add dash salt and pepper. Form into small balls—a little more than 1 tablespoon per dumpling.

Boil liver dumplings in salted water about 10 minutes.

Makes about 16 dumplings.

Katherina Moershel, Homestead

Note: It is customary to serve liver dumplings topped with a generous sprinkle of toasted bread crumbs and a side dish of applesauce.

Zunge
Boiled Beef Tongue

1 fresh beef tongue
1 medium onion,
    quartered
½ cup chopped celery
Salt and pepper

Ask your butcher to select a nice beef tongue, not too big or too small. In a very large pot, boil enough water to cover tongue, adding the onion, celery, and salt and pepper. Add the tongue, whole. Turn the heat down and simmer until meat is tender—this may take anywhere from 2 to 3 hours. You cannot, however, over-cook a beef tongue, so assume it will take at least 3 hours to simmer and plan your meal accordingly.

Once the meat is tender, remove and allow to cool about 10 minutes before peeling off the tough outer skin of the tongue. Slice meat about ¼ inch thick; arrange on platter and serve.

Serves six to eight people.

Note: In communal Amana, steers were usually slaughtered only during the autumn or winter months, and so boiled beef tongue was a cold weather dish. Each kitchen, in turn, was given beef tongue when available, and the village butcher kept note of the delivery so that no kitchen would be forgotten during the course of the butchering season.

Boiled tongue was served with side dishes of hot horseradish sauce, creamed spinach, and fried potatoes. In Amana homes today, where colony culinary traditions survive, beef tongue is relished with its customary side dishes or is chilled and sliced for sandwiches.

Schweinebraten
Sour Pork Roast

2 cups vinegar

1 onion, chopped

4 cloves

1 bay leaf

¼ cup water

2 to 4 pounds pork roast
   or loin

Salt and pepper to taste

1 to 2 tablespoons flour

Combine vinegar, onion, cloves, bay leaf, and water. Place roast in earthernware or glass bowl; pour vinegar mixture over roast and refrigerate two days, turning roast and basting occasionally.

Remove roast from marinade. Reserve 1 cup marinade. Place meat in roasting pan and add 1 cup marinade and dash salt and pepper. Roast as usual—approximately 40 minutes per pound at 325°. Remove roast from pan, place pan on heat, and stir in flour to make gravy. Cook over low to medium heat until gravy is smooth.

Serves four to eight.

Note: Serve pork roast with mashed potatoes or crumbed potatoes, sauerkraut, and applesauce.

Karbonade
Baked Breaded Pork Loins

½ cups dried bread
   crumbs

2 eggs, beaten

2 tablespoons milk

8 pork tenderloins

⅓ cup vegetable
   shortening

Salt and pepper

Preheat oven to 325°.

Place crumbs in a pie pan. In a second pan or bowl beat eggs and add milk. Dredge loins in egg, then in crumbs and salt and pepper, coating well. Melt vegetable shortening in a large skillet. When hot, brown tenderlions in skillet. Place browned tenderloins in ovenproof casserole or pan and bake, covered, 1 hour.

Serves four.

Erna Pitz, High Amana

Boiled Spareribs

2 pounds spareribs,
   trimmed of fat

1 onion, quartered

2 stalks celery, chopped

1 teaspoon fresh parsley

In a large kettle bring to boil spareribs, onion, chopped celery, and parsley in enough water to cover. Simmer, covered, until tender, about 2 hours.

Drain and serve hot spareribs alongside sauerkraut or red cabbage.

Serves four.

Pot Pie mit Spätzle
Boiled Chops and Bratwurst with *Spätzle*

For boiled chops and
bratwurst
8 cups boiling water
4 pork chops
1 sliced onion
1 bay leaf
2 to 3 cloves
Several peppercorns
2 medium potatoes,
    peeled and sliced in
    half
4 bratwurst, cut in
    thirds or quarters

For Spätzle
2 ½ cups flour
1 teaspoon salt
Pinch baking powder
1 cup milk
2 eggs, beaten lightly

For browned bread
crumbs
2 tablespoons butter or
    margarine
½ cup dry bread crumbs
A little salt, if you like

In a very large kettle, boil water, pork chops, onion, bay leaf, cloves, and peppercorns. Turn down heat; cook 25 minutes. Add potatoes and bratwurst; cook an additional 20 minutes. While pot pie is cooking, prepare browned bread crumbs and *Spätzle* batter.

For *Spätzle,* measure flour and sift with dry ingredients. Form a well and add milk. Mix a smooth, soft batter or dough, blending in beaten eggs, one at a time, mixing well after each addition.

Add *Spätzle* to pot pie using *Spätzle* slicer or the traditional method as follows: While tilting bowl over boiling water, use a sharp knife to cut batter as you very slowly pour it into the boiling water. The sliced batter should be about the size of your little finger. Dip knife into water to keep the batter from sticking to the knife. Boil *Spätzle* in pot pie about 5 minutes.

For browned bread crumbs, melt butter or margarine in a medium or a small skillet. Add bread crumbs and stir or turn with fork or spatula. Allow crumbs to brown evenly, turning or stirring frequently. Add dash salt if you wish. Crumbs tend to burn so monitor heat. Once mahogany brown, remove from heat or leave on very low heat until ready to use.

Drain pot pie. Place in very large serving dish or on a platter and top with browned bread crumbs.

Serves four.

Dorothy Zuber, Middle Amana

Poultry

Chickens were raised by each kitchen house, and the size of the flock depended upon the number needed to keep the kitchen in eggs throughout the year with enough additional eggs to take to the village general store for trade. Flocks numbering 300 or 400 chickens were common. Geese and ducks were not raised in communal Amana, nor were domestic turkeys raised here until after the end of the communal era.

In the spring a number of pullets were killed, plucked, and dressed for roasting or baking. Unless something out of the ordinary happened, baked or roasted chicken was a spring dish, and because it provided a much-needed respite from the usual beef or pork, everyone looked forward to and savored a chicken dinner.

Quite often throughout the year, an old hen found her way into a soup kettle, and eggs, either scrambled or fried, were served regularly during spring and summer. In late summer and autumn, excess eggs were "calcified" in crocks in a heavy gelatinlike solution and stored for winter use.

In the Chicken Yard

My mother was a *Küchebaas,* and in our chicken yard we had 350 to 400 chickens, and those were laying chickens, and pullets, one year olds and two year olds. . . . The first year we were in the kitchen house, we had a small chicken house, and in there we had a brooder stove, and one spring we had 400 little chickens. My mother said, "What are we going to do?" I told my mother, "If you don't want to raise chickens, I will." . . . But it was not free gratis. When I raised the chickens, my mother washed the dishes all summer while I tended chickens. I was 14 years old. I remember I had luck; out of 408 chickens, I lost only 10 little baby chicks. There is a saying, "*Da dummste Bauer* raises *da meerste Kartoffel*!" [The dumbest farmer raises the most potatoes.] I had that kind of dumb luck, and I remember I had much rather tend chickens than wash dishes.

I had a tame little rooster that I called Martin, and Martin broke his leg, so what did I do? I picked him up and took him to Dr. Noé's office and asked him to fix the broken leg, and Dr. Noé said later to the druggist, Mr. Miller, "that is the first chicken leg I've set." And Martin got well again; he limped a little bit.

Elizabeth Schoenfelder, Amana

Hühnersosse
Creamed Chicken

2 tablespoons butter

¼ cup flour

3 cups chicken broth

2 cups cooked chicken
  cut into bite-sized
  pieces

⅛ teaspoon nutmeg

Salt and pepper to taste

¼ cup cream (optional)

In a large saucepan, melt butter. Stir in flour to form white paste. Slowly add chicken broth, stirring to form sauce. Add chicken. Heat until thick and bubbly, stirring in nutmeg and salt and pepper to taste. Simmer 20 minutes, stirring occasionally. For a richer, more flavorful sauce, add cream while simmering.

Serves four.

Note: *Hühnersosse* is served over noodles, *Spätzle,* or potato dumplings and is topped with browned bread crumbs.

On Christmas Day, when young and old anticipated the joyful unfolding of holiday events, chicken sauce over noodles was the traditional main dish in communal kitchens. Rice soup, *Hühnersosse,* noodles, mashed potatoes, coleslaw, stewed plums and prunes, and slices of sweet *Stollen* (yeast bread laced with citron and raisins) made up the menu for the holiday meal.

CHAPTER 12 *MEHLSPEISEN:* FRITTERS, PUFFS, AND PUDDINGS

Pfüttele

*Let 3 ½ quarts milk come to a boil and then add
1 pound butter. Add gradually 5 ¾ pounds flour
until batter separates from pot. When cool, add 60
eggs, a small hand-full of salt. Fry in hot fat.*

Enough for us.

Louise Herrmann Noé, *Baas*, Noé Kitchen House, Amana
Translated by Louise Miller DuVal

On Tuesdays or Thursdays at noon villagers looked forward to *Mehlspeisen:* delicious cream puffs, light-as-air *Schneeküchlein,* sweet rice pudding, or dessert waffles. The variety of *Mehlspeisen* recipes was such that the *Küchebaas* could choose from among many delicious desserts.

The word *Mehl* means flour in German, and *Mehlspeisen* refers to desserts made with flour, namely fritters and puffs. Puddings, which contain no flour but are sweet and filling, were included in this category of dessert dishes. In a few kitchens, puddings, particularly rice or starch (*Eis*) pudding, were served occasionally on Saturdays as well as on a *Mehlspeisen* day.

Recipes that called for a quantity of fresh eggs were made in the spring or summer when the hens were most productive. Puddings that required a lot

of milk, such as *Eispudding,* were also summertime fare. In the winter when the villagers needed extra-filling meals to fuel hours spent working in frigid weather and neither eggs nor milk was plentiful, the cooks relied on dessert pancakes, waffles, *Hefeklösse* (yeast dumplings), and recipes for bread pudding, farina pudding, noodle pudding, and other baked puddings.

Many of the recipes call for only those ingredients commonly found in a well-stocked pantry. Most of the recipes are very easy to prepare. However, one or two of the recipes, particularly the *Hefeklösse* (yeast dumplings), require an experienced hand and a few trial runs to perfect. In the communal kitchens, *Hefeklösse mit Zimmetsosse* (yeast dumplings with cinnamon sauce) were considered a meal in itself. When the cooks took the time to prepare dumplings with cinnamon sauce, the usual meat course was not served. A true colony delicacy, *Hefeklösse* are worth the effort. In communal Amana, a cook who learned to prepare the perfect yeast dumpling was sure to earn the praise of her diners and the respect of an entire village.

Hefeklösse mit Zimmetsosse
Dumplings with Cinnamon Sauce

For dumplings
1 cake yeast
3 cups milk
2 pounds (7 cups) flour
1 ¼ teaspoons salt
½ cup vegetable
   shortening

For steaming dumplings
1 to 2 cups water
1 tablespoon vegetable
   shortening
Dash salt

*For browned bread
   crumbs*
2 tablespoons butter or
   margarine
¾ cup bread crumbs

For cinnamon sauce
¾ cup sugar
¾ cup flour
2 teaspoons cinnamon
½ cup milk
2 ½ cups scalded milk

Dissolve yeast in warm milk. Combine with other dumplings ingredients to form a dough.

Give the dough a good long knead, at least 15 minutes. Cover bowl with a dish towel and set in a warm spot. Allow to rise until double in bulk—don't punch down!

Form dough into dumplings about 2 inches across. Place dumplings on cloth-covered board and allow to rise until double in size.

For steaming dumplings, boil water in a large heavy-bottomed skillet or kettle with tight-fitting lid. (Depending upon how large your skillet is, you will want enough water to allow a good boiling to occur but not enough to cover more than one quarter of the dumplings. Dumplings should sit, not float, in the pan. The point is to steam, not boil, the dumplings.) Add 1 tablespoon vegetable shortening and salt to the boiling water. Place dumplings in skillet, side by side. Cover with tight-fitting lid. Steam about 10 to 15 minutes. Do not remove the lid. After 10 to 15 minutes in a heavy steam, the dumplings should appear puffed with crusty, browned bottoms. They may need to be separated with forks.

For browned bread crumbs, in a small skillet, melt butter. Add bread crumbs and brown over medium heat, turning crumbs or stirring so that they brown evenly. Crumbs should attain a nice rich color. Top dumplings with bread crumbs before serving.

For cinnamon sauce, in a bowl combine sugar, flour, and cinnamon. Stir in $\frac{1}{2}$ cup cold milk and set aside. In a saucepan scald milk over medium heat, stirring constantly. Slowly add cold milk mixture to scalded milk and cook on top of double boiler for 20 minutes. Serve sauce hot over warm dumplings and bread crumbs.

If you don't plan to serve the dumplings immediately, place them in an ovenproof dish, top dumplings with bread crumbs, and place in the oven to warm. Dumplings should be served warm with browned bread crumbs and cinnamon sauce.

Serves six.

Emily Roemig, Amana

Easier *Hefeklösse*

1 tablespoon shortening
1 cup boiling water
1 teaspoon salt
1 package 12 unbaked frozen dinner rolls
Browned bread crumbs and cinnamon sauce (see preceding recipe)

In a heavy skillet with a lid or in an electric fry pan, melt shortening; add boiling water and salt. Place rolls in skillet; cover and simmer 15 minutes until crust forms on the bottom of the dumplings. While steaming dumplings, brown bread crumbs. When dumplings are done, serve immediately with bread crumbs and cinnamon sauce. Or place in an ovenproof dish, top with browned bread crumbs, and place in warm oven until ready to serve. Add sauce just before serving.

Serves six.

Dorothy Zuber, Middle Amana

Note: Dorothy Zuber, an accomplished Middle Amana cook who has manned the kitchen at Zuber's Restaurant in Homestead for many years, hit upon this idea when a hectic schedule forced her to look for shortcuts in the kitchen. She still loves the old-fashioned *Hefeklösse* but has found this to be a happy alternative when time is short.

On a Winter Tuesday Noon in 1916

Middle Amana *Küchebaas* Marie Reihmann kept track of the *Mehlspeisen* served in her kitchen so that she would not repeat the same dish twice in the same month. In the winter of 1916 she wrote in her kitchen journal:

Tuesday

January 4—*Griespudding* [farina pudding]

January 11—*Pfannkuchen* [dessert pancakes]

January 18—*Peistengel* [rhubarb pie]

January 25—*Gries cakes* [farina cakes]

February 1—*Reispudding* [rice pudding]

February 8—*Brotpudding* [bread pudding]

February 15—*Matte Kuchen* [cottage cheese pie]

February 22—*Hefeklösse mit Sosse* [dumplings with cinnamon sauce]

Because pie baking was a labor-intensive effort, pies were baked every four to six weeks on *Mehlspeisen* day.

Rupfklösse
Torn Dumplings

This dessert is prepared precisely the same way as *Hefeklösse* (page 138), however, when the dumplings are taken from the steaming kettle, the puffed top of each dumpling is torn open with two forks, the air is released, and the *Hefen* (mounded top) diminishes. Serve with browned bread crumbs and cinnamon sauce.

Although no one remembers quite why, *Rupfklösse* were preferred in some kitchen houses.

Amana Apple Fritters

¼ cup sugar
6 apples, peeled, cored, and cut into rings
1 cup flour
1 teaspoon baking powder
½ cup milk
3 egg whites, beaten until nearly stiff
Lard or vegetable shortening for deep fat frying
Powdered sugar

Sprinkle ¼ cup sugar over the apples and set aside. Mix flour, baking powder, and milk. Fold egg whites into this mixture and combine to form a light batter.

Dip each apple ring into the batter and deep fat fry. Communal cooks used lard, but vegetable shortening works nearly as well. Fry until golden brown. Sprinkle with powdered sugar and serve warm.

Serves four.

Note: It's best to use sweet, firm Jonathan or McIntosh apples.

Apple Fritters II

6 eggs, separated
1 cup whole milk
1 ½ cups sifted flour
½ teaspoon baking powder
½ teaspoon salt
4 large apples, peeled, cored, and cut into very small chunks or rings
Lard or vegetable shortening for deep fat frying
Powdered sugar

Beat egg yolks and whole milk. Sift together flour, baking powder, and salt. Add flour mixture to beaten yolks and stir. Beat egg whites until stiff. Fold whites into batter. Stir apple chunks into batter. Deep fat fry large spoonfuls in hot lard or vegetable shortening. Fat should be hot enough to brown a bread cube in 60 seconds—no hotter. Sprinkle with powdered sugar and serve warm.

Serves four.

Note: If the apples you are using are not quite fresh, chopping rather than cutting them into rings works best. For a simple variation sprinkle cinnamon on top as well as sugar.

Tante Lizzie's Fritters

2 cups flour

⅓ cup sugar

Pinch salt

2 eggs

½ cup buttermilk

½ cup milk

1 teaspoon baking soda

4 medium-sized firm
   apples, peeled,
   cored, and chopped
   into small chunks

Vegetable shortening or
   lard for deep fat
   frying

Powdered sugar and
   cinnamon

Sift together flour, sugar, and salt. Break in eggs and stir. Add buttermilk, milk, and baking soda, stirring well. Stir apple chunks into batter. Heat shortening or lard in a deep skillet (cast iron works best). Drop batter by large spoonfuls into hot fat and fry until golden brown. Top with powdered sugar and cinnamon.

Serves four.

Lizzie Siegel, lower South Amana

Note: Lizzie Siegel was the cook at the lower South Amana Hotel. When folks traveled by train and two major railroad lines converged in South Amana, one in upper and one in lower South Amana, the twins prospered. Each had its train station, hotel, and general store. Lower South was the bigger of the two and boasted a full complement of homes, kitchen houses, and barns, but on its hill upper South, with just a few brick homes standing in a row, seemed above all such things having, after all, the best view of the river valley.

For a few days each autumn (and again at Christmas and summer break) the village experienced a migration of sorts. University of Iowa students passed through the village on the railway heading east to Iowa City. Those who had to change railways and trains were transported from one rail station to the other via a horsedrawn "taxi." If the young men and women were lucky enough to pass through the village during the noon hour, they stopped at the lower South Amana Hotel for lunch, where fresh, hot apple fritters dusted with cinnamon and sugar were served to hungry travelers.

Apfelküchlein: The Swabian Fritter

 Look through any cookbook on German regional cuisines, and apple fritters will be among the many desserts favored in Swabia, Hesse, and the Rhineland. Swabian cooks, however, are credited with "inventing" the apple fritter.

Swabia is in southwestern Germany and claims Stuttgart as its principal city. In Germany, Swabian cuisine is noted for its tender noodles and fritters, and it's here that a great German favorite, the Swabian pocket, or *Maultaschen,* was born. A large raviolilike pasta with a filling of seasoned meat and bread crumbs, the Swabian pocket is close kin to our Amana *Gefülltenudlen.* And no wonder, since many residents of Swabia joined the Community of True Inspiration and made the journey to Ebenezer and later to Amana. These transplanted Swabians brought their recipes along to America and modified them for use in the communal kitchens. The apple fritter, *Gefülltenudlen,* and another Swabia invention that took Germany by storm, *Spätzle,* were served in the communal kitchens and readily adopted by the community.

The apple fritter was a particular favorite in communal Amana. Although peeling and coring the apples was a chore, the dish was relatively easy to make in large quantity with inexpensive ingredients ready at hand.

Schneeküchlein
Snow Cakes

6 eggs, separated

6 tablespoons flour

6 tablespoons milk

Lard or vegetable
   shortening for deep
   fat frying

Powdered sugar

Maple syrup or fresh
   fruit

Separate eggs and beat egg yolks until light and fluffy. Stir in flour and milk, mixing until batter is smooth. Beat egg whites until very stiff. Fold egg whites into batter. Deep fat fry spoonfuls of batter until golden. Remove and drain. Sprinkle with powdered sugar and serve warm. Should be topped with maple syrup or fresh fruit.

Serves four.

Elizabeth Schoenfelder, Amana

Pfüttele
Puffs

1 ¼ cups milk
½ cup butter
1 ¾ cups flour
1 tablespoon sugar
Pinch salt
¼ teaspoon baking
    soda
¼ teaspoon baking
    powder
6 eggs
Lard or vegetable
    shortening for deep
    fat frying
Powdered sugar

Bring milk to a boil; add butter and stir until the butter is melted. Take off the heat and stir in flour, sugar, salt, baking soda, and baking powder. Allow mixture to cool a bit; then add eggs, one at a time, stirring well. Deep fat fry by large spoonfuls. (Communal cooks used lard, but vegetable shortening will do.) Fry until golden brown. Remove and drain. Sprinkle puffs with powdered sugar and serve warm.

Serves four.

Noé Kitchen House, Amana
translated by Louise Miller DuVal

Windbeutel
Wind Bags or Cream Puffs

For dough
2 cups water
½ pound butter
2 ½ cups flour
8 eggs
Pinch salt

For vanilla filling
⅓ cup sugar
⅛ teaspoon salt
¼ cup cornstarch
2 ¾ cups milk
2 tablespoons butter or
    margarine
1 teaspoon vanilla

Preheat ovent to 425°.

Simmer water and butter until butter is melted. Stir in flour and pinch salt and cook 1 minute. Allow to cool a bit and then stir in eggs, one at a time. Drop batter by rounded tablespoonfuls onto a greased baking pan and bake at 425° for 15 minutes. Then decrease heat to 350° and bake 20 minutes longer or until well browned. When cool, cut puffs and fill with vanilla filling.

For vanilla filling, mix sugar, salt, and cornstarch with milk. Stir. Bring to a boil over medium heat, stirring constantly. Boil 1 minute. Remove from heat and stir in butter or margarine and vanilla. Allow to cool and set before spooning into puffs.

Makes about 1 dozen large puffs.

Pfannkuchen
Pancakes

1 cup milk
½ teaspoon salt
1 cup flour, sifted
2 eggs
⅛ to ¼ cup vegetable
    shortening, melted
Powdered sugar
Maple syrup or fresh
    fruit

Slowly stir milk and salt into flour. Batter should be smooth. Add eggs, one at a time, beating well after each.

Heat a heavy skillet and melt a bit of shortening so that the shortening coats the bottom of the skillet. Pour just enough batter to cover bottom of skillet. When pancake is nicely browned, turn and brown second side. Sprinkle with powdered sugar. Place pancakes in a warm oven until ready to serve. Serve with maple syrup or with fresh fruit and a sprinkle of powdered sugar.

Yields about 4 pancakes.

Note: This dessert pancake is very much like a crepe and can be served with sliced strawberries, raspberries, or a light fruit sauce.

Bettelman (Begger Man)
Bread Pudding

5 slices bread, at least
    three days old
Butter
½ cup raisins
    (optional)
3 cups milk
⅓ cup plus 2 table-
    spoons sugar
Pinch salt
3 eggs, beaten
¼ teaspoon cinnamon
Pinch nutmeg

Preheat oven to 350°.

Toast bread lightly, butter bread, and break into pieces. Arrange in a 9 × 9-inch baking dish. Should be fairly full of bread; if not, add another piece. Sprinkle raisins over bread.

In a heavy saucepan, scald milk. Stir in ⅓ cup sugar and pinch salt. Slowly pour scalded milk mixture over eggs. Pour milk and egg mixture over bread and stir just a bit so that all bread pieces are moist. Combine 2 tablespoons sugar, cinnamon, and nutmeg (fresh grated nutmeg is best). Sprinkle over bread pudding. Set baking dish in a pan of hot water; bake for 1 hour or until knife inserted comes out clean. Serve warm with grape sauce or vanilla sauce (see following recipes).

Traubensosse
Grape Sauce

1 ½ cups grape juice
2 teaspoons cornstarch
2 tablespoons sugar

Combine ingredients in saucepan or double boiler and cook over medium heat until sugar dissolves and mixture thickens. Serve warm over bread pudding.
Yields enough for eight to nine servings.

Marietta Moershel, Homestead

Sosse
Vanilla Sauce

2 cups milk
½ cup sugar
1 tablespoon cornstarch
1 egg, beaten
1 teaspoon vanilla

Simmer milk. Mix sugar, cornstarch, and beaten egg and then stir into milk. Simmer until sauce thickens (usually just a few minutes). Remove from heat. Stir in vanilla. Refrigerate until ready to serve. Warm a bit before serving over bread pudding.
Yields enough for eight to nine servings.

Chocolate Bread Pudding

Occasionally, when the *Küchebaas* saw fit, chocolate bread pudding was served and was a great favorite, especially among the children. Simply add 1 square melted chocolate to scalded milk and omit raisins, cinnamon, and nutmeg from bread pudding recipe (page 145). Chocolate bread pudding requires no sauce.

Chocolate Pudding

6 cups milk

1 ½ cups sugar

½ cup cornstarch

¾ cup cocoa

½ teaspoon salt

½ teaspoon vanilla

In a bowl, mix ½ cup milk, ¾ cup sugar, cornstarch, cocoa, and salt. Set aside. Pour 5 ½ cups milk into a large saucepan and stir in ¾ cup sugar. Cook milk and sugar over medium heat, stirring constantly until boiling. Using eggbeater or wire whip, beat other mixture into milk and sugar. Stir in vanilla. Cook 1 minute more. Pour into serving dishes. Cool and serve. Serves four to six.

Susanna Hahn, Middle Amana

Note: Mrs. Hahn almost never makes boxed instant puddings. "Once you get the hang of this, it's easy and it tastes so much better!" she maintains.

Eispudding mit Sosse
Ice Pudding with Sauce

For pudding

4 cups milk

6 tablespoons corn-
    starch

¼ teaspoon salt

⅔ cup sugar

1 teaspoon vanilla

For sauce

1½ squares chocolate

4 cups milk

¾ cup sugar

1 tablespoon cornstarch

Scald 3 cups milk in top of double boiler (or in a heavy saucepan directly on stove, stirring constantly). Combine cornstarch, salt, and sugar with remaining cup milk. Pour very slowly into scalded milk. Stir and cook over moderate-high heat for about 5 minutes more. Remove from heat. Stir in vanilla. Pour into 9 × 13-inch glass baking dish. Cover and refrigerate at least 5 hours before serving.

For sauce, melt chocolate in a double boiler (or in a heavy saucepan directly on burner, stirring constantly). Scald 3 cups milk. Combine sugar, cornstarch, and melted chocolate with 1 cup milk. Very slowly stir this mixture into scalded milk. Simmer 5 more minutes. Pour into glass jar, bowl, or similar container. Cover and refrigerate.

When the *Eispudding* is firm, cut into squares and place on a serving dish or in a dessert bowl. The *Eispudding* should be firm enough to hold its shape. Pour a generous dollop of chocolate *Sosse* over the *Eispudding*. The chocolate sauce may have thickened while refrigerated; if so, simply stir well before pouring it over the *Eispudding*.

Yields about 12 servings.

Note: This was a favorite summer dessert; cool and sweet, the very name implied refreshment. And since the recipe calls for a quantity of milk, communal cooks could use the extra portions allotted them when village dairy herds were at peak production.

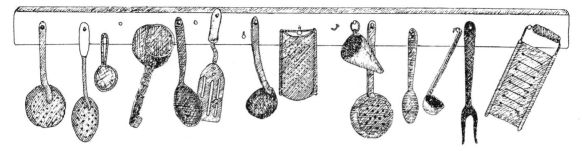

Tapioca Pudding

4 cups milk
⅓ cup tapioca, small
    pearl
2 eggs, separated
½ cup sugar
Pinch salt
½ teaspoon vanilla

    Soak tapioca per box instructions or use quick-cooking tapioca. Combine milk and tapioca in a heavy-bottomed saucepan. Cook, stirring constantly, until tapioca is clear. Beat egg yolks; add sugar and salt. Add ½ cup hot milk and tapioca to beaten egg mixture. Return all to saucepan. Heat again to boiling point. Boil 2 minutes, stirring all the while. Remove from heat. Beat egg whites until stiff. Fold egg whites and vanilla into pudding. Pour into serving dish.

    Yields about four to six servings.

Rote Grütze
Red Fruit Tapioca

2 cups cranberry juice
    cocktail
¼ cup sugar
4 tablespoons tapioca

    Soak tapioca per box instuctions or use quick-cooking tapioca. Combine juice and sugar in large saucepan or double boiler. Cook over low heat and stir until sugar is dissolved. Add tapioca and continue cooking until tapioca is clear and pudding has thickened. Cool. Serve with vanilla sauce (page 146).

    Yields two to four servings.

Marietta Moershel, Homestead

    Note: This communal Amana recipe has been updated by Mrs. Moershel who uses cranberry juice cocktail rather than the home-canned plum or cherry juice a *Küchebaas* would have had on hand.

Reispudding
Rice Pudding

4 cups milk
½ cup rice
2 tablespoons butter
¼ cup sugar
¼ teaspoon salt
2 eggs, beaten
1 teaspoon vanilla
Cinnamon

Stir together milk, rice, butter, sugar, and salt. Pour into double boiler and cook slowly until rice is soft (about 1 hour).

Beat eggs well. Remove 1 cup hot milk and rice mixture and gradually add to beaten eggs. Then return to rice mixture. Stir in vanilla. Serve warm topped with a sprinkle of cinnamon.

Yields about six servings.

Baked Rice Pudding

⅔ cup rice
2 cups milk
2 tablespoons butter
4 eggs, separated
½ cup sugar
½ teaspoon vanilla
Cinnamon

Preheat oven to 350°.

Combine rice and milk in double boiler. Cook slowly until rice is soft (about 1 hour). Allow to cool. Cream butter, egg yolks, and sugar and stir into cooled rice. Beat egg whites until nearly stiff. Fold egg whites and vanilla into rice. Pour into a buttered 2-quart baking dish or casserole and bake at for 45 minutes until pudding is firm and top is browned. Serve warm with a sprinkle of cinnamon.

Yields about six servings.

Elise Zuber, West Amana

Note: When raisins were available, the communal Amana cook added a handful just before folding in the egg whites.

Reis mit Citronsosse
Rice Balls with Lemon Sauce

For rice balls
1 ½ cups rice
½ teaspoon salt
5 cups water

For lemon sauce
3 tablespoons corn-
    starch
¾ cup sugar
3 cups water
2 egg yolks, beaten
Juice of 1 lemon

Combine rice ball ingredients and boil in top of double boiler for about 1 ½ hours or until water is absorbed and rice is tender. Chill rice.

Form rice into small balls and arrange in a 2-quart glass dish.

For lemon sauce, combine cornstarch and sugar; add water slowly until cornstarch is dissolved. Bring to a boil over medium heat, stirring constantly until mixture is smooth. Cook for about 5 minutes, stirring all the while. Cool slightly; add well-beaten egg yolks and lemon juice. Cool. Pour over rice balls and chill at least 2 hours before serving.

Serves six.

Elizabeth Schoenfelder, Amana

Note: A popular summertime dessert served on *Mehlspeisen* day or, perhaps, Saturday at noon.

Griespudding
Farina Pudding

2 ⅔ cups milk
½ cup farina
1 ½ tablespoons butter
⅓ cup sugar
½ teaspoon salt
4 eggs, separated

Preheat oven to 350°.

Scald milk, add farina and butter, and cook in a double boiler (or heavy saucepan, stirring constantly) until thick. Remove from heat. When cool, add sugar, salt, and beaten egg yolks. Beat egg whites until foamy and nearly stiff. Fold egg whites into mixture. Pour into a greased 2-quart baking dish or casserole and bake for about 1 hour. Do not open oven door until nearing completion.

Serves six.

Note: Although it seems too much to ask of a "grits pudding," it should be light and puffy, very much like a soufflé. While no communal Amana cook would have known about soufflés, they did, however, strive to attain a dish as delicate as a French chef's best effort.

Flour Pudding

You might imagine that something that sounds as bland as flour pudding would be easy to make. However, as every young Amana kitchen girl knew, the production of a decent flour pudding was not to be taken lightly.

This recipe, for 35 servings, was written by Louise Herrmann Noé and tucked in the Noé Kitchen House recipe collection. It was translated from German to English by Louise Miller DuVal.

Flour Pudding

2 pounds flour, sifted
1 ½ pounds butter
1 ½ quarts milk
6 teaspoons baking powder
50 eggs, separated
1 pound powdered sugar

There were few instructions given in Mrs. Noé's journal, but a former communal cook explained that first the careful cook weighed the flour on her scale. Each kitchen was equipped with a simple scale, and cooks would have been hard pressed to do without it. After measuring the flour and the butter, the cook sifted the flour, at least twice. In a cooking pot, the butter was melted. In a second pot, the milk was brought nearly to a boil. While keeping a wary eye on the milk, the cook stirred the flour into the melted butter. Finally the milk was added to the flour and butter, the whole was beaten smooth, the baking powder was added, and the pot taken off the hearth.

While the batter was cooling, 50 eggs were separated. With a quick, strong stroke, the egg yolks were beaten until frothy. With an equally strong hand, sugar was stirred into the yolks, and the mixture was added to the cooled batter. Beating the batter until it was light and airy, the cook probably asked for someone else in the kitchen to take a turn with the spoon. Meanwhile, the cook took up her eggbeater and began whipping 50 egg whites. Finally, after the egg whites had formed stiff, moist peaks, the whites were ever so gently folded into the pudding. The pudding was poured into several large buttered pudding forms and baked in a moderate oven (about 350°) for 1 hour, or just long enough for the cook to recover the use of her arm.

Standing in front of the oven, tempted to open the door, the cook might have said a little prayer for a perfect flour pudding: feather light and puffed with air, a sweetly tender pudding.

Scherben
Shards

3 ½ cups flour
½ cup plus 3 table-
spoons butter
3 tablespoons sour
cream
2 tablespoons sugar
½ teaspoon vanilla
mixed with 2 to 3
tablespoons water

Pinch salt
2 eggs
3 egg yolks
Lard or vegetable
shortening for deep
fat frying
Powdered sugar

Combine flour, butter, sour cream, sugar, vanilla, salt, eggs, and yolks. Work into a smooth dough. Refrigerate about 1 hour. Roll out on a floured board until about ⅓ inch thick. Cut into triangles or rectangles—2–3 inches across. Deep fat fry in hot lard or shortening until golden brown. Drain, pat dry, and sprinkle with powdered sugar while still warm. Serve warm.

Serves six.

Kuchenschnitten
French Dessert Toast

1 cup milk
2 eggs, beaten
¼ cup sugar
½ teaspoon vanilla
Cinnamon
Nutmeg
6 slices day-old coffee
cake, unfrosted
½ cup flour
Melted vegetable
shortening or
vegetable oil, 1 inch
deep in skillet
Fruit, fresh or canned,
or powdered sugar

Stir together milk, beaten eggs, sugar, vanilla, and a dash of cinnamon and nutmeg (fresh grated nutmeg is best). Dredge sliced coffee cake through milk mixture and place in a colander or a dish. Take leftover milk mixture and add ½ cup flour—beat into a batter. If the batter seems too thick, add milk, 1 tablespoon at a time. Dip slices of coffee cake into the batter.

Fry in inch-deep hot vegetable shortening or oil until light brown. Turn once. Serve with fresh or canned fruit: strawberries, raspberries, peaches, or plums. Or serve plain with a sprinkle of powdered sugar.

Serves four to six.

Louise Wendler Noé, High Amana

Note: Of course, communal cooks lived in the pre-frozen foods era and relied on canning or drying to preserve fruits. If they had had access to a freezer, they certainly would have used it. We can take advantage of such modern conveniences, and frozen blueberries, strawberries, and raspberries are delicious on this old-fashioned dessert.

CHAPTER 13 PIES AND *KUCHEN*

When the cooks made pie, they made enough so that everyone could have half a pie. You got a half a pie. You could eat a piece for dessert and save another piece for later. . . . My brother, when he was a boy, sometimes he would eat the whole thing—he didn't wait!

Elise Zuber, West Amana

Every few weeks, pies were baked in the communal kitchens, and the aroma of spiced apple, sweet rhubarb, or grape pie filled the kitchen house. Pie baking, a labor-intensive job, was usually done on *Mehlspeisen* day, and enough pies were baked so that every kitchen house patron was given half a pie. In some kitchens this meant that 20 or more pies were baked and set upon the long dining room tables or on the *Altan* (porch) benches to cool.

Two kinds of piecrust were favored: the typical pastry crust made with lard and a thicker, more flavorful *Mürbeteig* crust made with yeast. *Mürbeteig* pies were standard kitchen house fare since the crust was quick and easy to beat together and press into the pie plates. When making 20 or more pies at a time, ease of preparation is a consideration. Yeast pies were made with fruit, often rhubarb, plum, peach, or cherry. Once in a while, the cooks made *Zwiebelkuchen*, onion pie with a rich custard filling, which they served warm, fresh from the oven.

One West Amana cook recalled the laughter and uproar in her kitchen when two of the *Zwiebelkuchen* were stolen from the *Hausgang* (foyer) bench, where they were cooling. The culprit turned out to be the shepherd's collie, an intelligent and able dog, who carried first one pie, and then a second, from the bench out the open door, down the stairs, and behind the woodshed, where he was discovered sleeping contently in the sunshine by two sparkling clean pie pans.

Pie Crust

2 cups flour, sifted
1 teaspoon salt
¾ cup vegetable
  shortening
¼ cup water

Sift flour and salt together. Cut shortening into flour until grain is nearly pea sized. Add water . Blend together lightly. Form dough into two balls. Roll out.

Makes one 9-inch double-crust pie. You may want to double or triple recipe and freeze crusts for future use. To freeze: Roll out crust and place in pie pan. Cover pan with waxed paper and seal in freezer bag.

Note: Communal Amana cooks used lard, and traditionalists insist that lard results in the most tender, flaky crusts imaginable. Today's diet-conscious cooks prefer using vegetable shortening and can achieve excellent results if they are careful not to overhandle the dough or use too much flour, as either practice can result in tough pastry.

Traubenpie
Double-Crust Grape Pie

1 cup sugar
1 egg yolk
1 teaspoon flour
3 teaspoons cornstarch
3 tablespoons half and
  half or cream
2 cups seeded grapes
  with skins
1 9-inch pie shell with
  top, unbaked (see
  preceeding recipe)
1 tablespoon butter

Preheat oven to 325°.

Combine sugar, egg yolk, flour, cornstarch, and half and half or cream. Fold in seeded grapes. Pour in unbaked pie shell. Dot with butter. Place top crust, crimp edges, pierce top to allow steam to escape. Bake about 15 minutes. Raise heat to 350° and bake an additional 15 to 25 minutes.

Emilie Steele, High Amana

Traubenpie
Concord Grape Pie

1 cup Concord grape
    pulp
¾ to 1 cup sugar
1 tablespoon flour or
    quick-cooking
    tapioca
1 egg, beaten
Pinch salt
1 9-inch pie shell,
    unbaked (page 156)

Preheat oven to 375°.

You will need more than 1 cup of grapes to obtain 1 cup pulp. Separate skins from grape pulp. Reserve grape skins. In a medium saucepan, bring grape pulp to a boil, stirring constantly. Cook until soft. Remove from heat and run pulp through a strainer or sieve to remove seeds.

Add ¾ to 1 cup sugar to grape pulp depending upon the sweetness of the grape pulp. Blend in flour or tapioca, 1 beaten egg, and a pinch of salt. Add grape skins. Fill unbaked pie shell. Bake until set, about 30 minutes.

Jennie Reihmann, Middle Amana

Himbeerenpie
Red Raspberry Pie

3 cups raspberries
3 tablespoons tapioca,
    small pearl, quick
    cooking
1 ½ cups sugar
2 tablespoons flour
1 9-inch pie shell with
    top, unbaked (page
    156)
1 to 2 tablespoons
    butter

Preheat oven to 450°.

Mix fruit, tapioca, sugar, and flour. Pour into 9-inch unbaked pie shell. Dot with butter and place top crust. Crimp edges. Pierce top to allow steam to escape. Bake for 15 minutes; reduce heat to 350° and bake an additional 30 minutes.

Emilie Steele, High Amana

Piestengelpie
Rhubarb Pie

3 cups rhubarb, cut into
   small pieces
3 eggs, beaten
1 ¼ cups sugar
1 teaspoon vanilla
⅓ cup milk or half and
   half
1 9-inch pie shell,
   unbaked (page 156)
Powered sugar

Preheat oven to 400°.

Chop rhubarb into ½- to ¼-inch-long pieces. Beat eggs well; add sugar, vanilla, and milk or half and half. Fold in rhubarb. Pour into pie shell.

Bake for 10 minutes. Reduce heat to 350° and bake an additional 35 to 40 minutes or until custard is set. When nearly cool, sprinkle top with powdered sugar.

Janet Zuber, High Amana

Making Coconut Pie in the Communal Kitchen

Louise Herrmann Noé, *Küchebaas* of the Noé Kitchen House in the village of Amana, recorded in German some of her kitchen recipes including recipes for chocolate cream pie and coconut custard pie. Here is her list of ingredients and basic instructions for making coconut custard pie, and although there is no mention as to how many pies this recipe produces, we can assume that it was quite a few. Translation by Louise Miller DuVal.

Coconut Pie

30 cups milk
10 cups coconut
32 tablespoons flour
40 tablespoons sugar
20 egg yolks

Place milk and coconut on the fire. When boiling, stir in flour and sugar. When cool, beat in egg yolks.

Mürbeteig
Yeast Crust

2 cups flour

¼ teaspoon salt

1 envelope yeast

2 teaspoons baking
   powder

½ cup sugar

¼ cup vegetable
   shortening

¾ cup milk

Combine flour, salt, yeast, baking powder, and sugar. Cut in shortening. Stir in milk and knead a bit. Divide dough in two. Lightly grease two pie pans. Using well-floured fingers, press dough into bottom and up sides of greased pie pans.

Makes two 9-inch single-crust pies.

Mürbeteig Kuchen
Fruit and Custard Filling for Two Yeast Crust Pies

2 to 3 cups, or enough
   for two pies, your
   choice of fresh or
   canned fruit: apples,
   cherries, plums,
   raspberries, ground-
   cherries, rhubarb, or
   peaches

2 9-inch yeast crust pie
   shells, unbaked (see
   preceding recipe)

1 cup sugar

1 cup milk

2 tablespoons flour

2 eggs, beaten

Preheat oven to 425°.

If using fresh fruit, pit and pat dry. If using canned fruit, drain juice. Arrange fruit evenly on pie dough.

Beat together sugar, milk, flour, and beaten eggs. Pour over fruit.

Bake pies for 10 minutes. Reduce temperature to 350° and bake an additional 35 minutes, approximately, or until custard is set. Different fruits do require slightly different baking times. Custard should be firmly set, and crust should be golden.

Wilma Rettig, South Amana

Note: Many colony cooks dust the top of the cooled *Mürbeteig Kuchen* with powdered sugar.

Mattekuchen
Cottage Cheese Filling for Two Yeast Crust Pies

1 ½ cups cottage cheese

2 tablespoons flour

3 tablespoons cream

3 eggs, well beaten

½ cup sugar

½ teaspoon vanilla

¼ cup raisins

2 9-inch yeast crust pie
   shells, unbaked
   (page 159)

Preheat oven to 425°.

Combine all ingredients. Fill two yeast crust pie shells. Bake as you would a *Mürbeteig Kuchen* or until custard is set and crust is lightly browned.

Schaefer Kitchen House, East Amana

Zwiebelkuchen
Onion Pie

3 to 4 cups onion, sliced

1 tablespoon butter

Salt and pepper to taste

3 eggs, beaten

1 9-inch yeast crust pie
   shell, unbaked (page
   159)

Preheat oven to 350°.

Fry onion in melted butter until golden brown. Add dash salt and pepper. Let onion cool for about 5 minutes. Beat eggs until frothy and combine with onions. Pour into one *Mürbeteig* pie shell and bake about 30 minutes or until set. Serve while still warm.

Betty Christen, Amana

Sweet Yeast Doughs

Streusel (a square or rectangular sugar-topped coffee cake), braided loaves, or sweet rolls were baked in the communal kitchens every Saturday and occasionally on Wednesdays. The preparation of sweet yeast doughs was a full-scale effort that required the *Küchebaas* and her helpers to mix the dough the afternoon before and set it to rise through the night. Early the next morning the sweets were baked and ready to serve.

Sweet Yeast Dough for Coffee Cake

For dough

2 envelopes yeast

1 ½ cups warm milk

1 heaping teaspoon salt

2 eggs

1 ¼ cups sugar

½ cup vegetable shortening, melted

5 heaping cups flour

2 tablespoons butter, melted

For topping

¼ cup butter, softened

½ cup brown sugar

½ cup sifted flour

1 ½ teaspoons cinnamon

Preheat oven to 350°.

Combine yeast and 1 cup warm milk and let it stand for a minute or two. In a large bowl, combine the rest of the milk, salt, eggs, and sugar. Stir in melted shortening and beat well. Add dissolved yeast. Add half the flour, beating until smooth. Blend in remaining flour to form dough.

Turn dough out on lightly floured board. Knead about 15 minutes. Place in a greased bowl and allow to rise until double in bulk .

Punch the risen dough. Using a portion of the dough roll out to ½ to ¾ inch thickness and place in greased square or rectangular 8- or 9-inch pan. Repeat with remaining dough. Allow to rise a second time. Brush top with melted butter.

Combine topping ingredients and mix until crumbly. Sprinkle on top of yeast dough. Bake for 25 to 30 minutes.

Schaefer Kitchen House, East Amana

Note: The ingredients for this sweet yeast dough were listed in the Schaefer Kitchen House recipe journal kept by *Küchebaas* Lena (Magdalena) Schaefer of East Amana. She wrote that the recipe was from her friend Johanna Werner. The original recipe called for "1 ½ cakes yeast" and has been updated to incorporate the dry yeast packaged in envelopes commonly available in today's supermarkets.

Everlasting Dough

1 potato, cooked and
   mashed
1 cup potato water
1 cup milk
1 cup water
1 cup melted vegetable
   shortening
1 cup sugar
2 teaspoons salt
1 envelope yeast
   dissolved in ¼ cup
   warm water
8 cups flour

Cook potato in boiling water. When fully cooked, remove potato and mash. Reserve 1 cup potato water.

Bring milk very nearly to boil. Add potato water, mashed potato, and water. Beat well. Add melted vegetable shortening, sugar, and salt, beating after each addition. Stir in dissolved yeast and 2 cups flour. Beat well until foamy—about 5 minutes. Set this mixture in a warm place. Let it work about 3 hours. Blend in remaining flour (6 cups) and knead by hand.

Now store the dough in the refrigerator until you are ready to bake.

Remove as much dough as you think you will need to form doughnuts, coffee cake, or braided sweet bread. Add cinnamon, raisins, and other spices as desired. The rest of the dough may be kept in refrigerator until needed.

Katy Gunzenhauser, Amana

Note: This recipe was very popular in communal kitchens where doughnuts were a popular treat, and several different, although very similar, versions of it exist and are still used in Amana today.

Election Cake

For cake
2 ¾ cups flour, sifted
¾ teaspoon salt
1 teaspoon nutmeg
1 cup milk
¾ cup sugar
1 envelope yeast
¼ cup warm water
½ cup shortening
1 egg
½ cup citron
½ cup raisins
½ cup chopped nuts

For sugar glaze
1 cup powdered sugar
2 tablespoons water or
   milk
½ teaspoon vanilla

Preheat oven to 350°.

Sift flour, salt, and nutmeg. In a saucepan scald the milk; then add ¼ cup sugar and stir until dissolved. Cool to lukewarm.

In a large bowl, sprinkle dry yeast into warm water. Stir in lukewarm milk mixture. Add 1 ½ cups sifted flour mixture and beat with wooden spoon until smooth. Cover with towel and set in a warm place. Allow to rise—about 1 hour. Dough should be light and bubbly.

In a second bowl, cream shortening and remaining ½ cup sugar. Add egg, beating well.

Using your hands, mix dough with creamed shortening and sugar. Add remaining 1 ¼ cups flour. Knead in citron, raisins, and nuts. This must be thoroughly blended, so take your time.

Place dough in a well-greased 10-inch tube pan and cover. Set in a warm place and allow to rise about 1 hour. Bake for 45 to 55 minutes or until toothpick inserted comes out clean. Cool in pan before inverting.

Combine ingredients for sugar glaze. When cake is still slightly warm, drizzle with sugar glaze.

Marie Reihmann, Middle Amana

Note: Mrs. Reihmann did indeed make this cake on election days.

Given to You

Marie Reihmann, a former Middle Amana *Küchebaas* and the daughter of a *Gartebaas*, died in 1975. Her children, grandchildren, and great-grandchildren remember her well as a loving woman who enjoyed minding children, baking, and needlework.

In her Middle Amana home there was always work in progress—baskets of rags ready to be braided into rugs, trousers to be mended, and socks to be darned. And more often than not, there were children playing there while she worked.

Betsy Trumpold Momany of Amana can tell you how she, as a young girl, helped her great-grandmother, "Reihmann's *Oma*," lay out the intricate patchwork quilts. "She would sit in her rocker and have all the pieces spread on the floor in front of her. She would point with her crutch at what she wanted where, and I would move the pieces of fabric, and then we would sit back and look. Then she would say, 'No, that gold doesn't go there by the blue; it should be over here,' and we would move them all around until she was satisfied, which usually took quite a while."

Mrs. Reihmann gave her quilts to her kin, and now they are her legacy. Done in mossy greens, rosy pinks, or autumn gold and bronze, or in the clearest blues and yellows, her quilts are treasured by her children who can look at one and say, "Look, here is a piece of *Tante*'s draperies and *Onkel*'s brown shirt . . . and here's Janet's summer dress, remember, with the white collar . . . and isn't that a square of Mom's old kitchen curtains?" A family history, of sorts, is stitched in her quilts, piece by piece, square by square, a domestic history of baby bunting and new spring jackets, old grey suits and silk ties.

You can lay your hand upon a quilt and touch the maker's life—the colors she beheld, the things she liked, the people she loved—stitched together by her hands and given to you.

WINTER

Gently falls the glist'ning snow,
Cov'ring all the world below;
Snow that disappears so fast,
Springlike breezes come at last.

All life knows the time and year,
Ruler over seasons here;
Summer, winter, spring and fall,
All await Thy glorious call.

Joachim Neander,
"In the Quiet Solitude" [1650],
translated by Louis Marz,
The Amana Church Hymnal

CHAPTER 14

WINTER

Those sleigh bells, that's what I think of now.
The horses all had those brass bells on their harnesses,
and when we brought wood in from the timber
or brought in the ice, you know, when we worked with
the horses, those bells would ring,
and that's what I think of now, the bells.

Fred Schinnerling, Middle Amana

Come winter, life in communal Amana eased into a slower, cold weather routine that seemed to keep pace with the drift of smoke from the chimneys and the sound of sleigh bells. The first village bell rang at 7:00 A.M. rather than at 6:00 A.M., and those men who did seasonal farm work spent winter days occupied in the furniture shop, the wagon shop, or some other craft shop. In the kitchens workdays were generally shorter, allowing women more time to quilt and do needlework.

Making Quilts

Some of the garden workers, now unemployed, spent time in the village sewing room, or *Nähstube*. There they had access to fabric and sewing machines and sewed clothing and linens for any single men or elderly folks living in the village. Cotton quilts were made in the *Nähstube* for bachelors or anyone else who had need of a new quilt and no female family members to supply it.

Most quilting was done at home by family members, and winter did not pass without the wooden quilting frame being set up at least once or twice in the parlor and a few friends and relatives gathering to "sew quilt." Quilting was so much a part of communal colony life that the lovely patterns used and the simple techniques employed are still very much a part of Amana today. Although the craft is intact, few really old Amana quilts have survived the years. In communal times, worn-out quilts were recycled; the cotton or sateen outer fabric was removed, and the wool batting was cleaned and recarded at the woolen mill for a new quilt.

Amana quilts are really comforters, made from two or more large pieces of fabric sewn together with a wool or cotton batting. A few piecework or patchwork quilts were made in the Amanas, but generally the comforter style was favored as a practical means of quilt construction. The beauty of an Amana quilt is in its sewn pattern, with some of the patterns as old as time. The tiny patient stitches following the *Karo* (diamond pattern), the *Schlangekranz* (serpent's wreath), the *Pfeife* (circle of pipes), or any of the other designs tell a story of sorts. They tell of the virtue in selfless labor, the grace in simplicity, and the joy in friendship.

Doctors and Midwives

As tranquil as these communal days may have been, every home saw, at one time or another, the kind of emergency that disturbs and disrupts. When these emergencies occurred, when someone was hurt or ill, they sent for the doctor. Free medical care was provided to the Amana people during the colonies' communal era (1855–1932). Usually there were three or four physicians in residence in the Amana Colonies to provide medical treatment to Amana residents. When one doctor neared retirement age, a likely young man was selected by the *Grossebruderrat* and sent away for university and medical training. All his expenses were paid by the community with the understanding that the young doctor would return to his home and establish a practice under the tutelage of his older, more experienced colleagues.

Doctor offices were located in Homestead, Middle Amana, and the village of Amana, but house calls were frequent, and an Amana doctor spent much of his time on home visits. Medicines were available from the doctor and at the pharmacies located in Homestead and Amana. Many of the medicines, including a patented headache remedy, were made on site. Residents from neighboring towns and farms called for and visited Amana doctors as well, and the nominal fees charged to "outsiders" were added to the community treasury. The colony doctor, like his colony neighbors, did not receive a wage or a salary.

Occasionally, the Amana doctor had to refer patients to out-of-town hospitals and specialists. Hospital care and referrals were paid for by the community. For instance, one South Amana girl born with a defective hip and unable to walk was sent with her mother to Chicago, where she received care from an eminent German surgeon who surgically repaired her hip, enabling her to walk. Now nearing age 90, she tells the story.

I was only 4 or 5 years old, and the doctor, he said to my father, "I have read about someone who can help her and we're going to send her to Chicago for this special surgery.". . . My mother and I we went by train, and it was something for my mother! We had to stay several weeks, and when I came home, the doctor came all the time to see me and to do the exercises, the therapy. Had the doctor not found that German doctor and had he not sent me, I would not have walked, ever.

Until about 1940 in the Amana Colonies (and elsewhere in the rural Midwest), mothers delivered their babies at home. In Amana, midwives, or *Hebammen* as they were called, were selected and trained by the colony doctors to assist them in home births and to care for mothers and infants following delivery. Of course, a midwife had to be prepared to deliver a baby without the doctor's help, and midwives did so when the doctor did not reach the home in time to attend the birth.

Understandably, midwifery was an awesome responsibility that few women felt comfortable assuming. When Emma S. Setzer, a South Amana midwife for over 30 years, was first asked by Dr. William Moershel to become a midwife, she had yet to have her first child. She expressed her reservations to the doctor, "I told him, 'I don't want to. In the first place they will say, 'What does she know!' I haven't even had a baby!' He said to me, 'That's all right, neither have I.' "

Emma S. Setzer went on to assist in the delivery of many Amana babies. Her duties included providing nursing care for the new mother and the infant for at least nine days following the delivery and making regular reports on their progress to the doctor. As she once said, "One time we had Sunday school confirmation, and of the 30 children there to be confirmed, 15 were my babies. Someone said, 'You shouldn't call them your babies.' But after those nine days they felt like my babies very much."

Home Remedies

Colonists used home remedies for those aches and pains that did not merit a doctor's visit. The following remedies were contributed by Madeline Roemig, Marietta Moershel, Betty Wetjen, Maureen Thalacker, and Elizabeth Schoenfelder.

For earaches: Make a thick pancake batter consisting of flour and vinegar. Brown in a hot skillet. Wrap the hot *Essigpfannkuchen* (vinegar pancake) in a small dishcloth or a square of flannel and place on the sore ear. Rest awhile with this hot compress on the ear.

Also for earaches: Gather and dry chamomile. Using two small squares of soft flannel, sew a sachet and stuff with crushed chamomile. Warm the sachet on the stove or in the oven (do not wet) and place on the sore ear. Reheat sachet as necessary.

For sore throats: Spread warm bacon fat on a soft cloth or an old stocking and wrap poultice around the neck. Also try drinking hot tea laced with 1 teaspoon honey and $\frac{1}{8}$ teaspoon ground clove.

For head colds and chest colds: String camphor ice on thread and wear like a necklace until the fever subsides.

For warts: Rub the sap of a milkweed plant on the wart.

To prevent tapeworms: Eat toasted pumpkin seed.

For sores: Gather leaves from the "pig ear" plant and steep in boiling water. Drench a soft cloth in the resulting brew; place on the sore.

For boils: Soak a slice of day-old bread or coffee cake in warm milk and place on the boil.

For dry or chapped skin: Gently rub skin with olive oil.

For bee or wasp stings: Make a thick paste of baking soda and water. Smear on sting and wrap with clean cloth.

For upset stomach: Drink warm peppermint tea or chamomile tea.

For chills: Mull grape wine with a little water and a dash of sugar, cinnamon, and clove. Wrap yourself in a thick blanket; drink warm spiced wine while resting with your feet near the stove. If you are preparing this remedy for children, add a bit more water.

For insomnia: Count your blessings, every one.

From the Bakery

When the air was very cold, it was easy to catch the scent of baking bread, for each village had its bakery where bread was baked six days a week for the kitchen houses. The bakeries produced enough round 4-pound loaves (in East Amana they had 3-pound loaves) of white bread to feed the entire village. In the village of Amana over 60 4-pound loaves were needed daily, and the bakeries used nearly 100 pounds of flour from the mill down the street to accomplish one day's bread baking. The Amana Flour Mill provided for the bakeries in Amana, East Amana, Homestead, and Middle. Bakeries in South, West, and High Amana received their flour and other ground grains from the West Amana Flour Mill. Both mills sold flour to outside markets.

They made their own yeast in communal Amana bakeries. Once a week hops were boiled in a copper kettle with a measure of cracked Amana-grown barley. When the brew was cool enough to allow the baker to insert his finger without risking a burn, a dipper of yeast from the previous week's supply was added as a starter. Then the new yeast was left to ferment overnight before being transferred to a stone crock in the cellar. The bakery kept a large supply of active yeast on hand, because it provided liquid yeast by the jarful to the kitchen houses for their weekly coffee cake and other yeast dough baking. Originally in Amana, hops were grown for yeast and for beer brewing. However, since the quality of the hops was not up to standard, the attempt was abandoned, and hops were purchased from sources in Washington or Oregon.

The daily routine in the bakery was so well rehearsed that an Amana baker was said to be able "to bake in his sleep if need be." Using a starter dough made the day before and left to rise overnight, additional salt, water, and flour were added. The dough was mixed by hand in a 10-foot-long wooden trough and allowed to rise twice. Then with the graceful, economical movements learned through time and repetition, the baker deftly shaped the dough and placed it in round rye baskets sprinkled with a little flour and cornmeal. The flour and cornmeal kept the dough from sticking to the rye baskets and added texture to the bottom crust. Meanwhile, a fire was built in the stone hearth. Once it burned down to red coals, the coals were spread evenly on the floor of the hearth and left for 30 minutes or so. Then the cinders were carefully removed and the stones swept with a long moplike tool. There were no temperature gauges in colony stone hearth ovens, so the bakers had to judge how hot the oven was and adjust baking times accordingly. After years spent at this job, the baker knew by observing the color of the stone in the hearth whether or not to open the oven draft or to proceed with baking. Using the long wooden peel, the baker placed the loaves in the hearth and removed them about an hour later when the perfectly brown crusty loaves were ready. From racks in the bakery to the back of the bakery wagon, the bread was carried and then delivered to the kitchen houses by the baker's apprentice.

Making the Coffee Cake

Louis Schmieder, a former Amana baker, remembered well the recipe for making coffee cake dough. He and the other Amana bakers made coffee cake once a week and just prior to holidays. From this rich yeast dough flavored with raisins, several different kinds of coffee cakes were made. Sometimes the bakers braided the loaves making *Zopfkuchen,* or the cakes were baked in round fluted molds and were called *Ratonkuchen,* or the dough was shaped into small buns, or *Wecke.* The recipe for colony coffee cake is as follows:

Colony Coffee Cake

3 gallons milk
6 pounds sugar
4 pounds lard
3 ½ ounces salt
36 pounds flour
½ pound yeast
4 pounds raisins

This recipe produced 63 pounds of dough, which was cut, shaped, placed in molds or pans, and baked in the stone hearth oven until fragrant and crusty brown.

Wasserweck and Other Breads

In addition to white bread and coffee cake, the bakeries made rye bread and the occasional few loaves of whole wheat bread. During World War I, when flour consumption was cut due to quotas, cornmeal and oatmeal bread were baked and served to colonists who undoubtedly longed for their usual yeasty 4-pound loaves.

When the community doctors prescribed special diets for their patients, breads were baked accordingly. Whole wheat bread was baked for those with diabetic or digestive conditions. Nursing mothers and invalids were given *Wasserweck,* or water buns. The recipe for *Wasserweck* has been lost or forgotten it seems, although residents recall that the buns, really small loaves, were made with milk, not water, and were especially fine grained like French bread. New mothers and sick children also received *Zweibeck* (twice-baked), slices of bread or coffee cake toasted in the stone hearth to a deep mahogany hue. *Zweibeck* and cocoa was the treat given to youngsters too ill to go to school.

Tradition Continues

Like the making of wine, beer, and fine cured and smoked meats, the baking tradition lives on in the Amana Colonies, where bakeries produce breads, coffee cakes, and rolls. The Hahn Bakery in Middle Amana, built in 1865 and operated by Jack and Doris Hahn, has the only remaining original stone hearth oven. The Hahns employ recipes and techniques very much in the communal baking tradition as Jack's father was the Middle Amana baker for many years and took the time to pass on his expertise to his son.

Brewing Beer

Prior to 1884, when the state of Iowa passed a prohibition law, beer was brewed at several locations in the Amanas. The village of Amana had the largest and most productive brewery, but breweries were also located in South Amana, West Amana, and Homestead. A brewery in Middle Amana closed about 1870, according to original brewing records now in the Museum of Amana History, Archive Collection.

Although a number of men served as brewers for the village of Amana, in 1867 Benedict Elzer signed the Amana brewery's monthly production report, the earliest available record of brewing in the Amana Colonies. In Amana the brewery was located on the "back street" in a brick structure adjoining the cooper shop. It was located likewise in West Amana, where a brick brew house and cellar were located on the northern-most street adjoining the cooper shop. This made it convenient for West Amana cooper Adam Kircher to attend to his responsibilities as village brewmaster. The South Amana cooper, John Schnetzler, also served as village brewmaster working in the *gewölbt* (vaulted) cellars of the South Amana brewery located on the west edge of the village. In Homestead the brewery adjoined the meat shop and was managed for a number of years by brewmaster, Jacob Klipfel. In Middle Amana August Koch, church elder and schoolteacher, served as the Middle brewmaster, having had experience in the community's first American brewery in Ebenezer, New York. Later on, P. L. Lippold, a community newcomer from Saxony, took on the Middle brewery, which was located in a brick building annexed to the "butcher shop."

Like wine, beer was made cooperatively, in quantity, and shared among adult community members. According to brewery tax records, from 1872 through 1883, colony breweries produced an average of 1,826 barrels (56,606 gallons) per year. Brewing took place in the village of Amana through all but the hottest months of the year. In the other, smaller breweries, beer was made October through April with the peak brewing season in February, March, and April. For instance, in February of 1869, records indicate that 133 ½ barrels were brewed; 80 of these barrels were brewed in the Amana brewery. In March of 1869 they racked 273 ½ barrels; 170 of these were brewed in the Amana brewery. Consumption, of course, increased in the summer. In June of 1869, Amana storekeeper and secretary Peter Winzenried tallied beer consumption in the seven villages at 103 ¾ barrels or 3,296 gallons. The good Germans of Amana obviously enjoyed the refreshment of a cool brew at the close of day.

Although the 1884 legislation was eventually repealed, organized community brewing was not resumed in the colonies, perhaps because of the expense. In addition to the annual federal permits and bonds required for breweries, a federal tax in the form of a stamp was affixed to each barrel. From 1879 through 1881 the Amana community paid an average of $1,758 per year for federal beer stamps. The taxes, plus other expenses, made beer brewing a costly venture. Presumably taxes were also paid on wine. Perhaps the colonists felt they could not afford both brewing and wine making and simply chose to concentrate on producing wine.

Beer making did continue on a much smaller scale as residents made their own home-brewed beer. Bottled home brew was a favorite at colony wedding receptions, and making the beer was the special responsibility of the groom and his friends. One Middle Amana groom recalled having to wash and return to his friends nearly 300 borrowed bottles following the wedding.

Cutting Ice

When temperatures hovered near 0° and the ice on the lake and on the Iowa River was thick, it was time to cut ice. Block ice, of course, was a necessity, and cutting a large quantity of ice and storing it properly were matters of great concern to the men of the community. On a day determined by the *Ökonomiebaas* (agriculture boss) and the man in charge of the icehouse, the ice making would begin and continue for several days. Nearly every man in the village joined the effort. The teamsters were up early harnessing the horses and preparing the wagons outfitted with special sleighlike runners. A second group of men spent the morning straightening up the icehouse and readying it for the first load. The majority of men were taken by sleigh to the Lily Lake or the Iowa River. Generally, East Amana, Amana, and Middle Amana men cut ice on the Lily Lake. Homestead made ice on the Iowa River, but later the men of Homestead built a small

pond near Homestead where ice could be cut closer to home. High Amana and South Amana crews cut their ice on the Iowa River, and West Amana men traveled upstream to a deep oxbow known as Watt's Pond.

It must have been a long day out on the flat with the wind blowing in your face and the ice underfoot and a lot of hard work to be done. As Carl Schuerer of East Amana put it, "That lake, in winter that was a pretty nippy place, I tell you. If we would have a wind like we had a couple of days ago, boy, you couldn't stand it up there. No, it was a cold place."

To begin the task, draft horses pulled snow blades across the ice to remove the snow. Then the ice was scored with a sharp blade, a task that demanded precision as each block had to be uniform. The ice was cut by hand and pulled or floated to the bank, where it was winched up a ramp to the bed of a wagon. Once loaded with ice, the wagon, fitted with runners, started for the village, a slow, cold ride for the teamster, to be sure. To beat the cold, the men built a fire on the ice and fried potatoes in a heavy black skillet along with thick slices of *Schwartenmagen* (headcheese). There probably was a jug of wine around, and certainly a big pot of coffee brewing on the grate; such were the provisions when making ice in the colony.

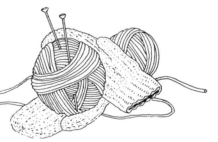

Strickschule and Other Wintertime Pursuits

When cutting ice or accomplishing some other outdoor task, colony fathers were happy to have the woolen mittens and socks knitted by their children. Young boys and girls were taught to knit in

Strickschule classes led by one or two of the older women of the village. *Strickschule* followed the regular schooltime and must have been a trial to youngsters who had spent all day indoors and were ready to get out and play. Their parents, however, forbade skipping *Strickschule* and cheerfully wore the results, appreciating just how much diligence was required of an earnest six year old to produce a pair of nubby mittens.

Following knitting class and chores, youngsters rode sleds, played in the woodshed, or skated on nearby ponds. The Mill Race was a dangerous but popular place to skate, and more than one colony youth was drowned, or very nearly drowned, while attempting to cross too-thin ice on the canal. Susanna Hahn said that as a teenager she once skated nearly three miles from Middle Amana to West Amana in order to buy a crochet hook at the West Amana Store and that Middle Amana youngsters often skated to Amana to visit friends. South Amana and West Amana youths held evening skating parties on a slough located in the forest between the villages; there they skated by lantern light, skimming on luminous pools from a dozen kerosene lanterns, casting shadows into the forest, where hoarfrost hung shimmering on the tree branches.

CHAPTER 15 CAKES FOR EVERY DAY

*Most Amana folks had a sweet tooth, and we
didn't get a chance to buy candy or anything like that,
so in the kitchen they made pies and cake,
and everyone always enjoyed them!*

Henry Schiff, Amana

Cakes were regularly baked and served in the communal kitchens. Unlike the very special wedding day cakes, these were made with less-costly ingredients. Since they were made in quantity, perhaps six or more cakes at a time, the less-compli- cated recipes were favored, and since all the beating and whipping was done by hand, nearly everyone in the kitchen helped prepare the cakes, taking turns beating the batter with a large wooden spoon, wire whisk, or eggbeater.

Schnee Kuchen
Snow Cake

1 cup butter
1 cup sugar
½ cup milk
1 ½ cups flour, sifted
    several times
Juice from 1 lemon
4 egg whites, beaten till
    stiff
Powered sugar

Preheat oven to 375°.

Lightly cut together butter and sugar. Then add milk and sifted flour, alternately. Beat vigorously. Flavor with juice of 1 lemon. In a second bowl beat egg whites until stiff. Fold beaten egg whites into batter. Pour into 9 × 13-inch greased and floured pan. Bake until cake springs back when touched (about 20 minutes, but be careful not to overbake). When cool, remove from pan and sprinkle top with powdered sugar.

Noé Kitchen House, Amana,
translated by Louise Miller DuVal

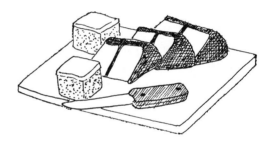

Yellow Cake

1 cup sugar
3 eggs
1 egg-sized lump of
    butter (¼ to ½ cup
    butter)
1 cup flour
2 teaspoons baking
    powder
8 tablespoons milk

Preheat oven to 350°.

Beat together sugar and eggs until foamy. Then add butter and beat well. Sift together flour and baking powder. Stir in milk and flour, alternately. Pour into 9 × 9-inch pan. Bake mixture, for 20 to 25 minutes. When cool, frost with chocolate frosting or simply dust with powdered sugar.

Noé Kitchen House, Amana,
translated by Louise Miller DuVal

Devil's Food Cake

Scant $\frac{1}{2}$ cup butter,
    softened
2 cups sugar
2 eggs
4 tablespoons melted
    unsweetened
    chocolate
$\frac{1}{2}$ cup buttermilk
2 cups flour
$\frac{1}{2}$ cup hot water, into
    which a scant
    teaspoon of baking
    powder has been
    dissolved

Preheat oven to 350°.

Cream together butter and sugar. Beat in eggs. Add melted chocolate and buttermilk, beating well after each addition. Sift flour and add to batter alternately with hot water. Pour batter into 9 × 13-inch greased and floured pan. Bake until top springs back to touch. Frost with your favorite chocolate frosting or cocoa frosting (see following recipe).

Cocoa Frosting

2 to 3 cups powdered
    sugar
$\frac{1}{4}$ cup butter
$\frac{1}{4}$ cup cocoa
$\frac{1}{4}$ cup milk

Whip sugar and butter until creamy. Stir in cocoa and milk. Beat until smooth.

Sour Cream Cake

2 cups flour, sifted
1 teaspoon baking
  powder
½ scant teaspoon
  baking soda
1 cup sour cream
1 egg, beaten until very
  light
1 cup sugar
½ cup milk
1 teaspoon vanilla

Preheat oven to 350°.

Sift together flour and baking powder and set aside. Then stir baking soda into sour cream and set aside.

In a mixing bowl, beat egg and sugar. Blend in flour mixture, alternating with sour cream mixture and milk. Add vanilla. Pour batter into greased and floured 9 × 9-inch pan. Bake about 30 minutes or until top is golden and cake springs back when touched. Dust with powdered sugar or serve with fresh strawberries or raspberries.

Louise Wendler Noé, High Amana

Blitzkuchen
Lightning Cake

¼ cup butter
½ cup sugar
4 eggs, separated
1 cup flour, sifted
2 teaspoons baking
  powder
¼ cup milk
¾ cup powdered sugar
½ cup chopped nuts

Preheat oven to 350°.

Cream butter and sugar. Beat egg yolks into creamed mixture. Then beat in flour and baking powder, alternating with milk. Pour batter into a greased 9-inch glass pie dish.

Beat egg whites until stiff peaks are formed and then gently fold in powdered sugar. Spread egg white mixture on top of batter and sprinkle with nuts.

Bake for about 1 hour.

Noé Kitchen House, Amana,
translated by Louise Miller DuVal

Note: This easy layered "cake" was a summer favorite in the kitchen house, when eggs were plentiful and a "light" dessert was especially pleasing.

Crumb Cake

3 cups flour

2 cups brown sugar

½ cup shortening or
   margarine

1 egg, beaten

1 cup buttermilk

1 teaspoon baking soda

1 teaspoon cream of
   tartar

Preheat oven to 375°.

In a large mixing bowl, mix flour and brown sugar. Cut in shortening or margarine. Reserve 1 cup for topping.

To remaining crumbs, stir in beaten egg and buttermilk. Add baking soda and cream of tartar, beating well after each addition. Pour batter in 9 × 13-inch greased baking pan. Top with reserved crumbs. Bake for 25 to 30 minutes.

Elise Zuber, West Amana

Shortcake

2 cups flour

2 tablespoons sugar

½ teaspoon salt

2 ½ teaspoons baking
   powder

4 tablespoons margarine
   or butter

1 cup milk

Fresh fruit or preserves

Preheat oven to 325°.

In a large bowl stir together dry ingredients. Cut in margarine or butter. Add milk and beat—batter will be a little stiff.

Spread batter in a greased and floured round 9-inch cake pan or a 9 × 9-inch cake pan. Bake until top springs back to touch and is golden in color.

Serve with fresh fruit or preserves.

CHAPTER 16 # CAKES FOR SPECIAL OCCASIONS

Before the wedding, a girl would make her hope chest. . . . I think I made and embroidered a dozen pairs of pillowcases. And she had to have four quilts; two for summer and two for winter.

Louise Blechschmidt, East Amana

In Amana we have a custom: at wedding receptions we serve a variety of homemade cakes baked by friends and relatives.

This custom began in communal Amana, where weddings boasted no bride in white lace, no organ prelude, no grand procession down the church aisle, no fancy tiered cake or bridal supper. The communal wedding, like most things associated with old Amana, was very simple.

At a communal Amana wedding, the bride wore her very best church dress, her black cap with tatted trim, her apron and shawl. She and her groom stood alone at the front of the *Saal* and faced the elder, a man the pair had known all their lives, who nonetheless represented all that was benevolent and resolute within the church. After asking them a few well-phrased questions, the good brother admonished them to cleave to one another in love, to build a home together in God's sight, and to seek God's grace always. No kiss concluded the ceremony; instead the pair received the quiet congratulations and good wishes of all present.

After the wedding service, the bride and groom dined at a family luncheon in a nearby kitchen house. The kitchen house meal was organized and the menu selected by the *Küchebaas* who took pains to make it a special occasion. Verona Schinnerling of Middle Amana remembered her wedding day in 1926. Her friends in the kitchen house brought potted plants from home and decorated the dining room with geraniums, cyclamen, and violets. Even the icebox doors were opened, and it was filled with blooming cyclamen.

Although a festive meal, the kitchen house dinner was select; only immediate members of the family were invited. Later a much larger and more boisterous party was held at the groom's family home. Friends and relatives from other villages were invited, and everyone, from the youngest child to the oldest *Oma,* celebrated merrily. The children played and ran about. The young folks gathered on the lawn for a game of "Happy is the Miller Boy" or "The Cutest Pig in the Parlor." Guests swapped gossip and family news. Courting couples stole away to the

Gartehäuschen, the arbor in the garden where the grapevines entwined. Even there, in the fragrant garden, away from the house, you could hear the laughter and the singing. Members of the *Sängerbund* (men's choir) would begin a song, and the women would join in, and the songs, German folk songs, hymns, and classical melodies, would continue for as long as the singers had voice.

Sweet fruit juice, grape and cherry *Saftwasser,* was served. A small barrel of grape wine or *Peistengel* (rhubarb wine) was brought up from the cellar and tapped. Bottles of homebrew beer stood in tubs of cold water. But the featured item on the menu was cake, all kinds of cake. There was *Sternkuchen,* baked by the *Küchebaas* in the large star-shaped tin made by the village tinsmith. There were nut cakes, chocolate cakes, feather cakes, pound cakes, and angel food, each cake contributed by the kitchen house cooks. It wasn't unusual for a bride to receive 30 or more cakes on her wedding day. These were displayed for all the wedding guests to admire and then sliced and arranged on large trays so that it was convenient for everyone to help themselves to several slices of their favorites.

This is an Amana tradition that continues to this day. The morning before the wedding, Amana ladies, in their aprons and housedresses or blue jeans and sweatshirts, stop at the bride's home bearing Tupperware containers or fancy cake plates. The precious cakes are accepted gratefully by the bride or her mother. If the reception is to be held elsewhere, those groomsmen deemed most levelheaded and trustworthy are appointed to take carloads of cake to the restaurant or hall where they are sliced and arranged on large trays for all to admire and enjoy. Although modern brides usually have at least a small tiered wedding cake, it's mostly for show, and slices of white cake go begging while wise guests select the delicious homemade cakes.

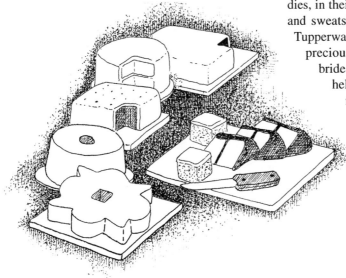

Sternkuchen
Marbled Star Cake

For white cake batter
1/2 cup butter
2 cups sugar
3 cups flour
1 cup milk
2 teaspoons baking
  powder
8 egg whites, beaten
  stiff

For pink cake batter
1/3 white cake batter
2 to 4 drops red food
  coloring

For yellow cake batter
1/2 cup butter
1 1/2 cups sugar
2 cups flour
2 teaspoons baking
  powder
1/2 cup milk
8 egg yolks
2 teaspoons vanilla

*For chocolate cake
  batter*
1/2 yellow cake batter
1/2 cup cocoa

Preheat oven to 325°.

This marble cake has four different-colored batters. For the white cake, cream first two ingredients of white cake recipe. Stir in flour alternately with milk. Add baking powder. Mix well then fold in beaten egg whites.

For pink batter, take 1/2 of white cake batter and pour into a bowl. Add small amount of red food coloring. Set aside white and pink batters.

For yellow batter, cream butter and sugar for yellow cake batter. Stir in flour, baking powder, and milk. Add egg yolks and beat well. Blend in vanilla.

For chocolate batter, take 1/2 of yellow cake batter and pour into a bowl—beat in cocoa.

This recipe was meant to fill a traditional star-shaped cake tin made by the Amana tinsmiths. To insure a perfect star, trace form on waxed paper, cut out waxed paper, and line tin before greasing and flouring. Cut this recipe in half for a large-sized bundt pan. Carefully pour yellow batter into well-greased and floured star tin, then add white batter, chocolate batter, and finally the pink batter. Don't fill your bundt pan or star tin to the top—leave 1 inch headroom. Excess batter may be poured into a greased and floured cake pan or cupcake pan.

Bake 40 to 50 minutes. Remember, less time is required for a smaller pan. When cool, carefully remove the cake from the pan and frost or sprinkle with powdered sugar.

Note: There is disagreement in the Amanas as to whether a *Sternkuchen* should be frosted. Some Amana cooks would never frost a *Sternkuchen.* At the most, they would dust it with powdered sugar. Some colony cooks prefer to drizzle the cake with a simple sugar glaze. Still others frost the *Stern* with a butter-cream frosting and even go so far as to decorate the top with halved walnuts or pecans. You may do just as you wish. The important thing is to be happy with your cake and to serve it proudly.

Fluff Cake

9 eggs, separated
1 ¾ cups sugar
⅛ teaspoon salt
1 cup sifted cake flour
1 teaspoon vanilla
Powdered sugar

Preheat oven to 325°.

Beat egg whites until foamy; then fold in 1 cup sugar and salt and continue beating until stiff. Fold in cake flour. Next add ¾ cup sugar to egg yolks and beat until thick and lemon colored. Add egg yolk mixture to egg white mixture. Add vanilla. Bake in an ungreased angel food cake pan (10-inch tube pan) for 1 hour. Invert pan to remove cake. Allow to cool completely before dusting with powdered sugar.

Katy Gunzenhauser, Amana

Nuzskuchen
Hickory Nut Cake

2 cups flour, sifted
2 ¾ teaspoons baking
    powder
¼ teaspoon salt
3 eggs, separated
⅔ cup vegetable
    shortening
1 ½ cups sugar
1 teaspoon vanilla
¾ cup milk
1 ½ cups ground
    hickory nuts (or
    walnuts, if you
    prefer)

Preheat oven to 350°.

Sift flour, baking powder, and salt together. Beat egg whites till stiff. Cream shortening, sugar, and vanilla until fluffy. Add beaten egg yolks and mix. Add sifted dry ingredients alternating with milk, beating well after each addition. Stir in nuts. Fold in stiff egg whites. Grease and lightly flour two 9-inch layer cake pans. Pour in batter and bake for about 25 minutes. Makes one double-layer cake. When cool, frost with your favorite butter-cream frosting or Mrs. Steele's caramel frosting (see recipe at end of chapter).

Emilie Steele, High Amana

Funeral Lunches

In communal Amana when a death occurred, the village elders and the family planned a funeral in the village where the deceased had lived. Friends and relatives from other villages made the trip by horse and buggy, and large, well-attended funerals were common. A luncheon of bread, sausage, cheese, pickles, and a variety of cakes was served at one or more kitchen houses following the funeral. Those who had attended the funeral were invited to lunch, and the event, however quiet and reflective, provided an opportunity to visit with friends from other villages and to talk with the family of the deceased.

This tradition continues in the Amanas where the family of the deceased hosts a simple buffet lunch at a local restaurant following the funeral. Friends and relatives bring home-baked cakes and other foods—a gesture of kinship and comfort, an expression of love.

Missouri Walnut Cake

1 cup sugar
½ cup margarine
2 eggs
2 cups flour
1 teaspoon salt
1 teaspoon baking soda
⅔ cup buttermilk
1 cup chopped walnuts

Preheat oven to 350°.

Cream sugar and margarine. Beat in eggs. In a separate bowl sift together flour, salt, and baking soda. Alternating with the buttermilk, beat flour mixture into the creamed mixture. Add chopped nuts. Pour batter into greased and floured 13 × 9-inch pan and bake about 55 to 60 minutes. Cool and frost with a fudge or maple frosting (see recipes at end of chapter).

Susanna Hahn, Middle Amana

Tante's Feather Cake

For cake

4 tablespoons butter or
   margarine
1 ¼ cups plus
   1 tablespoon sugar
4 large eggs (reserve
   whites from two
   eggs for frosting)
1 ¼ cups plus
   1 tablespoon flour
2 heaping teaspoons
   baking powder
Pinch salt
½ cup milk

For frosting

2 squares unsweetened
   chocolate, melted
1 heaping cup powdered
   sugar
2 egg whites (reserved
   from batter), beaten
   until stiff (don't
   overbeat)

Preheat to 375°.

Cream butter or margarine and sugar. Add 2 whole eggs plus the yolks of 2 more eggs (reserve 2 whites for frosting) and beat well. Sift together dry ingredients. Alternately add milk and dry ingredients to creamed mixture. Pour into two greased and floured 8- or 9-inch round layer cake pans. Bake for 15 to 20 minutes. Top should spring back at touch, and toothpick inserted should come out clean.

For frosting, melt chocolate. Add powdered sugar to beaten egg whites and blend. Then very slowly whip in a thin stream of warm, melted chocolate. Frost bottom layer, top layer, and sides when cake is completely cool.

Verona Schinnerling, Middle Amana

Note: Seven nieces and nephews and three times as many grandnieces and grandnephews of Verona Schinnerling count her feather cake among their favorite desserts. Mrs. Schinnerling bakes feather cakes for birthdays, weddings, holidays, and funerals.

Since this frosting contains uncooked egg whites, it is sensible to refrigerate the cake before and after serving.

Mrs. Seifert's Feather Cake

1 cup shortening

2 cups sugar

3 eggs, separated

3 teaspoons baking powder

3 cups flour

1 cup milk

1 teaspoon vanilla

Preheat oven to 375°.

Beat shortening and sugar until creamy. Add egg yolks to creamed mixture and continue beating. Sift together baking powder and flour; add this to batter, alternating with milk. Stir in vanilla. Beat egg whites until stiff peaks are formed; then fold whites into batter. Pour batter into three standard round layer cake pans, greased and floured. Bake for 30 minutes, then reduce heat to 350° and bake 15 minutes more. Test for doneness. Ice with chocolate frosting (see recipe at end of chapter).

Dorothy Seifert, Homestead

Spice Cake

½ cup vegetable shortening

1 cup sugar

2 eggs

2 cups flour

1 teaspoon baking soda

¾ teaspoon cinnamon

¼ teaspoon cloves

¼ teaspoon nutmeg

½ cup cocoa

1 cup buttermilk

½ cup raisins

Preheat oven to 350°.

Cream shortening and sugar. Stir in eggs; beat well. Sift together flour, soda, spices, and cocoa. Added sifted ingredients and buttermilk to creamed mixture, alternately, beating well. Stir in raisins. Pour batter into 8-inch square pan. Bake for 35 to 40 minutes. Dust top with powdered sugar or frost with vanilla frosting.

Hickory Nut Cake

½ cup shortening

1 ½ cups sugar

1 teaspoon vanilla

2 ⅔ cups flour, sifted

3 teaspoons baking
  powder

¼ teaspoon salt

1 cup milk

1 cup chopped hickory
  nuts

3 egg whites

⅛ teaspoon salt

Preheat oven to 350°.

Cream shortening and sugar until light and fluffy. Add vanilla, beating well. Sift together flour, baking powder, and salt. Sift three times. Add flour mixture to batter, alternating with milk. Beat well after each addition. Stir in nuts. In a second bowl beat egg whites and salt until stiff, but not dry. Fold into batter. Pour batter in two greased and floured 9-inch layer cake pans. Bake for about 30 minutes. Allow to cool. Frost top layer, bottom layer, and sides with maple frosting or caramel frosting (see recipes at end of chapter).

Janet Zuber, High Amana

Chocolate Chip Cake

6 eggs, separated

1 cup sugar

¾ cup flour (Note:
  measure flour, then
  sift)

1 teaspoon baking
  powder

1 teaspoon vanilla

2 squares unsweetened
  chocolate, grated

Powdered sugar

Preheat oven to 350°.

Beat egg whites and ½ cup sugar until stiff, but not dry. Beat egg yolks and ½ cup sugar until frothy. Combine. Sift together flour and baking powder. Stir in flour, baking powder, and vanilla. Finally add the grated chocolate. Pour into angel food cake pan. Bake for 45 minutes. Dust with powdered sugar.

Schaefer Kitchen House, East Amana

Chocolate Cake

2 cups flour, sifted

2 cups sugar

¾ cup cocoa

2 teaspoons baking soda

1 teaspoon baking
  powder

Pinch salt

½ cup vegetable oil

1 cup hot coffee

1 cup milk

2 eggs

Preheat oven to 350°.

Stir together flour, sugar, cocoa, baking soda, baking powder, and salt. Make a well inside dry ingredients and add oil, coffee, milk, and eggs. Beat just enough to mix—batter will be lumpy. Pour into greased 13 × 9-inch pan. Bake for 35 minutes. Frost with your favorite icing.

Black Walnut Cake

¾ cup butter or
    margarine
1 ½ cups sugar
3 eggs
1 teaspoon vanilla
3 cups flour
3 teaspoons baking
    powder
1 12-ounce can evapo-
    rated milk
3 cups ground walnuts

Preheat oven to 350°.

Cream butter and sugar. Add eggs, one at a time, beating well after each. Beat in vanilla. Sift together flour and baking powder. Add sifted flour mixture to creamed mixture, alternating with evaporated milk. Add nuts, reserving ¼ cup. (Reserved nuts should be sprinkled on top after cake is frosted.) Pour batter into three greased and floured 9-inch layer cake pans or one large tube pan or molded bundt pan. Bake the layer pans 30 to 35 minutes, the large tube pan 40 to 45 minutes. When cool, frost with your favorite vanilla or butter-cream frosting. Sprinkle nuts on top.

Linda Selzer, Homestead

Sunshine Cake

7 eggs, separated
2 teaspoons grated
    lemon peel
¼ teaspoon salt
1½ cups powdered
    sugar
1 cup flour

Preheat oven to 325°.

Beat egg yolks and lemon peel until frothy. Set aside.

Beat egg whites and salt until foamy. Slowly add sugar and beat until egg white begin to stiffen. Gently fold egg white mixture into egg yolk mixture. Sift flour directly into bowl and fold. Pour batter in an ungreased 10-inch tube pan. Bake 30 to 40 minutes. When cool, sprinkle with powdered sugar or glaze with vanilla frosting.

Note: Different, though very similar, recipes for sunshine cake were found in recipe journals kept by communal cooks in South Amana and Amana.

Golden Angel Food Cake

¾ cup warm water
¼ teaspoon salt
12 egg yolks
1 cup sugar
1⅔ cups flour
½ teaspoon lemon
    extract
2 teaspoons baking
    powder

Preheat oven to 325°.

Add water and salt to egg yolks and beat until stiff enough to "stand up" when spoon is lifted from yolks. Gradually fold in sugar and beat until sugar is dissolved. Fold in the flour, lemon extract, and baking powder. Pour into ungreased angel food cake pan and bake 1 hour.

Lilly Zcherney, High Amana

Mrs. Noé's Fudge Cake

For fudge cake
1½ tablespoons
    vinegar
1¼ cups milk
7 eggs, room tempera-
    ture, beaten until
    frothy

Preheat oven to 350°.

This recipe makes two cakes 13 × 9-inch cakes: one to keep and one to give away.

Several hours before preparing the cake batter, pour vinegar in milk to make the milk sour.

In a large mixing bowl, beat eggs until frothy and blend in melted shortening or lard, sugar, and salt; cream mixture. Add cocoa and boiling water; beat well. In a second bowl, sift flour and then add baking pow-

7 tablespoons vegetable
    shortening or lard,
    melted
5 cups sugar
½ teaspoon salt
2 cups cocoa
2 ½ cups boiling water
5 cups flour, sifted
5 scant teaspoons
    baking powder
3 ¾ teaspoons baking
    soda
2 teaspoons vanilla

For fudge cake frosting
4 cups sugar
3 heaping tablespoons
    cocoa
¾ cup butter
1 cup milk
1 teaspoon vanilla

der to the flour and sift again. Add sifted flour mixture to batter, using spoon to scrape bowl. Stir in vanilla.

Combine baking soda and soured milk; stir until soda is dissolved. Add soured milk to batter and beat.

Grease and flour two 9 × 13-inch baking pans or three 10 × 8-inch pans. Pour batter into pans. Bake for 25 to 30 minutes for 9 × 13-inch pans and 20 to 25 minutes for 10 × 8-inch pans.

Turn cakes from pans and frost tops and sides with fudge cake frosting.

For frosting, cream together sugar, cocoa, and butter. Add milk. In a heavy-bottomed saucepan, boil until soft ball stage is reached. (You may want to use a candy thermometer, 234°–240°, or the old-fashioned method: a drop of fudge in cool water should be soft and pliable but well formed.) Remove from heat; add vanilla. Put pan in cold water to cool and stir fudge vigorously, until a nice spreading consistency is achieved.

Careful cooks test fudge frosting before they remove it from the heat. To do so, spread a tiny amount of frosting on a saucer to check consistency. When beaten and cool, it should appear smooth (no sugar crystals) and nonglossy.

Louise Wendler Noé, High Amana

Note: "I first had this cake at a sewing circle club meeting (1930s). My friend served it and said that she had just tried this recipe but wasn't pleased with it; it hadn't risen enough. Well, I got the recipe and tried it at home and kind of kept at it. I added a few things to the recipe, and it turned out for me. I've been making it ever since," Mrs. Noé explained.

Although not an original communal kitchen recipe, it has earned a place in Amana culinary folklore as a wedding reception favorite. One colony grandmother who has married off a daughter, a son, and several grandchildren reported, "Everybody loves Louise's cakes and asks for them. I was so happy when she would bring her cakes, two or even sometimes three cakes, for the wedding receptions."

Mrs. Moershel's White Chocolate Cake

⅓ pound white
   chocolate, broken
   into chunks
½ cup water
1 cup butter
2 cups sugar
4 eggs, separated
2 ½ cups cake flour,
   sifted
1 ½ teaspoons baking
   powder
½ teaspoon salt
1 cup buttermilk
1 teaspoon vanilla
½ cup flaked coconut
1 cup chopped pecans
   or almonds

Preheat oven to 350°.

Place white chocolate and water in top of double boiler: heat over hot water until melted. Beat until blended; cool.

Cream butter and 1 ½ cups sugar until light and fluffy. Add egg yolks; beat thoroughly. Sift flour, baking powder, and salt. Add to creamed mixture in thirds alternately with buttermilk. Stir in vanilla and melted white chocolate, beating until smooth after every addition. Beat egg whites until soft peaks form; gradually add remaining ½ cup sugar and continue beating until stiff, but not dry. Fold into batter. Then gently fold in coconut and nuts.

Bake in a greased 9 × 13-inch baking pan for about 50 minutes.

Frost as desired but best if frosted with a butter frosting flavored with almond and then sprinkled with finely chopped nuts.

Katherina Moershel, Homestead

Note: This recipe was discovered by Mrs. Moershel sometime after the Great Change of 1932, which ended the communal era. With such costly ingredients it would not have been a cake made by the very frugal communal cooks. It is, however, as much a part of Amana as any simple sponge cake, for Mrs. Moershel's White Chocolate Cake made an appearance at two generations of weddings, funerals, and birthday celebrations.

Mysteries of Life and Cake

 Born in Amana in 1892, Katherina Hofer was married to Fritz Moershel of Homestead. After moving into a roomy two-story brick home on Homestead's peaceful main street, Mrs. Moershel raised one daughter and one son and later helped care for two grandchildren. In her home she did all the things she loved best. She cooked and baked, sewed and gardened. She looked after the people she loved. In 1987 she died at the age of 95.

Among many other things, her family and friends fondly recall that Mrs. Moershel baked the most luscious cakes. A very rich white chocolate cake (see preceding recipe) and a date cake reputed to have been Queen Elizabeth's own recipe were among those Mrs. Moershel baked and gave to others.

"I have often wondered how many hundreds of cakes she baked in her lifetime," commented Marietta Moershel, her daughter-in-law. "She was a treasure. . . . For years she took the *Chicago Tribune* and used to read all of the recipes. She got so many good ones from there. And she liked the more-complicated recipes—really, if it required patience, she was good at it."

One of Mrs. Moershel's best-loved recipes was for mystery cake (see following recipe). The layered marble cake with chocolate and cream frosting (flavored with a hint of orange), topped with shaved dark chocolate, was a wedding reception standout and nearly everyone's favorite.

Marianne, Katherina Moershel's granddaughter, explained how the cake got its name. "Apparently a women's magazine published the recipe with only the designation 'Mystery Cake.' The magazine held a contest in which its readers were asked to bake the cake and submit names for the cake. The winning entry was 'Lady Golden Glow.' Somehow that didn't have the special ring of 'Mystery Cake,' so the original name stuck, at least in our family."

"A birthday wasn't a birthday unless *Oma* Moershel baked you a mystery cake," one Moershel cousin remarked.

Made with priceless ingredients and exquisite patience, that cake was a gift of love. The generations of Amana folk who grew up beloved by *Omas* and *Opas,* who grew up wearing *Oma*'s woolen mittens and darned socks, who heard *Opa*'s stories and jokes, who helped pick peas and pull weeds in their garden, and who played in *Oma*'s lilacs, we are who we are because of the time, attention, and love given by grandparents. We are who we are because we have eaten mystery cake in many forms.

Mystery Cake

For cake
½ cup shortening
1 ½ cups sugar
Grated rind of ½
  orange
2 eggs, separated
2 ½ cups flour
4 teaspoons baking
  powder
¼ teaspoon salt
1 cup milk
1 ½ squares unsweet-
  ened chocolate

For filling and icing
3 tablespoons melted
  butter
3 cups powdered sugar
2 tablespoons orange
  juice
Grated rind of ½
  orange and pulp of
  1 orange
1 egg white, beaten
  until stiff
3 squares unsweetened
  chocolate

Preheat oven to 350°.

Cream shortening and sugar; add grated orange rind. Separate eggs, reserving whites in two separate dishes. Beat yolks into creamed mixture.

Sift together flour, baking powder, and salt. Add flour mixture alternately with milk to creamed ingredients. Beat one egg white until nearly stiff and fold into batter (use second whites for icing).

Divide batter into two parts. To one part stir in melted chocolate. Spoon batter, alternating chocolate and white, into two greased layer cake pans. Bake until cake springs back at touch of finger—about 25 minutes. Cake will be dry if overbaked. Cool completely before icing.

For filling and icing, beat remaining egg white until stiff. Set aside. Put butter, sugar, orange juice, and rind into a bowl. Cut pulp from orange, removing seeds and skin. Add pulp to butter and sugar mixture. Beat together until smooth. Fold in beaten egg white. Spread about ⅓ or less of this icing on top layer of cake. Using a sharp knife, shave ½ square chocolate and sprinkle on top of icing.

To remaining icing, add 2 ½ squares melted unsweetened chocolate. Spread this thickly on top of unfrosted layer. Place yellow frosted layer on chocolate frosted layer and frost sides with the rest of the chocolate frosting.

Katherina Moershel, Homestead

Note: As the frosting contains uncooked egg whites, it would be best to refrigerate cake before and after serving.

Caramel Frosting

½ cup butter, softened
1 cup brown sugar
3 to 4 cups powdered
  sugar
⅓ cup milk
½ teaspoon vanilla

Place butter and brown sugar in a saucepan and heat, stirring constantly until mixture bubbles. Then cook 1 minute more. Stir until caramel mixture is cool; add 3 cups powdered sugar gradually with milk, beating well after each addition. Add more sugar if needed to attain spreadable consistency. Add vanilla.

Emilie Steele, High Amana

Fudge Frosting

4 tablespoons cocoa
½ cup butter or
  margarine
6 tablespoons milk
4 cups powdered sugar
1 teaspoon vanilla
½ cup chopped nuts, if
  desired

In a heavy saucepan combine cocoa, butter or margarine, and milk; bring to a boil. Stir in powdered sugar, blending well. Add vanilla and nuts. Beat with wooden spoon until smooth and spreadable. Use frosting while still hot.

Susanna Hahn, Middle Amana

Maple Frosting

1 cup sugar
1 cup maple syrup
⅓ cup water
¼ teaspoon cream of
  tartar
1 egg white, beaten
  until stiff

Place sugar, syrup, water, and cream of tartar in a saucepan. Cook over medium heat, stirring constantly, until a little of mixture dropped from a spoon spins a thread. While sugar mixture is cooking, beat egg white until stiff. Gradually pour sugar mixture over egg white, beating constantly until a spreading consistency is achieved. Enough for a 9-inch layer cake or a 13 × 9-inch cake.

Chocolate Frosting

1 cup powdered sugar
2 tablespoons cocoa
2 tablespoons hot coffee
1 tablespoon melted
   butter

Whip the sugar, cocoa, and coffee until spreadable. Add a little milk if too dry. Stir in melted butter. Enough for one 9 × 9-inch cake.

Noé Kitchen House, Amana,
translated by Louise Miller DuVal

CHAPTER 17 HOLIDAY BAKING

And teach Thou me, this Christmas Day
How I a child of light may be,
Aglow with light that comes from Thee.

Caspar Nachtenhöfer,
"This Night a Wondrous Revelation,"
translation by Anna Hoppe,
The Amana Church Hymnal

Weihnachten in Amana

Infused by a spirituality that embraced a love for celebration, Christmas was a joyful time in old Amana. On Christmas Eve, the *Weihnachtsbaum,* decorated with bits of colored glass, handblown European ornaments, and candles, was a focal point. If a colony family was of Saxon descent (from the region in central Germany west of the Elbe River), it might have had a 3-foot-tall white wooden *Pyramid* standing in the parlor. Each of the round tiers was decorated with crocheted, wooden, or celluloid figures, typically birds, deer, a shepherd with his flock, or the Magi. Candles set on the *Pyramid* were lit, and the rising heat turned paddles on its top, causing the tiers to slowly rotate. The flickering candles, the play of light and shadow on the *Pyramid,* created a magical scene, made more so by the display of long-dreamed-for gifts beside the *Pyramid.*

In communal Amana, no one received wages; housing, food, clothing, medical care, fuel, and all else was provided by the *Gemeinschaft* (the community). Consequently, no one had much money, and gifts were either inexpensive or handmade. A bowl of fruit and nuts was customary. A single orange was considered a fine Christmas treat. Each child usually received a pair of thick, itchy woolen mittens or a wool hat or vest knitted from yarn spun in the Middle Amana Woolen Mill. Ice skates, blades made by the blacksmith and uppers made by a handy grandfather, were sought-after gifts. Sleds constructed by the village wagon maker and hobbyhorses outfitted with tiny saddles stitched by the harness maker were especially beloved. A new doll was every little girl's dream, but most girls were thrilled to see their favorite doll sitting beside the *Baum,* dressed in a new gown with lace trim tatted by *Oma.*

German storybooks and puzzles were given, these having been bought at the general store, where each December a shipment of toys and books was received to fulfill holiday wishes. At the High Amana General Store, the *Weihnacht's Zimmer* (Christmas Room) was on the second floor of the store. Used only at Christmastime, the room contained all the toys, books, and candies and was off-limits to children. During the day or in the evening, after prayer services, parents would visit and select gifts for their children, choosing from the picture books and wooden blocks, windup toys and china dolls.

Christmas Baking

Candles lit and kerosene lanterns flickering helped to create the magical illusions of Christmas, but good food lovingly prepared added to the gaiety.

Of course, homes were not outfitted for cooking and contained no oven, so all holiday baking was done at the communal kitchen or at the village bakery. Because everyone loved Christmas cookies (we are, after all, talking about Germans), steps were taken by the elders and the village baker to insure that everyone got their baking done. In December each family was assigned a day on which the village stone hearth oven would be made available to them. Then mothers and grandmothers got busy mixing together the *Lebkuchen,* the *Pfeffernüsse,* the nut cookies and butter cookies, the *Marzipan*, the chocolate drops, and the *Wiesbader Brot.* Bowls and crocks of cookie doughs were packed and taken by coaster wagon to the bakery. After the day's bread baking was done, the stones were just right for cookies. Using the baker's wooden paddle and his huge baking pans, dozens of cookies could be baked at once, and soon the bakery was filled with the delicious aroma of sugar and cinnamon and Christmas.

After school, the women were joined by their offspring, for cookie-baking day was very special, and every child knew the day his mother and grandmother baked. Although it has been 60 some years, there are folks in Amana who can still tell you, *"Ja,* our day was December 14."

When the cookies had cooled, they were carefully packed in tins and crocks and stored in a cool, dry place until Christmas. Of course broken or misshapen cookies were eaten on the spot, and a few tempting samples were saved for Father and *Opa* (grandpa).

Communal women favored cookie recipes that were simple to bake in quantity and those that called for ingredients easily procured. Cookies that were "good keepers" were valued since baking day might be as early as the second week of December. Of all the cookies made at Christmastime, the honey cookie perhaps is most typical of communal Amana.

Lebkuchen, made with sweet blossom honey is an excellent keeper. The main ingredient, honey, was produced in the village apiary. Gathered by the village beekeeper, honey was divided equally among all of the residents. Having a good quantity of honey to enjoy year-round and still having enough for a double batch of Christmas cookies was cause for rejoicing and earned the beekeeper nothing more than the respect of his neighbors.

Christmas in the Kitchen

The *Küchebaas* ran her kitchen with splendid efficiency all year round, but at Christmas, an extra effort was made to produce foods worthy of the holiday.

First there was the Christmas dinner to consider and plan for. In every kitchen house the traditional holiday meal was the same: rice soup, creamed chicken over homemade noodles, mashed potatoes, coleslaw, stewed prunes and peaches, and *Stollen.* Served on Christmas Day, the holiday meal was highly anticipated, for it featured a chicken dish, and chicken was very rarely served in communal kitchens, where frugal cooks had to control costs.

Stollen, a sweet yeast bread, laced with nuts, raisins, and citron, was baked in the kitchens. Loaves of *Stollen* were distributed to each kitchen patron and savored during daily morning coffee breaks and meals. When comparing recipes, Amana's *Stollen* seems to be a less-complicated version of the traditional *Stollenrezept* (*Stollen* recipe) commonly found in central Germany.

New Year's *Pretzel*

On New Year's Day it was customary to serve *pretzel*. Actually, New Year's *Pretzel* is a pretzel-shaped coffee cake, very light and sweet, frosted with white icing. Baked just before New Year's Eve, the *Pretzel* is still very much an Amana tradition. Local bakeries produce it for nonbaking residents, while many colonists bake their own and share with family and friends. Some colonists like their *Pretzel* topped with shredded coconut; others prefer a sprinkle of chopped nuts and wouldn't dream of using coconut. The coconut versus nut debate continues in the Amanas, but everyone agrees that New Year's Day is no holiday without *Pretzel*.

Today *Stollen* and, of course, Christmas cookies are baked by the basketful, and many Amana families would not consider celebrating the holiday without plates of *Lebkuchen* and *Marzipan*, nut cookies and *Stollen*.

Lebkuchen
Honey Cookies

1 tablespoon baking
    soda
3 tablespoons whiskey
2 cups honey
½ pound (1 cup and
    1 tablespoon) sugar
2 eggs
1½ pounds (5¼ cups)
    flour
Vanilla frosting (page
    211)

Preheat oven to 350°.

Dissolve soda in whiskey. In a very large mixing bowl, stir together dissolved baking soda and whiskey, honey, and sugar. (If honey is hard or granulated, heat slowly in saucepan until fluid before combining with other ingredients.) Stir until foamy. Add eggs, beating well after each. Then slowly add flour. A soft dough will form. Cover and set bowl in a cool place or refrigerate overnight.

Turn out a portion of the dough on a floured board. Kneading the dough is very important to the quality of the finished product, so take your time and knead until the dough feels springy and light, but not dry. Roll into 1- to 2-inch-thick ropes. Cut ropes into 2- or 3-inch-long pieces and place on a greased baking sheet.

Bake 10 minutes. Cookies should be golden brown, oval shaped, and about ⅓ to ½ inch thick. When cool, frost with vanilla frosting.

Makes about 5 dozen.

Lina Unglenk, Amana

Note: Some Amana cooks add a handful of citron or chopped hickory nuts, but Lina prefers her honey cookies without embellishment. "My grandmother used this recipe, my mother used this recipe, and I do too. The cookies always turn out nice, and they keep so well. Of course, they don't last long; the kids like them so!"

Süd Amana Lebkuchen
South Amana Honey Cookies

4 cups honey
2 ⅓ cups brown sugar
¼ teaspoon allspice
¼ teaspoon cinnamon
4 eggs
3 teaspoons baking soda
¼ cup whiskey
9 ½ cups flour, sifted
½ pound ground
   hickory or walnuts
Vanilla frosting (page
   211)

Preheat oven to 325°.

In a heavy-bottomed saucepan on medium-low heat, warm honey, stirring in brown sugar. When lukewarm, add allspice and cinnamon.

Dissolve baking soda in the whiskey. In a very large mixing bowl combine honey mixture and baking soda and whisky. Slowly stir in eggs and flour. Blend in nuts. Cover and chill overnight. Using your hands or a wooden spoon, blend dough, kneading well until dough achieves a light, springy quality. This may take 10 minutes or more. Roll dough into several 1- to 2-inch-thick ropes. Cut ropes into 2- or 3-inch-long pieces and place on a greased baking sheet. Bake 10 minutes. Cookies should be golden brown, oval-shaped, and about ½ inch thick. When cool, frost with vanilla frosting.

Makes about 11 dozen cookies.

Henrietta B. Berger, South Amana

Note: With 55 communal kitchens in seven villages preparing essentially the same foods, it makes sense that more than one recipe for a common dish exists in Amana. This is also true of Christmas cookies, which were made by virtually all colony cooks. Five variations of the *Lebkuchen* recipe were seen in the course of preparing this book. Some recipe variances can be said to occur by village. For instance, it seems that in South Amana they preferred their honey cookies with nuts and spices, as several South Amana natives have reported. Mrs. Berger's recipe requires nuts, cinnamon, and allspice, unlike Mrs. Unglenk's version from the village of Amana, which does not.

Lebkuchen ohne Eier
Honey Cookies without Eggs

1 cup brown sugar

1 cup honey

1 cup margarine

1 heaping teaspoon
    baking soda

$\frac{1}{4}$ cup hot strong
    coffee

4 $\frac{1}{2}$ cups flour

$\frac{1}{2}$ teaspoon ginger

$\frac{1}{4}$ teaspoon cinnamon

$\frac{1}{2}$ teaspoon salt

1 teaspoon vanilla

Preheat oven to 350°.

Cream together brown sugar, honey, and margarine. Dissolve baking soda in hot coffee. Add to creamed sugar mixture, alternating with flour. Stir in ginger, cinnamon, salt, and vanilla.

Chill dough; then shape into rolls (1 $\frac{1}{2}$ to 2 inches in diameter) and wrap in waxed paper. Refrigerate overnight. Slice into $\frac{1}{4}$-inch slices and bake on greased cookie sheet for about 10 minutes. Cookies should be firm and chewy, but not crisp or dry. Frost, if desired, with your favorite vanilla icing.

Makes about 4 dozen cookies.

Dorothy Seifert, Homestead

Note: Cooks seeking to cut cholesterol and fats will enjoy this modern adaptation of an old Amana favorite.

Wiesbader Brot
Wiesbaden Bread (named for the German city)

1 cup butter, softened

2 $\frac{1}{3}$ cups sugar

4 eggs, reserve yolks
    from 2

5 cups flour

1 tablespoon cinnamon

2 teaspoons baking
    powder

Colored sugar

Preheat oven to 325°.

In a very large mixing bowl, cream butter and sugar until fluffy. Reserving 2 yolks, beat 2 whole eggs and 2 whites until very frothy and combine with creamed sugar and butter. Gradually add flour, cinnamon, and baking powder. Mix well. Cover and chill dough overnight.

On a large lightly floured board, roll out small portions of dough to $\frac{1}{4}$-inch thickness. (Hint: If dough is too sticky to work with, take portion of dough and knead in a bit of flour. Try rolling out on floured wax paper. Dough is easier to work with when very cold.) Using cookie cutters, cut into shapes or simply use a fluted pastry wheel to cut into diamond shapes. Place on a greased baking sheet and brush with beaten egg yolks and sprinkle with colored sugar. Bake about 10 to 15 minutes until light brown.

Makes about 4 to 5 dozen.

Marie Reihmann, Middle Amana

Nuss Platzchen
Hickory Nut Cookies

½ cup butter or
    margarine, softened
2 ⅓ cups sugar (equals
    1 pound)
1 ¾ cups flour
1 teaspoon baking
    powder
4 eggs
½ pound hickory nuts,
    chopped fine

Preheat oven to 350°.

Cream butter and sugar. In a separate bowl, sift together flour and baking powder. Beat in eggs, alternating with flour mixture. Add hickory nuts and stir well. Drop by rounded teaspoonfuls on lightly greased cookie sheet. Bake 8 to 10 minutes.

Makes 4 dozen.

Lena Schinnerling, Middle Amana

Note: Mrs. Schinnerling, a resident of Middle Amana, was a *Garteschwester* (garden sister) helping to tend one of the large kitchen gardens in Middle Amana. She and her husband, Carl, and two children lived in the apartment adjoining the Middle Amana *Saal* (church). At Christmas these hickory nut cookies were among those Mrs. Schinnerling shared with family and friends.

Nuss Platzchen
Nut Cookies

8 eggs, beaten until
    foamy
2 ⅓ cups brown sugar
2 ⅓ cups granulated
    sugar
3 ½ cups flour
1 teaspoon baking
    powder
1 pound nuts (hickory
    or English walnuts,
    as you prefer),
    ground

Preheat oven to 350°.

Combine eggs with brown sugar and granulated sugar. Stir in flour and baking powder. If dough seems too stiff, add just a bit of milk to soften. Grind nuts, being careful to remove any bits of shell. Stir nutmeats into dough. Drop by rounded teaspoons on greased cookie sheet. Bake until firm, about 8 to 10 minutes.

Makes 5 to 6 dozen.

Louise Selzer, Homestead

Butter Gebäck
Soft Butter Cookies

8 eggs

3 cups sugar

½ pound (2 sticks)
butter or margarine,
melted until foamy

1 teaspoon baking soda

2 teaspoons baking
powder

6 ½ cups flour

1 teaspoon salt

Preheat oven to 350°.

Cream eggs, sugar, and butter. Add flour, salt, baking soda, and baking powder, beating well after each addition. The batter may be divided and embellished with coconut or melted unsweetened baking chocolate to provide three different cookies from one recipe. For chocolate butter cookies simply add 1 teaspoon vanilla and 1 square melted, unsweetened chocolate.

Drop by tablespoonfuls on ungreased cookie sheet and bake 8 to 10 minutes. Cookies will be firm, but not brown. Try not to overbake.

Makes about 5 dozen.

Caroline Trumpold, Middle Amana

Note: When Caroline Trumpold submitted this recipe, she wrote that it had been her mother's favorite cookie and that she used to double the recipe and then divide the batter mixing one portion with shredded coconut, another with melted chocolate for a double variation of the classic butter cookie.

Von die Mittler (From the Middlers)

Here is an original communal recipe for butter cookies from Marie Murbach of Middle Amana, translated by her granddaughter, Susanna Hahn of Middle Amana, who happily makes this recipe each Christmas for her grandchildren and great-grandchildren, many of whom live in Middle Amana. It is the giant twin to the *Butter Gebäck* recipe offered by Caroline Trumpold, also of Middle Amana, whose parents were, as you might expect, Middle Amana born. This recipe makes about 10 dozen cookies.

Butter Gebäck
Butter Cookies

4 pounds sugar

4 pounds flour

1 ½ pounds butter

17 eggs

4 teaspoons baking powder

2 teaspoons baking soda

2 teaspoons salt

¼ pound shredded coconut

Drop Cookies

4 eggs, beaten until
    frothy

1 cup granulated sugar

1 cup brown sugar

3 tablespoons butter,
    melted

3 ½ cups flour

3 teaspoons baking
    powder

1 teaspoon vanilla

1 cup raisins (or
    coconut or nuts, as
    you prefer)

Preheat oven to 350°.

Combine eggs and granulated sugar and beat 5 minutes. Stir in brown sugar and melted butter. In a second bowl combine flour and baking powder. Add flour mixture and vanilla to batter and beat well. Stir in raisins, coconut, or nuts. Drop by rounded teaspoons onto greased cookie sheet. Bake about 8 minutes.

Makes about 4 dozen cookies.

Caroline Shoup Setzer, South Amana

Note: For a rich chocolate drop cookie, simply melt 3 squares unsweetened chocolate and add to batter.

Marzipan
White Marchpane

4 eggs, beaten 10 to 15 minutes

4 cups powdered sugar

1 teaspoon baking soda

1 teaspoon baking powder

3 ½ cups flour

3 tablespoons butter, softened

Preheat oven to 325°.

Beat eggs and powdered sugar with electric mixer until whipped. Blend in baking soda, baking powder, and flour. Add butter. Refrigerate at least 2 hours before rolling out. Roll out on a floured board to ½-inch thickness. Using old-fashioned cookie cutters with deep, sharp edges, cut into shapes (circles, stars, diamonds, simple Christmas trees). Place cutouts on cookie sheets or board. With the rim of a thimble or the tip of small spoon, pierce tops of cutouts with half-circles and circles (top must be punctured, or it will bubble). Cover sheets or board with clean dish towels and store in a cool, dry place two days. Do not freeze or refrigerate.

Bake for 20 minutes. Cookies should be baked through and firm, but not browned.

Makes about 3 to 4 dozen.

Helene S. Kraus, Middle Amana,
and Carol Schuerer Zuber, East Amana

Note: Curiously, the Amana *Marzipan* recipes do not include almonds or almond paste, which is the fundamental ingredient of the German confection. Perhaps it is not so curious when we consider that it would have been difficult and expensive to procure almonds or almond paste in communal Amana. The Amana cooks improvised and came up with a very delicious variation on the *Marzipan* theme.

Braun Marzipan
Brown Marchpane

4 eggs, beaten 10 to 15
    minutes
2 cups brown sugar
⅓ cup granulated sugar
3 ½ cups flour
1 teaspoon baking
    powder
1 teaspoon baking soda
1 teaspoon cinnamon
Pinch cloves
Pinch nutmeg

Preheat oven 325°.

Blend all ingredients, beating after each addition. Refrigerate at least 2 hours before rolling out. Roll dough out on a floured board to ½-inch thickness. Using old-fashioned cookie cutters with deep, sharp edges, cut into shapes (circles, stars, fish, diamonds, simple Christmas trees). Place cutouts on greased cookie sheets. With the rim of a thimble or the tip of small spoon, pierce tops of cutouts with half-circles and circles (top must be punctured, or it will bubble). Cover with clean dish towels and store board in a cool, dry place for two days. Do not freeze or refrigerate.

Bake for 20 minutes. Cookies should be baked through and firm, but not browned.

Makes about 3 to 4 dozen.

Helene S. Kraus, Middle Amana,
and Carol Schuerer Zuber, East Amana

The Cookies That Went to "Rapids"

Carol Schuerer Zuber makes her *Oma* Kraus's *Marzipan* each Christmas and concedes that finding just the right place to store cookie sheets or cutting boards of cookies for two days is no simple matter. *Oma* put them in her attic, but Carol's 100-year-old restored East Amana home does not have an attic so accessible. One Christmas, Carol decided that she might try placing the cookie sheets in the backseat of her car. Parked in the garage, the car would be perfect: cool, dry, and dust-free.

The next morning she was called upon to run an errand for her family, who manages the Amana Barn Restaurant, and hopped in her car for a drive to Cedar Rapids. A few miles down the road she began to wonder why her car smelled so wonderfully of cinnamon and suddenly remembered the cookies, nicely covered with dish towels and carefully balanced on the backseat. They survived the drive just fine, and that Christmas everyone in Carol's family chuckled about the *Marzipan* that went to town.

Anise Cookies

4 eggs
4 cups powdered sugar
1 teaspoon baking soda
3 ½ cups flour
Dash oil of anise or
   1 teaspoon anise
   extract

Preheat oven to 350°.

Using electric mixer, beat eggs and powdered sugar on high for 10 minutes (in the communal kitchens they did this by hand for 20 minutes). Blend in baking soda, flour, and anise. Roll out dough on floured board to ⅓-inch thickness. Cut with cookie cutters or pastry wheel. Using the rim of a thimble or the edge of a spoon, pierce tops of cutouts with impressions (top must be punctured, or it will bubble). Place cookies on cookie sheets, cover with clean dish towel, and set in cool, dry place overnight.

Bake 8 to 10 minutes or until bottoms of cookies are lightly browned.

Makes about 3 to 4 dozen cookies.

Lina Unglenk and Caroline Zscherny, Amana

Note: Mrs. Unglenk remembers helping her mother make these licorice-flavored Christmas treats. Preparing the batter at home prior to taking it to the village bakery, where all Christmas cookie baking was done in communal days, Lina and her mother used the brass key from the wall clock to decorate the cookie tops.

Icebox Cookies

2 cups brown sugar
1 cup granulated sugar
1 cup vegetable
   shortening
4 eggs, beaten
4 cups flour
1 teaspoon baking
   powder
1 teaspoon baking soda
1 teaspoon vanilla
1 cup nuts, hickory or
   walnut, chopped fine

Preheat oven to 350°.

Cream sugars and shortening, beating until fluffy. Combine eggs with creamed mixture—mix well. Slowly beat in flour, baking powder, baking soda, vanilla, and nuts. If dough seems too soft and sticky, add a bit more flour. Shape dough into rolls; wrap with waxed paper and refrigerate overnight. Slice and bake on greased cookie sheets about 10 to 15 minutes. Test for doneness. The cookie will be too dry if overbaked.

Makes 4 to 6 dozen.

Carrie Shoup, South Amana

Note: Carrie Shoup of South Amana gave this recipe to her friend, Lena (Magdalena) Schaefer of East Amana, who faithfully copied the recipe into the old Schaefer communal kitchen *Rezeptbuch*. Mrs. Schaefer noted that she added 2 tablespoons buttermilk if the dough seemed too dry.

Date Nut Cookies

1 cup vegetable
  shortening
1 cup granulated sugar
1 cup brown sugar
3 eggs, beaten
3 cups flour
1 teaspoon baking soda

½ teaspoon baking
  powder
½ teaspoon salt
1 teaspoon vanilla
1 cup nuts, chopped
½ pound dates,
  chopped

Preheat oven to 350°.

Cream shortening and sugars, beating until fluffy. Add beaten eggs. Stir flour, baking soda, baking powder, salt, and vanilla into batter, mixing well. Add chopped nuts and dates. It is best to stir these in by hand.

Drop by rounded teaspoonfuls onto greased cookie sheet. Bake about 10 minutes.

Makes about 4 dozen cookies.

Erma Kellenberger, West Amana

Christmas Cookies

1 cup butter, slightly
  softened
1 cup granulated sugar
2 eggs, separate 1 of
  them
1 teaspoon grated lemon
  rind
3 cups flour
½ teaspoon salt
Colored sugar and silver
  dragées (optional)

Preheat oven to 375°.

Cream softened butter and sugar. Add 1 whole egg and another egg yolk to creamed mixture, working until thoroughly blended. Add lemon rind to batter. Sift together flour and salt and work into batter gradually using a wooden spoon. Then as dough stiffens, work flour with your hands, until dough is smoothly blended and stiff enough to roll.

Wrap dough in waxed paper and refrigerate for several hours or overnight. Roll a portion of the dough (keep the rest in the refrigerator while you roll) on a floored pastry cloth to ¼-inch thickness. Using cookie cutters, cut shapes as desired. Place on ungreased cookie sheet, brush with unbeaten egg white and decorate with colored sugar, silver dragées, or as desired. Bake about 8 minutes. Remove from sheet and cool on wire racks.

Makes about 8 dozen if you use smaller cookie cutters.

Marietta Moershel, Homestead

Note: Using a poinsettia-shaped cookie cutter made by her husband, Mrs. Moershel makes these cookies each Christmas, and they have long since become a cherished part of the Moershel family Christmas.

Fenceriegel
Fencelatch Cookies

2 ½ cups flour
1 teaspoon baking soda
1 teaspoon salt
½ cup brown sugar
½ cup vegetable
    shortening
¾ cup buttermilk or
    sour milk (1 table-
    spoon vinegar added
    to ¾ cup milk)
1 egg white (optional)

Preheat oven to 350°.

Combine flour, soda, and salt. Add brown sugar and cut in vegetable shortening as you would a piecrust. Add buttermilk or sour milk to form a soft dough. (To sour milk: 1 hour before preparation time, add vinegar to milk and stir. Set aside until ready to prepare the dough.)

Roll out dough on lightly floured board to ½-inch thickness. Using a fluted pastry cutter, or *Rädel* as they were called in the communal kitchen, cut dough into 2-inch squares, diamonds, or any shape and size desired. On greased cookie sheets, bake at 350° for about 10 minutes. If desired, brush tops of cookies with egg white just before baking.

Makes about 3 to 4 dozen cookies.

Emily Roemig, Amana

Note: Although not considered a Christmas cookie, *Fenceriegel* occupy a special place in Amana folk culture as the one cookie baked only in the village of Amana. This not-too-sweet brown sugar cookie was a Hertel Kitchen House tradition and Emily Roemig, who trained as a cook in the Hertel Kitchen House, remembers *Küchebaas* Ida Hertel pulling trays of hot *Fenceriegel* from the oven. Mrs. Roemig, a colony cook who loves preparing the traditional dishes, still makes these cookies for her family.

Chocolate Icebox Cookies

2 ½ cups flour, sifted
⅓ teaspoon salt
2 teaspoons baking
    powder
2 squares unsweetened
    chocolate, melted
⅔ cup butter or
    vegetable shortening
1 ½ cups sugar
1 egg
⅓ cup milk

Preheat oven to 350°.

Sift together flour, salt, and baking powder—set aside. Melt chocolate squares and allow to cool.

Cream butter or shortening and sugar until fluffy. Add the egg and beat well. Stir in sifted dry ingredients, alternating with milk. Blend in melted chocolate. Form dough into a roll and wrap with waxed paper. Refrigerate overnight.

Slice thinly. Place on ungreased cookie sheets and bake about 10 minutes.

Makes about 4 dozen cookies.

Katherina Moershel, Homestead

Weihnachts Stollen
Christmas Stollen

For dough

2 cups warm water

4 envelopes dry yeast

2 ½ pounds granulated
   sugar

5 pounds flour

2 ¼ cups ground nuts,
   pecans or hickory

½ pound raisins

1 cup candied citron

2 teaspoons cinnamon

1 teaspoon freshly
   ground nutmeg

1 tablespoon salt

4 cups scalded milk

¾ pound butter, melted

½ teaspoon almond
   flavoring

For topping

1 cup powdered sugar

1 cup granulated sugar

2 teaspoons cinnamon

Preheat oven to 350°.

In very warm water, dissolve yeast and 1 tablespoon sugar. Stir in 1 cup flour. Cover and set aside in a warm spot. Allow to rise until double.

Sift remaining flour into a very large bowl. In a second bowl sprinkle 1 cup sifted flour over ground nuts, raisins, and citron. Blend with spoon until fruits and nuts are coated with flour. Pour fruit and nuts into remaining sifted flour and combine. Add sugar, cinnamon, nutmeg (freshly ground nutmeg is best), and salt.

Scald milk and allow to cool a bit. Stir in melted butter. Pour warm milk and butter into dry ingredients and blend. Add almond flavoring. Add yeast mixture, stirring well. Turn out on a large well-floured board and knead until ingredients are blended and dough is elastic—may take about 10 minutes of kneading. *Oma* would tell you to place a piece of thread in the dough and knead until it appears at least three times. Rub sides of extremely large bowl (or two large bowls) with vegetable shortening. Place dough in bowl and cover with a clean cloth. Place in a warm spot overnight.

Grease seven standard size loaf pans with vegetable shortening. Turn dough out on well-floured board. Punch down. As you would bread dough, separate into seven neat loaves and place carefully in loaf pans with ends tucked under. Cover with a cloth and place in a warm spot to rise. Allow to rise until doubled. Just before baking cut a deep gash into the top of each loaf.

Bake for 50 minutes (adjust baking time to size of loaf pan). Tops should be evenly browned. After removing from the oven, turn out loaves and brush tops with melted butter and sprinkle with a mixture of topping ingredients. Stollen keeps well wrapped in plastic wrap, or it can be frozen.

Makes 6 to 7 loaves.

Susanna H. Wendler, High Amana

Note: When no longer fresh, slice loaf, butter slices, sprinkle with sugar, and toast in a warm oven until deep golden brown for *Zweibeck* (twice-baked). Or use for French dessert toast recipe given in Chapter 12.

Pretzel
New Year's Pretzel

2 cups warm water

2 cakes yeast

6 cups flour

10 tablespoons sugar

1 ½ teaspoons salt

1 cup raisins (more, if
you like)

2 eggs

¼ cup vegetable
shortening, softened

1 cup shredded coconut
(optional)

In ¼ cup very warm water, dissolve yeast. In a very large bowl mix together flour, sugar, salt, raisins, and the rest of the water. Blend in shortening, eggs, and yeast. Turn out on floured board. Knead well for 20 minutes. Place in a very large bowl, cover with a clean cloth, and place in a warm spot overnight.

Preheat oven to 350°.

Roll four equal portions of dough into 2-foot-long ropes (about 1 ½ inches thick). Fold and twist ropes into pretzel shape, place on a large greased baking sheet, cover with cloth, and allow to rise again—about 3 hours. Dough should double in size. Bake till golden brown (exact time will depend upon the size of the pretzel), about 20 minutes. Allow to cool and frost with thick vanilla frosting (see following recipe) and sprinkle tops with coconut if desired.

Makes 4 pretzels.

Lina Moessner, Middle Amana

Vanilla Frosting

2 tablespoons butter or
margarine

1 cup powdered sugar

2 tablespoons milk

½ teaspoon vanilla

Combine butter and sugar in a small mixing bowl and beat well. Add milk and vanilla, beating until frosting is lump-free. This frosting is perfect on *Lebkuchen* and Christmas cutouts. Make a double batch, adding a bit more sugar to thicken, and it can be used on New Year's Pretzel.

Note: Several communal recipes call for the addition of a dash of rose water to the vanilla frosting. Rose water for baking can sometimes be found in gourmet food shops or health foods stores.

In the Quiet Solitude

There is a story in Amana of a Christmas Eve long ago when a young man, late for the evening prayer service, hurried to the *Saal* (meeting place) through the snow. Holding his lantern high, he walked fast. Snow was falling, and there was no wind to rattle the tree branches. Except for the crunch of his boots, it was so still he could almost hear the snow touch down upon the drifts.

The congregation inside had just begun to sing, and the melody seemed to roll from the old sandstone building into the night, sweeping heavenward. The song reached the young man, and the very power of its message made him stop.

> In the quiet solitude,
> my heart brings Thee gratitude.
> Mighty God, oh, hear my plea,
> for my soul is seeking Thee. . . .
> Gently falls the glist'ning snow,
> cov'ring all the world below.
>
> (Joachim Neander, "In the Quiet Solitude,"
> translation by Louis Marz,
> *The Amana Church Hymnal*)

Then the young man knew he need not enter the *Saal* to worship the Lord who was there with him in the motion of the snowflakes and the quiet of the night.

THE
GREAT
CHANGE

CHAPTER 18 # WHEN THE KITCHENS CLOSED

All that winter some of the ladies talked about having a kitchen in their own house—something new for everyone. Nobody had any pots or pans, no stove or maybe just a kerosene stove. So . . . people got ready.

Elise Zuber, West Amana

In 1932 the people of the Amana Colonies set aside the communal system, ending a way of life that had been theirs for 89 years. Amana residents refer to it as "the Reorganization" or "the Great Change." Indeed, that is the most appropriate way to refer to a series of events that completely reorganized community structure and significantly changed the lives of every man, woman, and child in Amana—over 1,300 people.

Prior to 1932 an Amana colonist could depend upon "cradle to grave" security, including three meals daily, free housing, and medical care. In exchange, residents were expected to contribute their time and talents whenever and wherever required and to make sacrifices for the good of the community. Sometime in the 1920s, that spirit of self-sacrifice began to diminish. As one South Amana resident explained, "In old Amana the wolf was never at the door," and no one feared poverty. But boredom, limited educational opportunities, and a narrowing sense of personal freedom undermined happiness. Talk of change among the young people be-

came common, and finally, even many of the older folks had to admit that communal life was restrictive.

Additionally, the community faced severe financial difficulties due to both internal and external factors. A poor farm economy on the very eve of the Great Depression created a gloomy financial picture. Inability to control internal costs added to the community's problems. Fearing a financial collapse that would topple the community, Amana's leaders began to talk of change.

In 1931 discussions were held to help determine the community's future course of action. An elected body of village representatives known as the "Committee of 47" met repeatedly and eventually came to a consensus that the communal way of life was a detriment to the future well-being of the church and the community. Seeking legal and financial advice from various quarters and painstakingly discussing every aspect of the issue, the Committee of 47, led by a core group of men, drew up a plan for dissolving the communal system and instituting a for-profit

215

corporation, the Amana Society, to manage the business enterprises of the community. The Amana Church Society was to continue guidance of spiritual matters and to oversee church properties.

In the winter of 1932, the people of Amana signed a charter creating the new Amana Society. As part of the reorganization plan, each adult member received one voting share of stock in the new corporation. Each member also received a specific number of Prior Distributive shares based upon a formula taking into account his or her years of service in the old communal order. Elderly or handicapped members were given living allowances, provisions were made for the care of orphans, and all stockholders were entitled to free medical care.

Because all homes were owned in common, a fair and practical method for transferring ownership to private individuals had to be developed. All through the winter of 1932 men tramped through the snow and measured and remeasured lot lines plat-

ting the villages of Amana. Each home and lot was assessed and a value fixed. Residents were encouraged to buy their homes from the Amana Society and did so by using their Prior Distributive shares as collateral for a loan. Sometimes two families bought a large house together. Those families not wanting to buy a home could rent from the Amana Society at a low rate. Private home ownership was a major change for the Amana people. For the first time ever, they had the opportunity and the responsibility to

The vine-covered Noé Kitchen House is now the Museum of Amana History in the village of Amana. Many of the kitchen houses were converted to private residences and nearly all remain so today. Reprinted with permission from the Museum of Amana History.

care for their own homes. When they could afford to do so, many homeowners added kitchens, bathrooms, and other improvements. And for the first time, Amana people had to pay personal property taxes, mortgages, fuel bills, and other home maintenance costs.

Employment changed as those who had worked for the community became employees of the Amana Society and earned an hourly wage or salary. Some residents established their own businesses or found jobs outside the community. Especially during those transitional years just after the Great Change of 1932, when many Amana families were learning to cope with expenses, finding employment for the women was a concern, so the Amana Society established a small wholesale business for hand-knit items and homemade preserves. Women also found work in the Amana Woolen Mills, the corporate offices of the Amana Society, and several new business ventures of the Amana Society.

Earning a high school or even a college degree became, for the first time, a real possibility for many of Amana's young men and women. Prior to 1932 only a few men, and no women, were allowed to advance beyond the eighth grade. Thirty-four Amana teens attended high school in nearby towns in the autumn of 1932. Sixteen of the 34 were women. In 1934 Amana opened its own high school in Middle Amana, and parents proudly sent their children to claim what had once been denied.

Amana Refrigeration: Leadership and Innovation

Amana Refrigeration, founded by George C. Foerstner of Amana, played a crucial role in sustaining the community following the Great Change and the transition years by offering employment to colony residents and economic opportunity for the community as a whole.

Under Foerstner's management, the Amana Refrigeration became a leader in the home appliance industry by successfully marketing such pioneer products as the home upright freezer, the combination refrigerator-freezer, and the frost-free refrigerator. In 1965, Amana Refrigeration, Inc., became a Raytheon Company, and two years later forever changed food preparation methods with the introduction of the home microwave oven.

In 1997 the Goodman Co. of Houston, Texas, air conditioning manufacturers, purchased Amana Refrigeration. Employing 2,800 people at its Middle Amana plant, Amana Refrigeration produces a line of home heating and cooling products, in addition to home appliances.

The Day the Kitchens Closed

The forsythia were blooming the day the communal kitchens closed in the seven Amana villages. The forsythia were blooming, the gardens lay ready for planting, spring fieldwork had begun, and although the Amanas looked no different, a change had occurred. From that spring of 1932 the Amanas would never be the same again. As Elise Zuber of West Amana said:

Following the Great Change of 1932, former communal cooks grew accustomed to preparing foods in their own kitchens and learned how to cook for a family rather than for a neighborhood. Photo by William Noé. Circa 1940. Reprinted with permission from the Museum of Amana History.

They said we'll close the kitchens in April. And we were all glad. All that winter some of the ladies talked about having a kitchen in their home—something new for everyone. Nobody had any pots or pans, no stove or maybe just a kerosene stove. So people rigged things up at home and got ready.

I was 32 years old then. I never knew anything different than what was. Nobody did.

Well, the big day came, and everybody was excited. We had talked about it at the kitchen, about what to cook for the last breakfast, dinner, and so on. The *Baas* she did like always, said the menu like always. I know we had new lettuce. And radishes, I think. Soup, and I forget what meat for dinner. We cooked, and then it was time for the ladies to come pick it up and take it home. *Schwester* [sister] was slicing bread, and I was pouring out the soup, and then I looked up, and she was crying. Then pretty soon so was old Mrs.___ and Lina and me

too. We just stood there and cried.

It was hard on the old ones. They didn't know what was going to happen. But the young ones they were excited; here was their big chance. For me, well, I didn't know how it would be. My husband was happy.

Well, that meal was the last one for the kitchens. I don't remember all what we ate, but it was good.

Eventually the kitchen houses were sold as private homes to former residents. In May equipment from each kitchen, the baskets, tinware, implements, and crockery, were divided among the former patrons or sold at auctions. Women who had been trained in the communal kitchens had to learn how to prepare meals for 5 people rather than 35. Older women who had long since left the kitchen had to begin cooking in their own kitchens. These household challenges proved difficult for some women, but many welcomed the chance to try new recipes or foods and to prepare just what they wanted when they wished. A Middle Amana cook remarked that

No longer having to "put up" fruits and vegetables for the communal kitchens, the women turned to stocking their own family larders with the bounty of their gardens. Reprinted with permission from the Museum of Amana History.

her very first home-cooked meal included store-bought canned pineapple, the first pineapple she and her family had ever tasted.

Although everyone experimented with new recipes and foods, nearly all cooks continued to prepare the foods once served in the kitchen houses. The old recipes meant to feed a small army had to be cut down to family size, and many colony cooks did so, experimenting with ingredients before sharing the resized recipe with friends. In 1945, the women of the Homestead Welfare Club tested and assembled a cookbook of family-sized Amana communal recipes. The book, *Amana Colony Recipes,* has been reprinted many times and is still available in colony stores and shops. Cooks from all over the world have prepared traditional colony foods via this volume of recipes. Most importantly, *Amana Colony Recipes* has allowed young Amana cooks easy access to their culinary heritage.

A Heritage of Delicious Foods

In the decades following the Great Change several Amana families opened restaurants. Jacob Roemig opened the Colony Inn in the former Amana Hotel in 1936 and later hired Walter Schuerer to manage the restaurant. The Ox Yoke Inn was established in an Amana kitchen house by Bill and Lina Leichsenring in 1940. In Homestead the old hotel was remodeled by Bill Zuber and his wife, Connie, who opened their restaurant, Bill Zuber's Dugout, in 1948, following Bill's retirement from professional baseball. In 1950 Helen Zimmerman Graichen, a former communal cook, and her family started the Ronneburg Restaurant in what had been the Zimmerman Kitchen House in Amana. While in 1968, Carl Oehl and his family opened the Colony Market Place in what had once been the South Amana meat shop and smokehouse. The kitchens of all five of these restaurants were "manned" by cooks who had worked in the communal kitchens. These former *Küchebaase* and *Küchemadle* (kitchen girls)

prepared foods just as they had done in the communal kitchens. The same delicious soups, pies, and puddings, the same hearty vegetable dishes and main courses. Other foods, such as fried chicken and steaks, were added to the menus and have since become a part of the now-famous Amana Colony restaurant scene, but the basis for the colony restaurant can be traced to the kitchens of old Amana, where all comers were served and no one left the table hungry.

We in Their Seasons Find

As of the spring of 1932 Amana residents entered mainstream American life, and they did so in the midst of the very turbulent Great Depression. Talk to the colony people who lived during those times, and they will tell you that they were willing to exchange the known for the unknown because they believed in the future. They were willing, and some were even anxious, to exchange a life of dependence for a life of independence, believing that with the risk came opportunities.

How they faced the risks and opportunities following the close of the communal era and the dawn of new Amana is characteristic of the Amana people. Prior to 1932 Amana folks spoke of loyalty to the "*Gemeinschaft*" (the community); after 1932 they spoke of loyalty to the "corporation." It did not matter which word they chose, for they were talking about the same thing. An adage appeared frequently in the *Amana Society Bulletin,* a local news sheet first published just after the Great Change, "Say brother, we're the corporation, so don't kick yourself. Let's go!" The group ethic upon which the communal order depended did not die when the communal order ended; it flourished even under the new set of circumstances. Nor did spiritual Amana die with the end of the communal order. The Community of True Inspiration, founded in Germany so long ago, continues as the Amana Church Society, whose members meet and sing:

Who built the lofty firmament?
Who spread th' expanse of blue?
By whom are to our pastures sent
Refreshing rain and dew,
Refreshing rain and dew?

Who warmeth us in cold and frost?
Who shields us from the wind?
Who orders it that oil and must
We in their seasons find,
We in their seasons find.

(Paul Gerhardt,
"O Lord, I Sing with Lips
and Heart,"
The Amana Church Hymnal)

This answer is clear to those who stand on the
dark hillside and watch the break of day scatter light
and shadow across the valley. The red-tail hawk
wheels overhead, the deer disappear like the fog, the
farmers tend their stock, the villages awaken; so the
day begins in Amana.

BIBLIOGRAPHY

Amana Arts Guild Interview Collection. Audiotapes of interviews by Mike Mintle and Gordon Kellenberger pertaining to Amana folk arts and culture. Amana Arts Guild Folk Life Center, High Amana.

Amana Church Hymnal, The. Amana: Amana Church Society, English edition, 1992.

Amana Colony Recipes: A Collection of Traditional Amana Recipes, Homestead, Iowa: Ladies' Auxiliary, Homestead Welfare Club, 1948.

Amana Society Bulletin. A weekly news bulletin published by the Amana Society since 1933. Museum of Amana History Library, Amana.

Andelson, Jonathon G. "Communalism and Change in the Amana Society, 1855–1932." Diss., University of Michigan, 1974.

Andelson, Jonathon G., and Marie L. Trumpold. *How It Was in the Community Kitchen.* Middle Amana, 1976.

Baumgartner, Wilhelmine. Recipe journals. South Amana. Private collection, Annie Kephart.

Glaubensbekenntniss (Profession of Faith). Translation by Janet W. Zuber. Darmstadt: Community of True Inspiration (Amana Church Society), 1839.

Hertzberg, Ruth; Vaughan, Beatrice; and Greene, Janet. *Putting Foods By.* Brattleboro, Vermont: Stephen Greene Press, 1975.

Holloway, Mark. *Heavens on Earth.* New York: Dover, 1966.

Kellenberger, Gordon; Kellenberger, Jean; Hoehnle, Barbara; Hoppe, Emilie. *Quilting, Basketweaving, Carpetweaving, Utilitarian Woodwork, Tinsmithing, Craftwork for the Kitchens and Gardens, Hooked Rugs of the Amana Colonies, Samplers and House Blessings of the Amana Colonies.* Amana Arts Guild Pamphlet Series. Middle Amana: Amana Arts Guild, 1982–.

Kraus, George, and Fritz, E. Mae. *The Story of an Amana Winemaker.* Iowa City, Iowa: Penfield Press. 1984.

Meier, Lina. *Echte Deutsche Kochkunst: Genuine German Cooking and Baking.* Milwaukee, Wisconsin: Wetzel Brothers Printing, 1909.

Museum of Amana History, Amana. Amana Heritage Society. Amana Brewing Records, 1873–1878.

Museum of Amana History, Amana. Amana Heritage Society. Archive Collection. Amana Coupon Books Pre-1932 No. 8; 1932 Reorganization No. 9; Prestele Family No. 26; Amana Poets and Poetry No. 28; Amana Foods and Gardening No. 43; Music Score and Lyrics No. 46; Emma S. Sctzcr No. 48; Amana School No. 68.

Museum of Amana History, Amana. Amana Heritage Society. Cemetery Records.

Museum of Amana History, Amana. Amana Heritage Society. Letters of John Heinemann.

Museum of Amana History, Amana. Amana Heritage Society. Maps of Amana.

Museum of Amana History, Amana. Amana Heritage Society. Oral History Collection. Transcripts cataloged OH-86, OH-44, OH-63, OH-92, OH-51, OH-6, OH-62, OH-40, OH-80, OH-27, OH-28, OH-34, OH-33, OH-10.

Murbach, Marie. *Gartebaas* journal. Middle Amana. Private collection, Susanna Hahn.

Noé, Louise Herrmann. *Küchebaas* recipe collection. Amana. Translation by Louise Miller DuVal. Museum of Amana History. Amana Heritage Society. Archive Collection No. 92:9:1.

Nordhoff, Charles. *The Communistic Societies of the United States.* New York: Dover, 1966.

Oral History Collection. Transcripts of various interviews, 1982. Museum of Amana History Library. Amana.

Peck, Megan. "Detours of Time." Typescript regarding cheese making in Amana.

Peck, Megan. "Interview with Henry Schiff." Typescript of interview notes.

Riotte, Louise. *Sleeping with a Sunflower*. Pownal, Vermont: Storey Communications, Garden Way Publishing, 1987.

Schaefer, Lena (Magdelena). Schaefer *Küchebuch* recipe collection. East Amana. Private collection, Lucille Kraus.

Scharfenberg, Horst. *The Cuisines of Germany*. New York: Simon and Schuster, 1989.

Scheuner, Gottlieb. *Inspirations—Historie 1714–1817*. Translation by Janet W. Zuber. Amana: Amana Church Society, 1977–1987.

Schoenfelder, Elizabeth. "From Three Cups to a Teaspoon." *Iowan* 2, No. 5, (June-July 1954):40–42.

Shambaugh, Bertha M. H. *Amana: The Community of True Inspiration*. Iowa City, Iowa: State Historical Society of Iowa, 1908: Reprint. Iowa City, Iowa: Penfield Press, 1988.

Shambaugh, Bertha M. H. *Amana That Was and Amana That Is*. Iowa City, Iowa: State Historical Society of Iowa, 1932: Reprint. New York: Arno Press, 1976.

Shoup, Carrie. Recipe collection. South Amana. Private collection, Wilma Rettig.

Trumpold, Cliff. *Now Pitching: Bill Zuber from Amana*. Middle Amana: Lakeside Press, 1993.

Webber, Philip E. *Kolonie-Deutsch: Life and Language in Amana*. Ames: Iowa State University Press, 1993.

Willkommen. A guide to the Amana Colonies by Emilie Hoppe. Five issues annually. West Amana: Willkommen, 1982–.

Interviews

Conducted by Julie LeClere, 1992:
   Kellenberger, Erma.
Conducted by Emilie Hoppe, 1986–1993:
   Berger, Daniel.
   Blechsmidt, Rudolph.
   Christen, Betty.
   DuVal, Louise Miller.
   Gunzenhauser, Katy.
   Hahn, Susanna.
   Kellenberger, Al.
   Kephart, Annie.
   Kippenhan, Helen.
   Krauss, Helen Seifert.
   Moershel, Henrietta.
   Moershel, Marietta.
   Moessner, Lina.
   Noé, Louise Wendler.
   Rettig, Wilma.
   Rind, Helene.
   Roemig, Emily.
   Schiff, Henry.
   Schinnerling, Fred.
   Schinnerling, Verona.
   Schoenfelder, Elizabeth.
   Schuerer, Carl.
   Schuerer, Leni.
   Selzer, Art.
   Unglenk, Lina.
   Wetjen, Betty.
   Zuber, Elise.
Conducted by Gordon Kellenberger, 1991–1992:
   Kellenberger, Al.
   Schmieder, Louis.

INDEX

History

Recipes

THE AMANA COLONIES

WEST AMANA

HIGH AMANA

MIDDLE AMA

MIDDLE AMANA

SÄGEMÜHLE

MILL RACE

MILL RACE

MILL RACE

MILL RACE

IOWA RIVER

SOUTH AMANA

CHICAGO ROCK ISLAND AND PACIFIC

TO UPPER SOUTH

RICE CREEK →

EAST AMANA

AMANA

ILY LAKE

WOOLEN MILL →

IOWA RIVER

HOMESTEAD

EIS POND

TANNEWALD

SOUP

French Veg - 47
Lentil - sausage 48
Soup dumplings - 49
Asparagus - 53

SALADS

(colony dressing)

Greens with Radishes, egg - 58
Raddish salad 59
Cucumbers in sour cream + mayo 61
Mothers salad 62
* Hot sweet-sour ENDIVE - egg 63
Hot Potato Salad - 85   egg 63

VEGETABLES

Hot Celeriac 79
Fried Potatoes - marjoram 80
Fried Potatoes + crumbs - 82
Mashed Pot Fingers - Fried 82
Raw potato pancake + egg - 85
* Creamed Potatoes + celery - 86
Potato dumpling
Fried Potatoes with vegetables 87
Potatoes cooked in broth - 88
* Green beans - tomato - herb sauce 90
* Green beans with mustard - 90
Green cooked Cabbage - 92

Misc.
Spaetzle with milk 51
chow-chow - 104

Beef, Pork,

Sauerbraten (No gingersnaps) 128
Sour Pork roast 132

Chicken

creamed chicken, noodles 135

Dessert

apple Fritters 141
Chocolate bread pudding 147
Blanc mange 148
Rice pudding (2) 150
Farina pudding 151
French Dessert "toast" (cake) 153
* Rhubarb Pie 158
fruit - custard Pie (Puff past) 159
Walnut cake 184, 185
White chocolate cake, 192
Caramel Frosting 195
Brown sugar nut cookies 202
Soft butter cookies 203 (drop)
XXX Brown sugar cinnamon Cookies 206
anise cookies   207
Ice Box cookies 207
* Date - nut " 208
XX Brown sugar Ice Patch " 209